Praise for **GHOSTLY MATTERS**

"Avery Gordon's stunningly original and provocatively imaginative book explores the connections linking horror, history, and haunting."
—George Lipsitz

"*Ghostly Matters* immediately established Avery Gordon as a leader among her generation of social and cultural theorists in all fields. The sheer beauty of her language enhances an intellectual brilliance so daunting that some readers will mark the day they first read this book. One must go back many more years than most of us can remember to find a more important book."
—Charles Lemert

"One of the most courageous works of the last decade, *Ghostly Matters* is nothing less than an eloquent demonstration not only that modern knowledge practices are embedded in social forms of domination but that such practices work to conceal, rather than to disclose, the relationship between knowledge and power."
—Lisa Lowe

"What this review cannot capture is the eloquence of Gordon's language, which at times approaches the poetic, and the insistence of her political engagement. The text is of great value to anyone working on issues pertaining to the fantastic and the uncanny."
—*American Studies International*

"Admirably, *Ghostly Matters* is itself a model of its subject matter, demonstrating with its many personal disclosures and considered reflections on others why the critical act is, in the last instance, a mournful one."
—*Quarterly Journal of Speech*

GHOSTLY
MATTERS

GHOSTLY MATTERS

*Haunting and the
Sociological Imagination*

Avery F. Gordon

With a New Introduction
Foreword by Janice Radway

University of Minnesota Press
Minneapolis
London

Published with assistance from the Margaret S. Harding Memorial Endowment honoring the first director of the University of Minnesota Press.

Portions of chapter 2 were originally published in *Social Problems* 37, no. 4 (1990): 495–500; reprinted by permission of the University of California Press on behalf of the Society for the Study of Social Problems; copyright 1990 by the Society for the Study of Social Problems.

Permission to reproduce images in this book was granted by Jaimie Lyle Gordon for "Time Honored Hands," "Employees must wash hands," "Guardian Angel," "I went pioneering," "Is there somewhere I should stand?" "Fighting the Horizon," "If you were me, and I were you," and "Migrant Mother"; by the New-York Historical Society for *Old Kentucky Home—Life in the South* by Eastman Johnson; by the Cincinnati Art Museum for *Fugitive Slaves on the Underground Railroad* by Charles T. Webber; by the Henry Lillie Pierce Fund, Museum of Fine Arts, Boston, for *Slave Ship (Slavers Throwing Overboard the Dead and Dying, Typhoon Coming On)* by Joseph Mallord William Turner; and by Wilberforce House, Hull City Museums, Art Galleries and Archives, U.K., for the plan and cross section of the slaver *Brookes* of Liverpool.

New University of Minnesota Press edition, 2008

Published by the University of Minnesota Press
111 Third Avenue South, Suite 290
Minneapolis, MN 55401-2520
http://www.upress.umn.edu

Library of Congress Cataloging-in-Publication Data

Gordon, Avery.
Ghostly matters : haunting and the sociological imagination / Avery F. Gordon, with a new introduction; foreword by Janice Radway. – New University of Minnesota Press ed.
p. cm.
Includes bibliographical references and index.
ISBN 978-0-8166-5446-8 (pb : alk. paper)
1. Postmodernism—Social aspects. 2. Sociology—Philosophy. 3. Marginality, Social.
I. Title.
HM449.G67 2008
301—dc22   2007049308

Printed in the United States of America on acid-free paper

The University of Minnesota is an equal-opportunity educator and employer.

15 14 13 12 11 10 09 08   10 9 8 7 6 5 4 3 2 1

Contents

Foreword

Janice Radway

It must have been a challenge for Avery Gordon and her editors at the University of Minnesota Press to settle on a subtitle for *Ghostly Matters*. How do you encapsulate a book whose intellectually expansive introduction begins by claiming *theoretical* significance for the banal commonplace that "life is complicated"? In fact, Gordon's claim is even more provocative. She asserts not merely that the proposition that life is complicated is "perhaps the most important theoretical statement of our time" (3) but that sociologists and social analysts specifically have failed to grasp the true significance of the claim. Her reader has to wonder immediately what dense particularities the abstraction "complicated" demarcates for Gordon and why those specificities have failed to figure in social analysis, which, she implies, is fatally weakened by simplification and generalization.

Explicating the meanings of complication, Gordon notes immediately that this folk theoretical statement has two dimensions. First, she observes, "the power relations that characterize any historically embedded society are never as clear as the names we give to them imply" (3). Abstractions like Racism and Capitalism, which are constitutive of virtually all sociological analysis, may name forms of power, but they do not fully convey "the ensemble of social relations that create inequalities, situated interpretive codes, particular kinds of subjects" and, most significantly for Gordon, "the possible and the impossible themselves" (4). To take the measure of the social ensemble in all its singular fullness, Gordon suggests, one needs to "move analytically between that sad and sunken couch that sags in just that place where an unrememberable past and unimaginable future force us to sit day after day" and those abstractions that name the structure of "monumental social architecture[s]" (4). Though she acknowledges the advantages of sociology's rhetoric of abstraction, Gordon is wary of the way such rhetoric renders unremarkable not merely the overdetermined densities and complexities of everyday life but, even more consequentially, the subjectively experienced limitations and constrictions as well as longings and desires that always animate it.

The theoretical claim that life is complicated has another dimension, therefore, in Gordon's view. Even those who live in the direst circumstances possess a rich, contradictory subjectivity, something she calls "complex personhood" (4). She would have sociologists attend more carefully to this fact in their efforts to understand power and the way it is inflected by race, class, and gender dynamics. Complex personhood means that all people "remember and forget"; they are "beset by contradiction"; they "recognize and misrecognize themselves and others"; they get "stuck in the symptoms of their troubles." Yet, they "also transform themselves." Significantly, as well, they "tell themselves stories about themselves and their society's problems" that "weave between what is immediately available as a story and what their imaginations are reaching toward" (4). It is the particular density, delicacy, and propulsive force of the imagination that Avery Gordon wishes to see figured in sociological analysis, which she believes is limited by its restrictive commitment to an empiricist epistemology and its supporting ontology of the visible and the concrete. To make sense of what people do and why—as well as to understand what they might do differently— sociology cannot simply describe the vast and abstracted structures that both compel and inhibit social action. Rather, Gordon believes sociology must seek also to detect how conditions in the past banished certain individuals, things, or ideas, how circumstances rendered them marginal, excluded, or repressed. Sociology must preoccupy itself with what has been lost. According to Gordon, the lost is only apparently absent because the forced "disappearance" of aspects of the social continues to shadow all that remains. Because the past *always* haunts the present, sociology must imaginatively engage those apparitions, those ghosts that tie present subjects to past histories: hence, the subtitle, "Haunting and the Sociological Imagination."

But this subtitle and even this first elucidation of its projected argument fail utterly to capture the theoretical sweep of Gordon's book or the richness of its subject. Though *Ghostly Matters* is certainly about haunting, and it does take up certain questions about the proper object and method of sociology, it seems to me that what the book really does is probe deeply into the historical consequences of two different but related phenomena. To begin with, *Ghostly Matters* is a meditation about the extended intellectual consequences of the historically constituted divide between the social and the individual, the abstract and the concrete, the analytical and the imaginary. At the same time and as a function of this larger topic, the book pursues the nature of the connection between a fully racialized capitalism that itself depends on the abstracting processes of the market and those platitudinous but deeply felt notions about freedom, property, and individuality that ground American culture in a deep faith in the private. What Gordon traces is the intricate process by which the reductive and universalizing powers of the market are lived at the level of the conceptual and the intellectual and how the resulting divide between the general and the particular, between the social and the individual, constrains our ability to recognize and to redress the profound human costs of a system that is utterly dependent on the repression of a knowledge of *social* injustice. The book thus joins a theoretical meditation on how "knowing" is disciplined in the contemporary age with a deeply affecting inquiry into the character of an economic and political system that depends essentially on practices of social disappearance and enslavement.

One might say that Avery Gordon's book is interdisciplinary in the finest, most rigorous sense, for she does not simply pursue the traditional object(s) of one discipline merely by using some of the language and practices of another. Rather, she seeks a new object by straining to "know" in wholly new ways. What propels her forward in this case is a pained sense that sociology as we have come to know it (and the various other human sciences) cannot tell the true history of the losses occasioned by the slavery and racism that have been so enabling for capitalism. It cannot precisely because its very definition of the social primes us to "see" and thus to describe the reality of certain obvious things, thereby blinding us to the ways in which those things are expressly produced and fundamentally enabled by a history of loss and repression. Sociology does not well attend, then, to the living traces, the memories of the lost and the disappeared. And those memories, Gordon argues eloquently, must be honored because they provide a different sort of knowledge, a knowledge of "the things behind the things," of the social conditions and their effects that need to be changed to ensure a more just society. As she writes, "The ghost is not simply a dead or missing person, but a social figure, and investigating it can lead to that dense site where history and subjectivity make social life" (8). Avery Gordon seeks a new way of knowing, then, a knowing that is more a listening than a seeing, a practice of being attuned to the echoes and murmurs of that which has been lost but which is still present among us in the form of intimations, hints, suggestions, and portents. She terms these echoes and murmurs "ghostly matters" and suggests that they haunt us at every turn. "To be haunted," as she puts it, "is to be tied to historical and social effects" (190). She calls for a new sociology that can attend to such queer effects and can negotiate the relationship between what we only see and what we actually know.

Sigmund Freud figures centrally in this book, as one might expect of any volume devoted to repressions and apparitions. But Gordon does not merely use Freud here nor does she build in any simple way on Jacques Derrida's book *Specters of Marx* (1994). Equally unimpressed by intellectual tradition or fashionable argument, Gordon's work does not derive from the questions or paradigms of others but rather emerges thoughtfully, indeed searchingly, in a quite literal sense, from the political perplexities and conceptual conundrums that trouble her. Fittingly, what becomes a significant critique of Freud's privatized and claustrophobic notion of the unconscious begins with an apparition, the ghost of Sabina Spielrein, a woman who first appeared to Gordon amid the pages of a collection of Spielrein's own writings portraying her "as a link, a point of exchange, between two great men," Freud and Jung (32). Perplexed by Spielrein's absence from the traditional history of psychoanalysis given the fact that she theorized the death drive some ten years before Freud and haunted by her absence from a photograph of the Third Psychoanalytic Congress at Weimar, which Spielrein was expected to attend, Gordon finds herself distracted enough from her work at hand to begin wondering about the history of psychoanalysis and the relation of women to it. Her second chapter traces the remarkable inquiry that results, an inquiry that leads her both to recommend psychoanalysis as bearing "lessons for those of us also undertaking analysis that we think is of a different kind" and to critique Freud's version of it for the way it individualizes the unconscious, enclosing it within the subject, rather than conceiving it "as the life of others and other things within us" (48). For Gordon, subjectivity is always and inevitably haunted by the social and most especially by those repressions, disappearances, absences, and losses enforced by the conditions of modern life. As she puts it, haunting is a mediation, "a process that links an institution and an individual, a social structure and a subject, and history and a biography" (19). This astonishing chapter launches Gordon on her quest for a way to answer the question she posed first in chapter 1, a question she believes should underwrite all social analysis: "How do we reckon with what modern history has rendered ghostly?" (18).

In her effort to pursue an answer to that question, Gordon is principally assisted on her quest by two companions in thought, Luisa Valenzuela and Toni Morrison. I call Valenzuela and Morrison "companions in thought" because the complex theoretical and political work they have done in their novels *He Who Searches* and *Beloved* provide a critical opportunity for Gordon to think with, alongside, and in response to them. She does so by reading their works with a skill and sensitivity that is seen rarely these days. Gordon does not read these novels for the way they illustrate the workings of a particular paradigm or theory; in her hand, novels are not machines that demand or dictate a certain use. Rather, by approaching them as sophisticated meditations in their own right, as conversational openings, she replies to them by taking up their offerings, by pursuing the many implications of the very form of their storytelling. In doing so, she enables us to understand just how these writers prepare us to see differently both the things of our world and the histories that have made them possible.

Gordon's readings of both novels are nothing short of brilliant. In effect, Gordon reads Valenzuela and Morrison *as* social theorists, which is to say, as intellectuals who use imaginative fiction both to diagnose the political *dis*-ease of our historical moment and to envision just what it will take to put things right. Thus she is able to present Valenzuela and Morrison as two of our most perceptive political commentators on the particular and pervasive depredations of modern capitalist states. Although Gordon suggests that they are the sources of the "theory of memory as haunting" that she develops in *Ghostly Matters,* I think the situation is actually more complicated. It seems that Gordon herself brings this theory into *material* being by reading the things behind the things of the novels themselves. That is to say, she actively *articulates* exactly what these novels unconsciously know by rendering with a certain systematicity the particular way of knowing the world that produces the characters, objects, and events that inhabit their fictional space. Gordon is able to do this precisely because she reads as if that historical divide between two cultures, one enabled by abstraction and the other grounded in the imaginary and the concrete, never happened. In effect, she restores to social theory that attentiveness to the textures and meanings of experience that was bracketed off at the moment the sciences embraced the quantitative and conceded the province of the qualitative and the imaginary to literature and the arts. What she seeks, finally, is a new sociology, one that can better "write the history of the present" by attempting to "imagine beyond the limits of what is already understandable" (195). This will require, she suggests, a joining of sociology's traditional penchant for conceptual abstraction and its real skill at classification with attentiveness to the affective, the cultural, and the experiential, those ghostly matters that haunt our houses, our societies, our bodies, and our selves. If we are lucky, such a sociology might foster the kinds of "profane illuminations" she describes using the language of Walter Benjamin, those moments at a crossroads where "ghostly signals flash from the traffic, and inconceivable analogies and connections between events are the order of the day" (204).

Ghostly Matters is so rich and elaborate a book that even the summary I have offered here doesn't do justice to its intricately woven fabric. Even as Gordon provides startling readings of these two novels, comments trenchantly on the history of intellectual production that effectively produced sociology as a truncated political project, and considers the consequences of this for our ability to think critically about capitalism, racism, and the modern state, so too does she think deeply about how political change can be effected. There is a critical undercurrent running beneath the main tide of the book, a preoccupation that is articulated as such only during a few key moments. Most prominently, Gordon labels this the question of "the something to be done." Indeed, throughout the book she thinks constantly about change, about what it is, how it can be brought about, and about the identity of the agents who would do so. Although she is deeply moved and motivated by the weight and the fate of the social, she is also, it seems to me, deeply invested in the question of the subject and in the prospects for critical agency. She is not so naïve as to believe that agency is a matter simply of recovering an individual will or intention to act, however. Rather, she implies, radical political change will come about only when new forms of subjectivity *and* sociality can be forged by thinking *beyond* the limits of what is already comprehensible. And that, Gordon suggests, will be possible only when a sense of what has been lost or of what we never had can be brought back from exile and articulated fully as a form of longing in *this* world. A desire to reanimate the utopian, then, resides at the very heart of this book. Social analysts cannot afford to rely complacently on a penchant for describing and categorizing the past; embedded in the terrifying present that surrounds us, we must seek to revivify our collective capacity to imagine a future radically other to the one ideologically charted out already by the militarized, patriarchal capitalism that has thrived heretofore on the practice of social erasure. As Gordon puts it, "To be haunted in the name of a will to heal is to allow the ghost to help you imagine what was lost that never even existed, really. That is its utopian grace: to encourage a steely sorrow laced with delight for what we lost that we never had; to long for the insight of that moment in which we recognize, as in Benjamin's profane illumination, that it could have been and can be otherwise" (57).

Introduction to the New Edition

It has been enormously rewarding and also surprising that *Ghostly Matters* has found enough readers to warrant republication. What the book has meant to those who have gainfully read it, what it will mean to you coming to it anew, I cannot say and feel sure that I would get it wrong if I presumed. It's difficult and often meddlesome for authors to account for why something they have made touches or instructs or inspires or goads its readers. I remain, nonetheless, honored by the respect and attention the book has received, because while there are indeed some books that are, independent of readers, works of great beauty or import, *Ghostly Matters* is not one of those. It was conceived of and written as a hand held out to those who would take it under protection and in solidarity against that other hand that appears in many guises in our world, one of whose scenes opens Luisa Valenzuela's novel *Como en la guerra (He Who Searches)* about the disappeared in Argentina: *an enormous hand approaches his face, about to explode.* I take here, then, only the opportunity to extend an invitation to read anew or again. And I do so, more than any other reason, because the main themes addressed in *Ghostly Matters* remain unfortunately all too relevant today.

In writing the book, I took on two major problems with which I have, in good company, long grappled. The first was how to understand modern forms of dispossession, exploitation, repression, and their concrete impacts on the people most affected by them and on our shared conditions of living. This meant trying to comprehend the terms of an always already racial capitalism and the determining role of monopolistic and militaristic state violence. In this way, the book reflects the type of Marxian inspired and inflected analysis, my intellectual training, that nonetheless has had to part company with the orthodoxies, reductions, and aggravating ongoing refusals to accept the incontrovertible facticity of racial capitalism itself.

Haunting was the language and the experiential modality by which I tried to reach an understanding of the meeting of force and meaning, because haunting is one way in which abusive systems of power make themselves known and their impacts felt in everyday life, especially when they are supposedly over and done with (slavery, for instance) or when their oppressive nature is denied (as in free labor or national security). Haunting is not the same as being exploited, traumatized, or oppressed, although it usually involves these experiences or is produced by them. What's distinctive about haunting is that it is an animated state in which a repressed or unresolved social violence is making itself known, sometimes very directly, sometimes more obliquely. I used the term *haunting* to describe those singular yet repetitive instances when home becomes unfamiliar, when your bearings on the world lose direction, when the over-and-done-with comes alive, when what's been in your blind spot comes into view. Haunting raises specters, and it alters the experience of being in time, the way we separate the past, the present, and the future. These specters or ghosts appear when the trouble they represent and symptomize is no longer being contained or repressed or blocked from view. The ghost, as I understand it, is not the invisible or some ineffable excess. The whole essence, if you can use that word, of a ghost is that it has a real presence and demands its due, your attention. Haunting and the appearance of specters or ghosts is one way, I tried to suggest, we are notified that what's been concealed is very much alive and present, interfering precisely with those always incomplete forms of containment and repression ceaselessly directed toward us.

Haunting is a frightening experience. It always registers the harm inflicted or the loss sustained by a social violence done in the past or in the present. But haunting, unlike trauma, is distinctive for producing a something-to-be-done. Indeed, it seemed to me that haunting was precisely the domain of turmoil and trouble, that moment (of however long duration) when things are not in their assigned places, when the cracks and rigging are exposed, when the people who are meant to be invisible show up without any sign of leaving, when disturbed feelings cannot be put away, when something else, something different from before, seems like it must be done. It is this sociopolitical–psychological state to which haunting referred.

And it is in large measure on behalf and in the interests of the some-thing-to-be-done that I have thought the main value of *Ghostly Matters* lay. To see the something-to-be-done as characteristic of haunting was, on the one hand, no doubt to limit its scope. At the same time it was a way of focusing on the cultural requirements or dimensions of move-ment and change—individual, social, and political. I was concerned with how to adequately understand the social-subjective material or matter of what Cedric Robinson shorthandedly called "the nastiness," without either reducing these matters to the epiphenomenal or detaching them from what we conventionally call the political economy, an analytic challenge that remains still unsatisfied today. I was trying to develop a vocabulary that registered and evoked the lived and living meeting, in their historical time, of the organized forces of order and violence and the aggrieved person when consciousness of that meeting was arising, haunting, forcing a confrontation, forking the future and the past. At this meeting point, I thought we might locate a profound and durable practice of thinking and being and acting toward eliminating the condi-tions that produce the nastiness in the first place. And it was, I thought, one of the most important tasks of social theory, as Herbert Marcuse taught in *One-Dimensional Man,* to be "concerned with the historical alternatives which haunt the established society as subversive tendencies and forces" and to embody the epistemological instruction and reality principle implied in Marcuse's argument that "the values attached to these alternatives . . . become facts when they are translated into reality by . . . practice" (xi–xii).

Ghostly Matters was thus also motivated by my desire to find a method of knowledge production and a way of writing that could represent the damage and the haunting of the historical alternatives and thus richly conjure, describe, narrate, and explain the liens, the costs, the forfeits, and the losses of modern systems of abusive power in their im-mediacy and worldly significance. It seemed to me that radical scholars and intellectuals knew a great deal about the world capitalist system and repressive states and yet insisted on distinctions—between subject and object of knowledge, between fact and fiction, between presence and absence, between past and present, between present and future, be-tween knowing and not-knowing—whose tenuousness and manipula-tion seemed precisely to me in need of comprehension and articulation, being themselves modalities of the exercise of unwanted power. To this end, I found my greatest inspiration in the novels of Toni Morrison and

Luisa Valenzuela, and I sought to translate their lessons into a different but sympathetic idiom.

To some, *Ghostly Matters* and the problems it raised about knowledge production appeared as a localized disciplinary critique of sociology. This was never entirely my intention, despite the fact that sociology was the disciplinary location from which professionally and academically I set out to find a way to reveal and to learn from subjugated knowledge. As Michel Foucault famously explained, subjugated knowledge names, on the one hand, what official knowledge represses within its own terms, institutions, and archives. And on the other hand it also refers to "disqualified," marginalized, fugitive knowledge from below and outside the institutions of official knowledge production. Foucault sought the collaboration and equality of these two types of subjugated knowledge on the grounds that the emergence, whether welcomed or not, of knowledge by subjugated peoples makes advances in scholarly critique possible. But sociology, like all its fellow academic disciplines, has never proved capable of grasping and welcoming as equal the two forms of subjugated knowledge.

When *Ghostly Matters* was conceived and written, there was an optimism in the humanities and social studies that the older institutional edifices were crumbling, that new knowledge and modes of knowledge production were possible, and that these would be led and crafted by the people who had long been excluded from the citadels of the university. It was this specific context, which has yet to achieve its promise, that produced in *Ghostly Matters* the invitation to sociology to find a better purpose. Needless to say, as a whole this invitation was declined, and, like most academic disciplines, sociology is mostly distracted by its own insular professional affairs and doomed to irrelevance or subservient collaborationism. It remained then, as now, a matter of finding a route, access to that which is marginalized, trivialized, denied, disqualified, taxed, and aggrieved *and* a matter of redistributing respect, authority, and the right to representability or generalizability—the right to theorize, one could say—which among other things entails the capacity to be something other than a local knowledge governed or interpreted by a putative superior. It remained then, as now, a matter of building a shared and practical standpoint for negating dispossessions, disabilities, and dehumanizations.[1]

Among the beliefs held by old-time religion southerners collected by Zora Neale Hurston during her travels and research trips and recorded in *The Sanctified Church* was that "Ghosts hate new things" (21). The reason why is because ghosts are characteristically attached to the events, things, and places that produced them in the first place; by nature they are haunting reminders of lingering trouble. Ghosts hate new things precisely because once the conditions that call them up and keep them alive have been removed, their reason for being and their power to haunt are severely restricted. When this book was first published, and certainly when I started writing it, security/dirty wars, torture, disappearance and captivity, state repression via the rule of military law, enslavement—these were, in the First World, treated as obsolete practices that required a special brief to be considered a living inheritance, much less as urgent social problems to be addressed. Justification for my attention to them was constantly solicited. Today, no such pleading is necessary in the United States as evidenced by the occupation war in Iraq; the Global War on Terror, with its military authoritarian legalities, culture of manufactured fear, offshore carceral complex, and imperial pretensions; the spectacle of a "public" "democratic" debate on the necessity of torture and permanent captivity without even the benefit of a corrupt legal conviction; the intensifying division between rich and poor; the concomitant forms of enslavement and indenture engendered and then, as if inevitable, managed by new poor laws and by new wars against the poor in the country and in the city and in the stream of migration itself and then in the ever-growing prisons; the reporting of the presence of CIA ghosts—ghost airplanes, ghost prisons, ghost "detainees"—on the front page of the newspapers. War, slavery, captivity, authoritarianism, the theft of culture and of the means for creating autonomous, sustainable life, the attachment to epistemologies of blindness, and the investment in ontologies of disassociation remain the key problems of our time. And though they transform, keeping old and gaining new forms, they are urgent challenges for the politically engaged intellectual, whose task is to "side with the excluded and the repressed: to develop insights gained in confrontation with injustice, to nourish cultures of resistance, and to help define the means with which society can be rendered adequate to the full breadth of its human potentialities."[2] To help define the means by which society can be rendered adequate to the full breadth of its potentialities is by necessity a collective ambition and undertaking, one that grows alongside the looming degradations and on its polymorphous own. To the extent that this book can still offer a hand to fellow travelers or even to those who detoured here, I offer it again in the hopes that you find a welcome hospitality.

May 2007

Notes

1. Michel Foucault, "Society Must be Defended." *Lectures at the Collège de France, 1975–1976,* ed. Mauro Bertani and Alesandro Fontana, trans. David Macey (New York: Picador, 2003), 1–13. See also Avery F. Gordon, "Exercised," in *Keeping Good Time: Knowledge, Power, and People* (Boulder: Paradigm Press, 2004).

2. Chuck Morse, "Capitalism, Marxism, and the Black Radical Tradition: An Interview with Cedric Robinson," *Perspectives on Anarchist Theory* 3, no. 1 (Spring 1999).

ghostly
matters

1

her shape and his hand

That life is complicated is a fact of great analytic importance.
PATRICIA WILLIAMS, *The Alchemy of Race and Rights*

That life is complicated may seem a banal expression of the obvious, but it is nonetheless a profound theoretical statement—perhaps the most important theoretical statement of our time. Yet despite the best intentions of sociologists and other social analysts, this theoretical statement has not been grasped in its widest significance. There are at least two dimensions to such a theoretical statement. The first is that the power relations that characterize any historically embedded society are never as transparently clear as the names we give to them imply. Power can be invisible, it can be fantastic, it can be dull and routine. It can be obvious, it can reach you by the baton of the police, it can speak the language of your thoughts and desires. It can feel like remote control, it can exhilarate like liberation, it can travel through time, and it can drown you in the present. It is dense and superficial, it can cause bodily injury, and it can harm you without seeming ever to touch you. It is systematic and it is particularistic and it is often both at the same time. It causes dreams to live and dreams to die. We can and must call it by recognizable names, but so too we need to remember that power arrives in forms that can range from blatant white supremacy and state terror to "furniture without memories."

One day, the students in my undergraduate course on American culture and I made a thorough list of every possible explanation Toni Morrison gives in *The Bluest Eye* (1970) for why dreams die. These ranged

3

from explicit externally imposed and internalized white supremacist standards of value, *the nature of white man's work,* and the dialectics of violence and hatred to *disappointment,* to *folding up inside,* to *being put outdoors,* to *the weather,* to *deformed feet and lost teeth,* to *nobody pays attention,* to *it's too late,* to *total damage,* to *furniture without memories,* to the *unyielding soil,* and to what Morrison sometimes just calls *the thing,* the sedimented conditions that constitute what is in place in the first place. This turns out to be not a random list at all, but a way of conceptualizing the complicated workings of race, class, and gender, the names we give to the ensemble of social relations that create inequalities, situated interpretive codes, particular kinds of subjects, and the possible and impossible themselves. Such a conceptualization asks that we constantly move within and between *furniture without memories* and Racism and Capitalism. It asks us to move analytically between that sad and sunken couch that sags in just that place where an unrememberable past and an unimaginable future force us to sit day after day and the conceptual abstractions because everything of significance happens there among the inert furniture and the monumental social architecture.

But this list also reminds us that even those who live in the most dire circumstances possess a complex and oftentimes contradictory humanity and subjectivity that is never adequately glimpsed by viewing them as victims or, on the other hand, as superhuman agents. It has always baffled me why those most interested in understanding and changing the barbaric domination that characterizes our modernity often—not always—withhold from the very people they are most concerned with the right to complex personhood. Complex personhood is the second dimension of the theoretical statement that life is complicated. Complex personhood means that all people (albeit in specific forms whose specificity is sometimes everything) remember and forget, are beset by contradiction, and recognize and misrecognize themselves and others. Complex personhood means that people suffer graciously and selfishly too, get stuck in the symptoms of their troubles, and also transform themselves. Complex personhood means that even those called "Other" are never never that. Complex personhood means that the stories people tell about themselves, about their troubles, about their social worlds, and about their society's problems are entangled and weave between what is immediately available as a story and what their imaginations are reaching toward. Complex personhood means that people get tired and some are just plain lazy. Complex personhood means that groups of people will act together, that they will vehemently disagree with and sometimes harm each other, and that they will do both at the same time and expect the rest of us to figure it out for ourselves, intervening and withdrawing as the situation requires. Complex personhood means that even those who haunt our dominant institutions and their systems of value are haunted too by things they sometimes have names for and sometimes do not. At the very least, complex personhood is about conferring the respect on others that comes from presuming that life and people's lives are simultaneously straightforward and full of enormously subtle meaning.

That life is complicated is a theoretical statement that guides efforts to treat race, class, and gender dynamics and consciousness as more dense and delicate than those categorical terms often imply. It is a theoretical statement that might guide a critique of privately purchased rights, of various forms of blindness and sanctioned denial; that might guide an attempt to drive a wedge into lives and visions of freedom ruled by the nexus of market exchange. It is a theoretical statement that invites us to see with portentous clarity into the heart and soul of American life and culture, to track events, stories, anonymous and history-making actions to their density, to the point where we might catch a glimpse of what Patricia Williams calls the "vast networking of our society" and imagine otherwise. You could say this is a folk theoretical statement. We need to know where we live in order to imagine living elsewhere. We need to imagine living elsewhere before we can live there.

The Alchemy of Race and Rights by Patricia Williams (1991) is a book that captured my attention because, among other things, here is a woman who does not know if she is crazy or not, who sees ghosts and polar bears and has conversations with her sister about haunted houses and writes all of it down for us while she is sitting in her bathrobe with disheveled hair. Patricia Williams is a commercial lawyer and a professor of contract and property law. Her great-great grandmother was a slave, property. Her great-great grandmother's owner and the father of her children was Austin Miller, a well-known Tennessee lawyer and jurist. What is Patricia Williams looking for?

> I track meticulously the dimension of meaning in my great-great-grand-mother as chattel: the meaning of money; the power of consumerist world view, the deaths of those we label the unassertive and the inefficient. I try to imagine where and who she would be today. I am engaged in a long-

term project of tracking his [Austin Miller's] words—through his letters and opinions—and those of his sons who were also lawyers and judges, of finding the shape described by her absence in all this.

I see her shape and his hand in the vast networking of our society, and in the evils and oversights that plague our lives and laws. The control he had over her body. The force he was in her life, in the shape of my life today. The power he exercised in the choice to breed her or not. The choice to breed slaves in his image, to choose her mate and be that mate. In his attempt to own what no man can own, the habit of his power and the absence of her choice.

I look for her shape and his hand. (19)

I look for her shape and his hand; this is a massive project, very treacherous, very fragile. This is a project in which haunting and phantoms play a central part. This is a project where *finding the shape described by her absence* captures perfectly the paradox of tracking through time and across all those forces that which makes its mark by being there and not there at the same time. Cajoling us to reconsider (if only to get some peace), and because cajoling is in the nature of the ghost, the very distinctions between there and not there, past and present, force and shape. From force to hand to her ghostly presence in the register of history and back again, this is a particular kind of social alchemy that eludes us as often as it makes us look for it. Patricia Williams is not alone in the search for the shape of force and lost hands; there is company for the keeping. Wahneema Lubiano (1992, 1993), too, is looking for the haunting presence of the state in the cultural zones where it seemingly excuses itself. Kimberlé Crenshaw (1991) is trying to raise the specter of the ghostly violence of law's regime of objects, its objectivity. Catherine Clément has for some time been trying to "remember *today*" the "zone" that "somewhere every culture has . . . for what it excludes" (Cixous and Clément 1986). Norma Alarcón (1990) is following the barely visible tracks of the Native Woman across the U.S.-Mexico border, as she shadows the making of the liberal citizen-subject. Hortense Spillers (1987a) is reconstructing the American grammatology that lost some subjects in one passage and found others in a phantasmatic family of bad mothers and absent fathers. Maxine Hong Kingston (1977) is mapping the trans-Pacific travel of ghostly ancestors and their incessant demands on the living. Gayatri Spivak (1987, 1989a, 1993) keeps vigilant watch over the dialectic of presence and absence that characterizes "our" benevolent metropolitan relationship to the subaltern women "over there."[1] *I look for her shape and his hand.*

Ghostly Matters is about haunting, a paradigmatic way in which life is more complicated than those of us who study it have usually granted. Haunting is a constituent element of modern social life. It is neither pre-modern superstition nor individual psychosis; it is a generalizable social phenomenon of great import. To study social life one must confront the ghostly aspects of it. This confrontation requires (or produces) a fundamental change in the way we know and make knowledge, in our mode of production. *Ghostly Matters* is a theoretical and conceptual book that I hope demonstrates the utter significance of well-placed (as opposed to misplaced) concreteness and conveys the relevance of ghostly matters to the sociological enterprise, an enterprise at once in sociology and eagerly willing to make it into something entirely different. *Ghostly Matters* is an interdisciplinary work and in this sense representative of our times and needs. But it is Roland Barthes's notion of interdisciplinarity that it strives to instantiate: "Interdisciplinary work, so much discussed these days, is not about confronting already constituted disciplines (none of which, in fact, is willing to let itself go). To do something interdisciplinary it's not enough to choose a 'subject' (a theme) and gather around it two or three sciences. Interdisciplinarity consists in creating a new object that belongs to no one" (quoted in Clifford and Marcus 1986: 1). Not owned by anyone yet, this interdisciplinarity is in the public domain, which does not guarantee anything except that there is still some room to claim rather than discipline its meaning into existence. *Ghostly Matters* looks for a language for identifying hauntings and for writing with the ghosts any haunting inevitably throws up.

Ghosts are a somewhat unusual topic of inquiry for a social analyst (much less a degreed sociologist). It may seem foreign and alien, marginal to the field that conventionally counts as living social reality, the field we observe, measure, and interpret, the field that takes the measure of us as much as we take the measure of it.[2] And foreign and alien it is, for reasons that are both obvious and stubbornly oblique. There is a long story of how I came to write a book about ghostly matters, much of which is relevant to an engaged sociology of knowledge and some of which is even perhaps interesting, but a good deal of it is not what my colleague Harvey Molotch would call news.

I came to write about ghostly matters not because I was interested in

the occult or in parapsychology, but because ghostly things kept crop-
ping up and messing up other tasks I was trying to accomplish. Call it
grounded theory: in one field another emerged to literally capture my
attention and become the field work. The persistent and troubling
ghosts in the house highlighted the limitations of many of our prevalent
modes of inquiry and the assumptions they make about the social
world, the people who inhabit these worlds, and what is required to
study them. The available critical vocabularies were failing (me) to
communicate the depth, density, and intricacies of the dialectic of subjection and subjectivity (or what in my business we call structure and
agency), of domination and freedom, of critique and utopian longing.
Of course, it is not simply the vocabularies themselves that are at fault,
but the constellation of effects, historical and institutional, that make a
vocabulary a social practice of producing knowledge.[3] A vocabulary
and a practice were missing while demanding their due. Haunted and, I
admit, sometimes desperate, sociology certainly—but also the human
sciences at large—seemed to provide few tools for understanding how
social institutions and people are haunted, for capturing enchantment
in a disenchanted world.

If haunting describes how that which appears to be not there is often
a seething presence, acting on and often meddling with taken-for-
granted realities, the ghost is just the sign, or the empirical evidence if
you like, that tells you a haunting is taking place. The ghost is not simply a dead or a missing person, but a social figure, and investigating it
can lead to that dense site where history and subjectivity make social
life. The ghost or the apparition is one form by which something lost,
or barely visible, or seemingly not there to our supposedly well-trained
eyes, makes itself known or apparent to us, in its own way, of course.
The way of the ghost is haunting, and haunting is a very particular way
of knowing what has happened or is happening. Being haunted draws
us affectively, sometimes against our will and always a bit magically,
into the structure of feeling of a reality we come to experience, not as
cold knowledge, but as a transformative recognition.

How I came to write a book about ghostly matters is a long story, and
some of that story has to do with postmodernism, its trail of associations, its often deafening white noise. In 1992 the president-elect of
the Society for the Study of Social Problems called the members to the

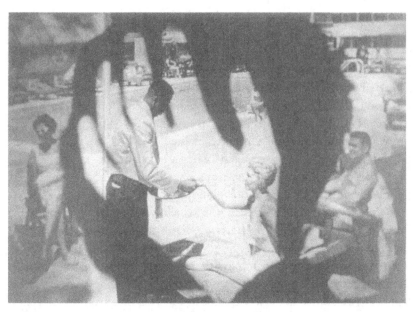

"Employees must wash hands" (copyright Jaimie Lyle Gordon, 1988–90, silver print, 16 × 20 inches)

annual meeting to discuss a new postmodern world order "structured around the dense and high velocity technological rituals of image management, informational CAPITAL, [and] cybernetic-like mechanisms of social control" (Pfohl 1991: 9) without forgetting that "it's not that the ghosts don't exist" (Pfohl 1992b: 7). The invitation linked a certain terminology of postmodernity with the critique of the social sciences' empiricist grounds of knowing. This was not inappropriate since over the past ten to twenty years there has been a veritable assault on our traditional ways of conceptualizing, studying, and writing about the social world and the individuals and cultural artifacts that inhabit this world. Whether the post-1945 period is conceived as the loss of the West's eminent metanarratives of legitimation or as a series of signposts announcing the arrival of significant reconfigurations of our dominant Western organizational and theoretical frames—poststructuralism, postcolonialism, post-Marxism, postindustrialism, postmodernism, postfeminism—many scholars across various disciplinary fields now are grappling with the social, political, and epistemological confrontations that have increasingly come to characterize it.

The claims and summons poststructuralism, in particular, has made on our traditional notions of the human subject, meaning, truth, language, writing, desire, difference, power, and experience have more recently "been placed in a larger context, or 'condition,' of which they have been seen equally as a symptom and as a determining cause. This larger condition—postmodernism—addresses a whole range of material conditions that are no longer consonant with the dominant rationality of modernism and its technological commitment to finding *solutions* in every sphere of social and cultural life" (Ross 1988: x). Situating postmodernism thus locates what is often construed as strictly philosophical or epistemological questions on a decidedly sociological and political terrain. As the invitation elaborated, and as Ross states, "postmodernist culture is a real medium in which we all live to some extent, no matter how unevenly its effects are lived and felt across the jagged spectrum of color, sex, class, region, and nationality" (ibid.: viii).

For the discipline of sociology, postmodern conditions have made their impact felt most strongly in the resurgence of "the ancient problem of the relationship between what in everyday language we call 'experience' of 'reality' and what we then decide to call 'knowledge' about it" (Jardine 1985: 145) and in the attendant dilemmas created for an empirical social science (see Agger 1989a, 1989b, 1990, 1991, 1992, 1993; Bauman 1992, 1993; R. Brown 1987, 1989; Clough 1992; Denzin 1986, 1991; Lemert 1990; Pfohl 1992a; J. W. Scott 1992; Seidman 1991, 1994a, 1994b). At the core of the postmodern field or scene, then, is a crisis in representation, a fracture in the epistemological regime of modernity, a regime that rested on a faith in the reality effect of social science. Such a predicament has led to, among other consequences, an understanding that the practices of writing, analysis, and investigation, whether of social or cultural material, constitute less a scientifically positive project than a cultural practice that organizes particular rituals of storytelling told by situated investigators. The promise of this postpositivist and, in a limited sense, post- or antimodern rupture for sociology is that rather than leading away from an analysis of the social relations of power (which is the presumed drawback of a concern with representation), it will lead to a different agenda for asking how power operates. Such an agenda could deliver, albeit with necessary improvements, on the unfulfilled promissory note given to sociology by Horkheimer and Adorno: namely, to link a thoroughgoing epistemological critique of modernity as what is contemporaneously ours with an insurgent sociological critique of its forms of domination (Frankfurt Institute for Social Research [1956] 1973).

Questions of narrative structuring, constructedness, analytic standpoint, and historical provisionality of claims to knowledge direct sociology to the ways in which our stories can be understood as fictions of the real. The challenge to the monopolistic assumption that sociology can provide an unproblematic window onto a more rather than less secure reality is both necessary and desirable in order to understand how the real itself and its ethnographic or sociological representations are also fictions, albeit powerful ones that we do not experience as fictional, but as true. At the same time, the increasingly sophisticated understandings of representation and of how the social world is textually or discursively constructed still require an engagement with the social structuring practices that have long been the province of sociological inquiry. It is these that draw our attention to the multiple determinations and sites of power in which narratives of and about our culture and its artifacts are produced and disseminated.

Part of the widespread ambivalence toward postmodernism and postmodernity stems from the complicated relationship between reality and its modes of production, a relationship crucial to the primary investigation of exclusions and invisibilities. Neither postmodernism nor postmodernity resolve this relationship by any means. (And, indeed, the common tendency to distinguish between postmodernism as a kind of voluntary idealism—a style or choice of approach—and postmodernity as a kind of crushing, all-encompassing materialism does not help matters at all. In fact, it sends social theorists back to the drawing board needlessly.) What some feminists and critical theorists have sensibly insisted on retaining is precisely a double structure of thought that links the epistemological and the social (see Flax 1992; Lubiano 1991). Feminism's presumed (and putatively paradigmatic) relationship to postmodernism rests on its participation in the critique of the transparency of language, objective causality, transnational generalization, and so on, all of which are part and parcel of the so-called crisis in representation (see Nicholson 1990; Butler 1992). But the critique of representation does not solve the problem of the continuing crisis of domination—coercive and consensual—unless it is linked to issues of governmentality, broadly understood (see Hennessy 1993; Mouffe 1992). Coupling problems with representation to an ongoing and aggressive concern with representability, in the political sense, is what enables epistemology to be properly situated in the ensemble of social relations of power in which such epistemologies are ensconced.

To say that sociology or social analysis more broadly must retain a double structure of thought that links the epistemological and the social, or, in other words, to say that sociology has to respond *methodologically* and not only as if from an autonomous distance begs the question of what exactly the novel postmodern social conditions to which we ought to respond are. Difficult diagnostic issues are at stake here, exacerbated by "the effort to take the temperature of the age without instruments and in a situation in which we are not even sure there is so coherent a thing as an 'age,' or zeitgeist or 'system' or 'current situation' any longer" (Jameson 1991: xi). It is no doubt true that some of the central characteristics of the modern systems of capitalism, state and subject formation, and knowledge production are undergoing significant modifications, and many are working to describe these changes and their implications (see Bauman [1988] 1994; Haraway 1985; Harvey 1989; Jameson 1991; Lash 1990). An equally powerful argument could be made, as Derrick Bell (1992) does in one of the more moving examples of Antonio Gramsci's maxim—optimism of the will, pessimism of the intellect—that things have hardly changed at all. I am simply not in a position to adjudicate the degree of continuity or discontinuity at such a grand scale and am inclined to consider most conclusions premature at this point, and perhaps at any point. In my own limited view, therefore, we are not "post" modern yet, although it is arguably the case that the fundamental contradictions at the heart of modernity are more exposed and much is up for grabs in the way we conceive the possibilities for knowledge, for freedom, and for subjecthood in the wake of this exposure. It is also arguably the case that the strong sense of living in "a strange new landscape . . . the sense that something has changed, that things are different, that we have gone through a transformation of the life world which is somehow decisive but incomparable with the older convulsions of modernization and industrialization" (Jameson 1991: xxi) so pervasive in many quarters is an influential and itself motivating social and cultural fact.[4]

Of one thing I am sure: *it's not that the ghosts don't exist.* The postmodern, late-capitalist, postcolonial world represses and projects its ghosts or phantoms in similar intensities, if not entirely in the same forms, as the older world did. Indeed, the concentration on haunting and ghosts is a way of maintaining the salience of social analysis as bounded by its social context, as in history, which is anything but dead and over, while avoiding simple reflectionism. Yet, in one particularly prominent framing of postmodernism, an overweening and overstated emphasis on new electronic technologies of communication, on consumerism, and on the spectacular world of commodities has, despite the rhetoric of exposing the new machinery, replaced conventional positivism with a postmodernist version that promotes the telecommunicative visibility of all codings and decodings. Crudely put, when postmodernism means that everything is on view, that everything can be described, that all "tacitly present means . . . [become] conscious object[s] of self-perfection" (Bauman [1988] 1994: 188), it displays an antighost side that resembles modernity's positivities more than it concedes.

Let me give you an example. Don DeLillo's 1985 best-selling novel *White Noise* is a paradigmatic postmodern text. Nothing much happens in it really. Jack Gladney, professor and inventor, in 1968, of Hitler studies, ruminates on American popular culture and family life while trying to learn German, which he doesn't speak. He has a hard time keeping his tongue in place, but does keep his competitive edge by refusing to really help his friend Murray set up a similar institutional program to promote Elvis studies. Jack loves his extended family, composed of children from various marriages, all of whom display a level of maturity Jack and Babette, his wife, lack. Babette is, like Jack, obsessed with a fear of dying, and all their shopping doesn't seem to help her, although it does "expand" her husband. Her fear leads her to covertly trade sex for drugs, which is all just fine until Jack and the children find her out. At this point, Babette becomes irrelevant and Jack plots to recover the drugs, his wife's sexual propriety, and his manhood. He never learns to speak German and the whole drama is interrupted by a toxic disaster that confuses the town, which had been simu-planning it for months. It is of no consolation to Jack that he might really die from postindustrial contamination, although the specter of "real" death provides him with enough justification to minimize his wife's "unreal" fears.

DeLillo's novel is a descriptively rich evocation of white suburban North America in the commodified landscape of late capitalism, full of clever insights and portable quotations. It conjures up some of the dominant and disturbing features of American life that are increasingly named postmodern: television-structured reality, the commodification of everyday life, the absence of meaning and the omnipresence of end-less information, the relentless fascination with catastrophes, and the circulating advertisements for the death of author, referent, and objective reality set within image upon image of the electric connections among life, death, and sex.

Notwithstanding my docudrama rendering of the plot, the familiar and familial noise of *White Noise,* a fiction, reads like a sociological map of white postmodern America, like an ethnography of sorts. Significantly, this reading effect is precisely related to those social conditions that the text itself identifies as challenging the distinctions between the fictive and the factual, and between the imaginary and the real. This is *White Noise*'s great strength as a social science fiction: it attempts to link the sociological and the epistemological dimensions of postmodernism. At the level of everyday language and procedure, DeLillo captures the optimistic cynicism of imploded meanings, empty memory banks, and televisual screenings. He is neither critical nor celebratory. Abandoning the terrain of politics, the contestation about and over power, he opts instead for a kind of market media effect where *everything was on television last night.*

White Noise is, however, a ghost-busting text that refuses to confront what has been rendered spectral by the twin hands of the social and the writer. At the close of *White Noise,* the language of enthusiasm for an American culture mediated and saturated by commodities whose hieroglyphics and secret codes fascinate and offer entrance into a world full of abandoned meanings and momentary ecstatic experiences gives way to a "sense of wandering . . . an aimless and haunted mood." *Smeared print, ghost images.* The members of DeLillo's television public find that the "supermarket shelves have been re-arranged . . . one day without warning":

> The men scan for stamped dates, the women for ingredients. Many have trouble making out the words. Smeared print, ghost images. In the altered shelves, the ambient roar, in the plain and heartless fact of their decline, they try to work their way through confusion. But in the end it doesn't matter what they see or think they see. The terminals are equipped with holographic scanners, which decode the binary secret of every item, infallibly. This is the language of waves and radiation, or how the dead speak to the living. (325–26)

At the end of DeLillo's novel, his story of contemporary white suburban everyday life (which in this novel is the virtual history of post-

World War II American culture) is figured by the rearrangement of the supermarket shelves. This is an apt metaphor for the social world *White Noise* articulates and orients around its protagonist, Jack Gladney: a commodified, post-Hiroshima landscape of late (night) capitalism where "everything was on television last night." Up until this point, Jack, who constantly interprets and theorizes (in perfectly encapsulated, spectacular one-sentence units) the popular culture that fascinates him, has been enthusiastic about the *waves and radiation* of an electronically simulated culture. *The myth being born right there in our living room* has its dark side, of course: *they believed something lived in the basement.* But neither the Airborne Toxic Event (Blacksmith's Bhopal), nor a world full of *abandoned meanings,* nor a wife fearful for her life for inexplicable reasons can shatter the smooth switching of channels that gives us *Family Ties* and *Guiding Light*(s). At the end all that remains is confusion, an inability to make out the words, and the postmodern surface sheen gone cynical and pessimistic. DeLillo's conclusion eerily encants: *But in the end it doesn't matter what they see or think they see.* The terminals can *decode the secret of every item.* No secrets, no gaps, no errant trajectories, only a passive scene of waiting and watching. From my point of view, and simply put, *But in the end it doesn't matter what they see or think they see* is the language of waves and radiation, a language in which the ghostly (or the living for that matter) cannot get a word in edgewise. *But in the end it doesn't matter what they see or think they see* is the postmodern positive language of power and indifference that is nothing more than the "second nature" of commodification speaking as our common culture (Jameson 1991: 314).

If the ghostly haunt gives notice that something is missing—that what appears to be invisible or in the shadows is announcing itself, however symptomatically—then in *White Noise* there are no ghostly haunts, or shadows, only the insistent visibility of fetishized commodity surveillance and that which masquerades as its absence. Indeed, one could argue that *White Noise* enacts a detour around just those issues of power it aggressively renders explicit. And it enacts that detour by its insistent emphasis, to the exclusion of a more dialectical way of seeing, on the hypervisibility of what could be called technological irrationality.

Visibility is a complex system of permission and prohibition, of presence and absence, punctuated alternately by apparitions and hysterical blindness (Kipnis 1988: 158). It is perhaps DeLillo's "hysterical blindness" to "apparitions" and to the "complex system of permission and prohibition, of presence and absence" that makes his book an example of postmodernist positivism, or hypervisibility. Hypervisibility is a kind of obscenity of accuracy that abolishes the distinctions between "permission and prohibition, presence and absence." No shadows, no ghosts. In a culture seemingly ruled by technologies of hypervisibility, we are led to believe not only that everything can be seen, but also that everything is available and accessible for our consumption. In a culture seemingly ruled by technologies of hypervisibility, we are led to believe that neither repression nor the return of the repressed, in the form of either improperly buried bodies or countervailing systems of value or difference, occurs with any meaningful result.

The representation of value or difference is indispensable for understanding the cleavages that power's divisive work accomplishes. To the extent that DeLillo's text performs some of the new ways in which difference, rather than simply being excluded or marginalized, is being staged or simulated, it tells an important story. For example, *White Noise* clearly puts the reader on notice that it will not (and then cannot) tell, with any sympathetic apprehension, the story of Jack's panicking wife, Babette, a powerful indicator of the way in which even silence and invisibility can be accessed. Such a narrative makes it difficult, if not impossible, however, to imagine her story as other than a kind of visible invisibility: *I see you are not there.* In other words, not much is left of Babette's value other than the fact that her absent life world can now be acknowledged, advertised, and consumed as background white noise. DeLillo's text may very well echo Jean Baudrillard's point that postmodern culture can increasingly bring within view (for consumption) that which previously remained at the margins, but it also reproduces the same features it describes. In so doing, it offers no place from which to challenge the ubiquity of that white noise and offer a countermemory. Indeed, the obsession with death in the novel is a substitute for dealing with the ghostly matter, the ghostly and haunting trouble. Rather, we are confronted with the morbidity of existence as a symptom of the inability to confront modernity's phantoms. Kept busy just surviving in the confusing supermarket of life, itself already having coded and decoded all exchanges, reification—the effacement of the traces of production—appears, in this milieu, to be the welcome relief one hopes for. Jameson (1991: 314–15) puts it well: "the point of having your own object world, and walls and muffled distance or relative silence all around you, is to forget about all those innumerable others for a while." To remember "would be like having voices inside your head" (315).[5] *It would be like having voices inside your head* because a postmodern social formation is still haunted by the symptomatic traces of its productions and exclusions. A different language than the one DeLillo offers is needed to even begin the work of writing a text that might have something more to say about *smeared print, ghost images.*

In a 1981 introduction to *Invisible Man,* Ralph Ellison wrote: "despite the bland assertions of sociologists, [the] 'high visibility' [of the African-American man] actually rendered one *un*-visible" (xii). Hypervisibility is a persistent alibi for the mechanisms that render one *un*-visible: "His darkness . . . glow[ing] . . . within the American conscience with such intensity that most whites feigned moral blindness toward his predicament." The difficulty for us now, as it was for Ellison when he published *Invisible Man* in 1952, is the extent to which the mediums of public image making and visibility are inextricably wedded to the cojoined mechanisms that systematically render certain groups of people apparently *privately* poor, uneducated, ill, and disenfranchised.

Ellison's *Invisible Man* gives double reference both to the unvisibility of the hypervisible African-American man and to the invisibility of "the Man" who persistently needs an alibi for the blindness of his vision. As a strategy of analysis, Ellison's insight underscores the need to conceptualize visibility as a *complex system of permission and prohibition, punctuated alternately by apparitions and hysterical blindness.* If Ellison's argument encourages us to interrogate the mechanisms by which the highly visible can actually be a type of invisibility, Toni Morrison's (1989) argument that "invisible things are not necessarily not-there" encourages the complementary gesture of investigating how that which appears absent can indeed be a seething presence. Both these positions are about how to write ghost stories—about how to write about *permissions and prohibitions, presence and absence,* about *apparitions and hysterical blindness.* To write stories concerning exclusions and invisibilities is to write ghost stories. To write ghost stories implies that ghosts are real, that is to say, that they produce material effects. To impute a kind of objectivity to ghosts implies that, from certain standpoints, the dialectics of visibility and invisibility involve a constant negotiation between what can be seen and what is in the shadows. Why would we want to write such stories? Because unlike DeLillo's indifference, *in the end* and in the beginning *it* does *matter what they see or think they see.* It matters because although *the terminals are equipped with holographic scanners,* they cannot *decode the secret of every item, infallibly.* Indeed, what is at stake here is the political status and function of systematic hauntings.

If the ghost is a crucible for political mediation and historical memory, the ghost story has no other choice than to refuse the logic of the unreconstructed spectacle, whether of the modern or postmodern variety. *White Noise* might bring us to the brink of establishing the necessity of reckoning with the instrumentality of hauntings. But because it does not invite us to make contact with haunting, to engage the shadows and what is living there, it does not help us to develop a form of historical accounting distinct from the diagnostics of postmodern hypervisibility. The purpose of an alternative diagnostics is to link the politics of accounting, in all its intricate political-economic, institutional, and affective dimensions, to a potent imagination of what has been done and what is to be done otherwise.

"Guardian Angel" (copyright Jaimie Lyle Gordon, 1992, silver print, 30 × 40 inches)

How do we reckon with what modern history has rendered ghostly? How do we develop a critical language to describe and analyze the affective, historical, and mnemonic structures of such hauntings? These questions have guided my desire to articulate, however insufficiently, a sense of the ghostly and its social and political effects. I use the word *sense* here deliberately to evoke what Raymond Williams called a structure of feeling—perhaps the most appropriate description of how hauntings are transmitted and received. I have not endeavored to establish transhistorical or universal laws of haunting per se[6] but rather to represent the structure of feeling that is something akin to what it feels like to be the object of a social totality vexed by the phantoms of modernity's violence. What does this mean? It means following the insights that come to those who see all these forces operating at once. Such a way of seeing can make you a bit crazy and imprecise and wary of shorthands. While it may be true that the constellation of social forces all collide in various ways, that social life's complication is, to use an often overused phrase, overdetermined, the obvious task of the critic or analyst is to designate the precise contours of experience and causality in particular instances. It is not a matter of accepting or rejecting any of a range of notions of social totality, and, academic common sense to the contrary, Marxists do not have a lock on this concept (Gordon 1992). Rather, it is a matter of exploring here the particular mediation that is haunting. As a concept, mediation describes the process that links an institution and an individual, a social structure and a subject, and history and a biography. In haunting, organized forces and systemic structures that appear removed from us make their impact felt in everyday life in a way that confounds our analytic separations and confounds the social separations themselves. Paying attention to the disjuncture between identifying a social structure (or declaring its determinate existence) and its articulation in everyday life and thought, I have hoped that working at understanding these gaps, the kinds of visions they produce, and the afflictions they harbor would enable us not to eradicate the gap—it is inevitable—but to fill in the content differently. Could it be that analyzing hauntings might lead to a more complex understanding of the generative structures and moving parts of historically embedded social formations in a way that avoids the twin pitfalls of subjectivism and positivism? Perhaps. If so, the result will not be a more tidy world, but one that might be less damaging.

It was in such a spirit that Horkheimer and Adorno ([1944] 1987) wrote a two-page note, appended to *The Dialectic of Enlightenment*, entitled "On The Theory of Ghosts." Despairing at the loss of historical perspective, at our "disturbed relationship with the dead—forgotten and embalmed," they believed we needed some kind of theory of ghosts, or at least a way of both mourning modernity's "wound in civilization" (216) and eliminating the destructive forces that open it up over and over again: "Only the conscious horror of destruction creates the correct relationship with the dead: unity with them because we, like them, are the victims of the same condition and the same disappointed hope" (215). One wonders what a completed theory of ghosts would have looked like had Horkheimer and Adorno actually written more than the note.[7] I have not written the Theory of Ghosts, a far too singular proposal for my purposes, but *Ghostly Matters* does attempt to describe, in homage to the viability of a Marxist concept of haunting, the ghostly haunt as a form of social figuration that treats as a major problem the reduction of individuals "to a mere sequence of instantaneous experiences which leave no trace, or rather whose trace is hated as irrational, superfluous, and 'overtaken'" (216).

And a problem it remains despite all that we can claim now to understand in the wake of what are, without doubt, major changes in who is permitted to make public knowledge and in the assumptions that direct and underwrite much contemporary inquiry. We have taken the legs out from under that fateful and deceptive Archimedean standpoint, substituting the view from somewhere for the old view from nowhere. We have become adept at discovering the construction of social realities and deconstructing their architecture, confounding some of the distinctions between culture and science, the factual and the artificial. We have rethought the relationship between knowledge and power, between text and context, highlighting the relationship between authorization and modes of authority. And we have made considerable representational reparations for past exclusions and silencings, making the previously unknown known, telling new stories, correcting the official records.

These are major accomplishments for work in universities, which change slowly and which, despite their ideology of invention, do not like too much of it. Yet I have wondered sometimes whether, for example, we have truly taken seriously that the intricate web of connections that characterizes any event or problem *is the story*. Warnings about relativism to the contrary, truth is still what most of us strive for. Partial and insecure surely, and something slightly different from "the facts," but truth nonetheless: the capacity to say "This is so." But truth is a subtle shifting entity not simply because philosophy says so or because evidentiary rules of validation are always inadequate, but because the very nature of the things whose truth is sought possesses these qualities. To tell the partial deconstructive truth of the thing that is the complex relation between subjection and subjectivity requires making common cause with the thing, requires what Michael Taussig calls sympathetic magic, that is, "granting . . . the representation the power of the represented" (1993a: xviii). Particularly for those who believe in the progressive quality of modernity's secularity, this is a somewhat remarkable claim. But a kind of sympathetic magic is necessary because in the world and between us as analysts and the worlds we encounter to translate into world-making words are hauntings, ghosts and gaps, seething absences, and muted presences. The political and affective modalities by which we gain access to the facticity of constructed power either reckons with or displaces these ghostly matters and the matter of the ghost, with consequences either way.

Bloodless categories, narrow notions of the visible and the empirical, professional standards of indifference, institutional rules of distance and control, barely speakable fears of losing the footing that enables us to speak authoritatively and with greater value than anyone else who might . . . Our methods have thus far been less than satisfactory for addressing the very nature of the things and the problems it is our responsibility to address, leaving us not yet making something new enough out of what are arguably many new ideas and novel conditions. A different way of knowing and writing about the social world, an entirely different mode of production, still awaits our invention. Such a mode of production would not reject the value of empirical observation per se, but might, to use Taussig's words, be more "surprised" by social construction, the making and making up of social worlds, thereby giving it the "respect" it "deserves" (1993a: xv-xvi). Indeed, we might expand the domain of the empirical considerably to include not only haunting and ghostly matters but also our own relations to social analysis. We might make common cause with our objects and subjects of analysis. Making common cause with our objects and subjects of analysis involves "understanding . . . the representation as contiguous with that being represented and not as suspended above and distant from the represented" (Taussig 1992: 10). Making common cause with our objects and subjects of analysis, which *is* to take social determination quite seriously, means "that one has to see oneself and one's shared modes of understanding and communication included in that determining. To claim otherwise, to claim the rhetoric of systematicity's determinisms and yet except oneself, is an authoritarian deceit, a magical wonder" (ibid.). Making common cause means that our encounters must strive to go beyond the fundamental alienation of turning social relations into just the things we know and toward our own reckoning with how we are in these stories, with how they change us, with our own ghosts.

Doing so is not easy because, among other things, knowing ghosts often shows up not as professional success, but as failure: the one whose writing/not writing only came together as she came together with the object, with the reality of fictions and the unrealities of the facts; the slightly mad one who kept saying, "There's something in the room with us," as those bloodless reified categories became animated through wonder and vexation. But it is also true that ghosts are never innocent: the unhallowed dead of the modern project drag in the pathos of their loss and the violence of the force that made them, their sheets and chains. To be haunted and to write from that location, to take on the condition of what you study, is not a methodology or a conscious-ness you can simply adopt or adapt as a set of rules or an identity; it produces its own insights and blindnesses. Following the ghosts is about making a contact that changes you and refashions the social relations in which you are located. It is about putting life back in where only a vague memory or a bare trace was visible to those who bothered to look. It is sometimes about writing ghost stories, stories that not only repair representational mistakes, but also strive to understand the con-ditions under which a memory was produced in the first place, toward a countermemory, for the future.

Sociology, in particular, has an extraordinary mandate as far as acad-emic disciplines go: to conjure up social life. Conjuring is a particular form of calling up and calling out the forces that make things what they are in order to fix and transform a troubling situation. As a mode of apprehension and reformation, conjuring merges the analytical, the procedural, the imaginative, and the effervescent. But we have more to learn about how to conjure in an evocative and compelling way. If haunting is a constitutive feature of social life, then we will need to be able to describe, analyze, and bring to life that aspect of social life, to be less fearful of animation. We ought to do this not only because it is more exact, but also because to the extent that we want our writing to change minds, to convince others that what we know is important and ought to matter, we need to be more in touch with the nature of how "the pieces of a world . . . littered all over a sociological landscape" (D. Smith 1987: 99) affect people. And we do not usually experience things, nor are affects produced, in the rational and objective ways our terms tend to portray them. The counterpart to reification, the conjur-

ing trick, might be better captured by Walter Benjamin's profane illumination or Marx's sensuous knowledge. Of course, the tricky thing is
that scholars too are subject to these same dynamics of haunting: ghosts
get in our matters just as well. This means that we will have to learn to
talk to and listen to ghosts, rather than banish them, as the precondition
for establishing our scientific or humanistic knowledge.

Ghostly Matters is thus, on the one hand, a modest book and, on the
other hand, quite ambitious. Its modesty lies in its very simple point.
Ghostly matters are part of social life. If we want to study social life
well, and if in addition we to want to contribute, in however small a
measure, to changing it, we must learn how to identify hauntings and
reckon with ghosts, must learn how to make contact with what is without doubt often painful, difficult, and unsettling. The book's ambition
lies in asserting that in order to do this, we will have to change the way
we have been doing things.

"I went pioneering" (copyright Jaimie Lyle Gordon, 1993, silver print, 16 × 20 inches)

I have many more questions than answers, a potentially disappointing
feature of this book, but endemic to the enterprise. In the chapters that
follow, I have tried to explore three broad questions. First, what are the
alternative stories we ought to and can write about the relationship
among power, knowledge, and experience? I have been particularly
troubled by the contrast between conceptual or analytical descriptions

of social systems and their far more diffused and delicate effects. Haunting occurs on the terrain situated between our ability to conclusively
describe the logic of Capitalism or State Terror, for example, and the
various experiences of this logic, experiences that are more often than
not partial, coded, symptomatic, contradictory, ambiguous. What is it
to identify haunting and follow its trajectory? Second, if the ghost's arrival notifies us of a haunting, how does the ghost interrupt or put into
crisis the demand for ethnographic authenticity—what Jacqueline Rose
(1986: 12) has called the "unequivocal accusation of the real"—that
we expect from those who can legitimately claim to tell the truth? The
intermingling of fact, fiction, and desire as it shapes personal and social
memory situates us on the border of the social sciences and makes me
wonder, What does the ghost say as it speaks, barely, in the interstices
of the visible and the invisible? And, third, we are part of the story, for
better or worse: the ghost must speak *to me* in some way sometimes
similar to, sometimes distinct from how it may be speaking to the others. How then can our critical language display a reflexive concern not
only with the objects of our investigations but also with the ones who
investigate? What methods and forms of writing can foreground the
conditions under which the facts and the real story are produced?

What is my method for answering these questions? The method here
is everything and nothing much really. (The question of method has
also gotten me into some trouble, as chapter 2 shows.) I do not devise
procedures for the application of theories because one major goal of
this book is to get us to consider a different way of seeing, one that is
less mechnical, more willing to be surprised, to link imagination and
critique, one that is more attuned to the task of "conjur[ing] up the
appearances of something that [is] absent" (Berger 1972: 10). A way of
seeing is not a rule book for operationalizing discrete explanatory theories. It is a way of negotiating the always unsettled relationship between
what we see and what we know (ibid: 7). I suppose you could say that
the method here involves producing case studies of haunting and ad-
judicating their consequences. What kind of case is a case of a ghost? It
is a case of haunting, a story about what happens when we admit
the ghost—that special instance of the merging of the visible and the invisible, the dead and the living, the past and the present—into the making of worldly relations and into the making of our accounts of the
world. It is a case of the difference it makes to start with the marginal,
with what we normally exclude or banish, or, more commonly, with

what we never even notice. In Gayatri Spivak's formulation, it is a case of "what . . . it [is] to learn, these lessons, otherwise" (1992: 775). It is not a case of dead or missing persons sui generis, but of the ghost as a social figure. It is often a case of inarticulate experiences, of symptoms and screen memories, of spiraling affects, of more than one story at a time, of the traffic in domains of experience that are anything but transparent and referential. It is a case of modernity's violence and wounds, and a case of the haunting reminder of the complex social relations in which we live. It is a case that teaches a lesson (or two) about how to write what can represent that haunting reminder, what can represent systematic injury and the remarkable lives made in the wake of the making of our social world.

Literary fictions play an important role in these cases for the simple reason that they enable other kinds of sociological information to emerge. In the twentieth century, literature has not been restrained by the norms of a professionalized social science, and thus it often teaches us, through imaginative design, what we need to know but cannot quite get access to with our given rules of method and modes of apprehension. Where else do we learn of the tremulous significance of *furniture without memories,* learning about it in the same moment as we are drawn in, hearts in hand, to a story told just so? In the broadest sense, sociology is concerned with both the production and the interpretation of stories of social and cultural life. Yet the division of the disciplines separates literature (story/fiction) and social science (fact). This disciplinary segregation is an uneasy one, however; the border is not quite as secure as institutional mandates presume. Not only is the origin of sociology as a unique discipline bound up with its relationship to literature (see Lepenies 1988), but sociology's dominant disciplinary methods and theoretical assumptions constantly struggle against the fictive.[8] By the fictive I mean not simply literature but that complication with which I began: the ensemble of cultural imaginings, affective experiences, animated objects, marginal voices, narrative densities, and eccentric traces of power's presence. For sociology, the fictive is our constitutive horizon of error; it is what has been and must be exiled to ordain the authority of the discipline and the truthful knowledge sociology can claim to produce.

As a mode of storytelling, sociology distinguishes itself from literature by its now historical claim to find and report the facts expertly. The maintenance of a disciplinary object, social reality, that meets something akin to the juridical strict scrutiny test is predicated upon a clear distinction between what is (socially) real and what is fictional. As Michel de Certeau puts it, "At the level of analytic procedures . . . as at the level of interpretations . . . the technical discourse capable of determining the errors characteristic of fiction has come to be authorized to speak in the name of the 'real.' By distinguishing between the two discourses—the one scientific, the other fictive—according to its own criteria, [sociology] credits itself with having a special relationship to the 'real' because its contrary is posited as . . . [fictive]" (1983: 128). To the extent that sociology is wedded to facticity as its special truth, it must continually police and expel its margin—the margin of error—which is the fictive. But these facts are always in imminent danger of being contaminated by what is seemingly on the other side of their boundaries, by fictions. Like a taboo that is always being approached in the act of avoidance, when sociology insists on finding only the facts, it has no other choice but to pursue the fictive, the mistake it seeks to eliminate. A marginal discourse, the story of how the real story has emerged, consistently shadows and threatens to subvert the very authority that establishes disciplinary order.

If "the margins of the story mark a border between the remembered and the forgotten" (Haug et al. 1987: 68), my use of fiction to designate this border intends to call attention to both the broader issues of invisibility, marginality, and exclusion, and also to the "twist[s] and turn[s], reinterpret[ations] and falsifi[cations], forget[tings] and repress[ings] [of] events" (ibid.: 40) that are part of the research and writing process. These are characteristically the elements an objective account attempts to minimize. But these are precisely what interest me. So, I have tried to make the fictional, the theoretical, and the factual speak to one another. In that conversation, if we can call it that, I have hoped to acknowledge and foreground as real and operative just those twists and turns, forgettings and rememberings, just those ghostly haunts that a normal social scientific account routinely attempts to minimize. I have hoped to find in writing that knows it is writing as such lessons for a mode of inscription that can critically question the limits of institutional discourse. More importantly, I have hoped to draw attention to a whole realm of experiences and social practices that can barely be approached without a method attentive to what is elusive, fantastic, contingent, and often barely there.

There is no question here of privileging Literature. Literature has its own problems or, rather, it has its own business. It has a history and a market that implicates it in the production of a highly ideological enterprise called Culture; part of its economy of literacy situates it within an academic discipline, literary criticism or now cultural studies, where particular struggles over value and access take precedence. My concern is unequivocally with social life, not with Literature as such (even if literature itself is, of course, riddled with the complications of the social life—my object of inquiry—it represents and sometimes influences). But fictions are what stand on the other side of the facts in our lingering Manichaean scheme, and so they have helped to highlight the problems with "logical and chronological frameworks" and "the simplicity of casual chains"; they have helped to show what "breaks through precisely where the [sociologist] assembles and joins" (Robin 1980: 234–35). It is precisely the relationship between what *assembles and joins* and what is gaping, detouring, and haunting that concerns me and is central to the cases I have analyzed. Fictionality and the inventiveness of social constructionism are not ends in themselves, however. They open the door to understanding haunting. Haunting is a part of our social world, and understanding it is essential to grasping the nature of our society and for changing it. Social life, especially when so fraught with ghosts, does not obey our rules of method and our disciplinary organization of it. We need not, however, find the loss of this deluding innocence so terribly frightening.

Ghostly Matters consists of five chapters that should be read sequentially, but can be read in any order you wish. In chapter 2, forced to take a detour, I go looking for a woman, Sabina Spielrein, who was not in a photograph in which she was supposed to be. I find her in psychoanalysis, the only human science that has taken haunting seriously as an object of analysis. But psychoanalysis does not know as much about haunting as it might seem. Chapters 3 and 4 venture to contemplate haunting and ghosts at the level of the making and unmaking of world historical events. Chapter 3, written around Luisa Valenzuela's novel *Como en la Guerra/He Who Searches*, is about the system of state terror known as disappearance in Argentina. Chapter 4, centered on Toni Morrison's novel *Beloved*, is about Reconstruction and the lingering inheritance of U.S. racial slavery. These chapters attempt to show how paying attention to ghosts can, among other things, radically change how we know and what we know about state terror and about slavery and the legacy of American freedom that derives from it. Chapter 5 concludes by way of a summary of the book's principal themes and lessons.

Specters are still haunting, not only in Europe and not only of communism. Our contemporary society is still a "society that has conjured up such gigantic means of production and of exchange . . . like the sorcerer, who is no longer able to control the powers of the nether world whom he has called up by his spells" (Marx and Engels [1888] 1973: 72). The task then remains to follow the ghosts and spells of power in order to tame this sorcerer and conjure otherwise.

The Weimar Congress, September 1911

2

distractions

Educated People

> All supposedly educated people have ceased to believe officially
> that the dead can become visible as spirits, and have made
> any such appearances dependent on improbable and remote
> conditions.   SIGMUND FREUD, "The Uncanny"[1]

Official suppositions give him away; Freud is not sure. After all, he is
trying to explain uncanny experiences and the haunted homes that they
are.[2] Haunted houses, frightening familiarities, animated doubles, words
and thoughts magically materialized into brute things, the effacement
of reality and imagination, involuntary repetitions. Freud is supposedly
an educated man. And that is why he will stick with all these ghostly
matters, elaborating them with keen precision and knowing, almost in-
tuitively, that the experience of the uncanny is not simply "intellectual
uncertainty." It is what I call being haunted, a state, I will emphasize
over and over again, that is not simply one of cognitive doubt, or of the
unknown, but something else. Psychoanalysis will have much to teach
us, then, about ghostly matters, obsessed as it is with the haunted lives
of modern supposedly educated Anglo-European people. And for this
singular obsession, oftentimes brilliant, we will pay our debt, even as
we long to be done with the inherited psychic life this imaginative science conjured up in the wake of "the *phantom objectivity* of capitalist
culture" (Taussig 1992: 4).[3] But Freud is an educated man, and on a
mission to create an official science, no less, and so he will, after entic-
ing us with marvelous and macabre stories, give up the ghost, so to
speak. I'll tell you a little story to show you what I mean.

31

The Pretense

> The creative writer can . . . choose a setting which . . . differ[s]
> from the real world by admitting . . . ghosts of the dead. So
> long as they remain within their setting of poetic reality, such
> figures lose any uncanniness which they might possess. . . . The
> situation is altered as soon as the writer pretends to move in
> the world of common reality. In this case he accepts as well all
> the conditions operating to produce uncanny feelings in real
> life; and everything that would have an uncanny effect in real-
> ity has it in his story.   SIGMUND FREUD, "The Uncanny"[4]

Some time ago, I was on my way to an official conference with an abstract and a promise. The path seemed straightforward. Challenges to
the traditional distinctions between fact and fiction, between truthful-
ness and falsity, between reality and fantasy, and between presenta-
tion and representation had beset the human sciences, arriving with a
double whammy, unsettling the basis of the sociological mission and
its methods. These challenges posed not only epistemological questions,
but also social ones of grave import. Under the sign of postmodernity,
paradigmatically new social realities—the collapse of Man and his
knowledge regimes, images of reality more real than the real itself, em-
pires speaking back, the dissolution of well-worn boundaries between
centers and margins, the migration of new peoples into established institutions and countries, the unprecedented mobility and flexibility of
capital, and so on—called for our attention. I promised to speak professionally about what kinds of methods could adequately study the cultural dimensions of these portentous events. I was on my way to a conference with an abstract and a promise. But then I got distracted by a
photograph and had to take a detour in order to follow the traces of
a woman ghost.

There's photographic evidence of her absence. I certainly would not
have noticed the fact that she was not there if I hadn't stumbled upon
her by accident. I found her in a book, entitled *A Secret Symmetry*, that
tells a somewhat remarkable story of her as a link, a point of exchange,
between two great men (Carotenuto 1984).[5] Remarkable, yet familiar,
an uncanny recognition of her story called out my desire to know more.
Feeling the abstract lose its grip, I began to search for the traces of a
ghost, a woman who, the book cover proclaimed, "changed the early
history of psychoanalysis"; changed that history by virtue of being there

between Carl Jung and Sigmund Freud and by virtue of not being in the photograph.

There's photographic evidence of her absence. The Third Psychoanalytic Congress took place at Weimar on September 21–22, 1911. The photograph, a group portrait resembling the kind usually taken once a year at school, displays around fifty well-dressed individuals, mostly men who seem indistinguishable from one another, the eight women sitting down in front. Sabina Spielrein is not there. In the past, she had refused to pose for the camera; there is another photograph of her surrounded by her father and brothers, shielding her face in that half-joking, half-serious way we have of looking when we are spoiling a good party. Far less jocular, even wrenching, is the description of Spielrein during her hospitalization for schizophrenia: she used to "cover her eyes with her hands—not even the world of images could get through, since all of her anxiety was projected onto them, transforming them into terrifying symbols" (S 151). Maybe she was afraid of her own image and the harm it might do her. Maybe she just did not want her picture taken. After all, she was supposed to be there. In a letter to Freud at the end of August 1911, Jung had listed her name—"Frl. Dr. Spielrein (!)"—as part of the "feminine element" representing Zurich (McGuire 1988: 440). In a diary entry written almost a year before the conference, Spielrein wrote, "In my imagination I already saw my friend [Jung] in love with her, I saw her sitting next to me at psychiatric congresses, she—proud and contented as wife and mother, I a poor psychopath who has a host of desires and can realize none of them; renouncing love, my soul rent with pain" (S 29).

The context for Spielrein's fantasy that Jung will fall in love with "her"—one of Spielrein's friends and fellow students—is Spielrein's anger at not being recognized as the source of the ideas presented in the other woman's dissertation: "The jewish girl forgets entirely that she owes her psychiatric knowledge to a large extent—if not completely—to me" (S 28). Here, the rivalry Spielrein experiences slips seamlessly between a desire for professional acknowledgment by Jung ("He will compare her analysis with mine, which, to be sure, is much more complicated, and he will think that mine is nothing special after all" [S 29]) and a desire for Jung himself. Spielrein had already "secretly" started to write her key work, "On the Death Instinct," and had already begun to "greatly fear that my friend [Jung], who planned to mention my idea in his article in July, saying that I have rights of priority, may simply borrow the whole development of the idea, because he now wants to refer to it as early as January. . . . I love him and hate him" (S 35). Spielrein's triangulated fantasies of love, ambition, knowledge, and rivalry, fantasies not entirely without basis given Jung's admission in *Memories, Dreams, Reflections* that "it was essentially because of them [the women patients] that I was able to strike out on new paths in therapy" (1965: 145), get increasingly complicated. From the treasonous girlfriend and the almost conventional by comparison threesome, she moves quickly in the diary to discuss the relationship between Freud and Jung, alternating between imagining Jung as her "little son" and imagining both herself and Jung as "married to Prof. Freud," and to express anxiety that Jung will fall in love with Freud's daughter, whom Spielrein considers another rival. It is no wonder Spielrein exclaims, "It is certainly a great relief to write a diary" (S 29).

A woman was supposed to be someplace, but she never arrived: "The Weimar Congress, organized by Jung and opening on 11 [*sic*] September 1911 was supposed to include Sabina Spielrein among its participants, as Jung himself informed Freud, but we know from a calm and lengthy letter written by Jung to Sabina that she had found a psychosomatic pretext for not going to Weimar" (S 182). A woman was supposed to be someplace, but only a pretext was woven and delivered.

Here is her story, seductively displayed on the back cover of *A Secret Symmetry,* an advertisement for a fascinating story, a story of fascinations: *Here is the fascinating story of Sabina Spielrein, a young Russian woman brought to Jung's psychiatric clinic in Zurich to be cured of a serious nervous disorder. Once cured of her illness, Spielrein falls deeply in love with her analyst. Despite his attraction to her, Jung chooses to break off the relationship when it threatens to cause a scandal. Spielrein then confides in Freud, Jung's mentor and father figure, and he becomes confessor to them both. Through Spielrein's diary and letters, published in paperback for the first time, the reader is presented with a rare glimpse into the essence of psychoanalytic work and into the lives of its key figures.* The advertisement does not mention that Spielrein wrote about the death drive ten years before Freud published his seminal work on the death instinct, *Beyond the Pleasure Principle* (1920); it does not mention that it might have been the love affair that "cured" her; and it does not mention the fact that Sabina Spielrein is not in the photograph of the participants at the Weimar Congress taken in the year she finished her dissertation.

The Photograph

The history of psychoanalysis and women's relation to it is inextricably bound up with the development and use of photography and the documentary image. For this we owe much to Jean-Martin Charcot's pioneering work on hysteria at the Salpêtrière clinic in Paris and his three-volume *Iconographie photographique de la Salpêtrière* (1876–80), a photographic-classificatory scheme of female hysteria. "But, as for the truth, I am absolutely only the photographer; I register what I see," said Charcot (quoted in Showalter 1985: 151). Charcot's early studies and public lectures on female hysteria were elaborately staged and theatricalized, documenting more than the signs of hysteria. As Elaine Showalter astutely points out, "Women were not simply photographed once, but again and again, so that they became used to the camera and to the special status they received as *photogenic subjects*" (1985: 152, emphasis added). Posed, stylized, and seductive, the hysterical image could have severe consequences: "During the period when [Augustine, a young girl who entered the hospital in 1875,] was being repeatedly photographed she developed a curious hysterical symptom: she began to see everything in black and white" (154).

Freud studied with Charcot from October 1885 to February 1886, but the replacement of the visual spectacle with the talking cure marks the transition, through Josef Breuer and Anna O, to psychoanalysis proper. The contradictory implications of the shift from the centrality of the visual and the spectacular to the oral and the interior have been well analyzed, especially by Clément (1987) and Rose (1983, 1986). Rose's argument is most apt here:

> [Freud] questioned the visible evidence of the disease—the idea that you could know a hysteric by looking at her body. . . . [B]y penetrating behind the visible symptoms of disorder and asking what it was that the symptom was trying to *say* . . . Freud could uncover . . . unconscious desires and motives. . . . Freud's challenge to the visible, to the empirically self-evident, to the 'blindness of the seeing eye' . . . can give us the strongest sense of the force of the unconscious as a concept against a fully social classification relying on empirical evidence as its rationale. (1983: 16)

There's photographic evidence of her absence. Sabina Spielrein is seemingly not in the photograph of the Weimar Congress participants taken in the year she finished her dissertation.

Repetition

> The factor of the repetition of the same thing will perhaps not
> appeal to everyone as a source of uncanny feeling. From what
> I have observed, this phenomenon does undoubtedly, subject
> to certain conditions and combined with certain circumstances,
> arouse an uncanny feeling, which, furthermore, recalls the
> sense of helplessness experienced in some dream-states.
>   SIGMUND FREUD, "The Uncanny"[6]

Sabina Spielrein saw spirits. *In my attacks of anguish it seemed to me
that an unknown force was trying to take me away. . . . I often had the
feeling of flying away, against my will. Animals and diseases, which I
imagined in the form of living beings, were trying to "do me harm" and
drag me into the fearful darkness of death* (S 152). Sabina Spielrein
haunts the institution of psychoanalysis. Her eerie story is haunting me,
an alibi of sorts for my concern with how we are going to inhabit, or
habituate ourselves to, what we think we already know about the delicate and fraught relation between the analyst and the analyzed, the subject and object of investigation, self and other, you and me, us and
them. Can a ghost really be a case?

   Some time ago, I was on my way to a conference with an abstract
and a promise, a woman also hoping to remember later that she too
was in the year she finished her dissertation. I was thinking about the
powerful appeal of Régine Robin's statement that "something crosses
over the disciplinary boundaries which only fiction can apprehend, like
a trace of unassumed contradictions, as the only way to designate the
locus of its own production" (1980: 235). The fictional, the made-up,
the invention that comes between me and my object of study and that is
the result of the encounter, a real thing. It is never fully ours for the
making, of course, and that is why those "unassumed contradictions"
come like traces, often remain as traces, the tracks of our fieldwork,
dragging all that construction into the relationship between me and
knowledge. That is also why we need to be careful not to forget the
institutional boundaries between a professional interest in facts and a
professional interest in fictions; why we need to be careful not to get
romantically attached to either literary criticism, another profession, or
to invention, constructionism, textuality, "the locus of [our] production[s]." Nonetheless a certain degree of impending helplessness was
troubling me. How in the world were we going to detect those unassumed contradictions materially, in a way that made them matter? And

so an abstract was written and it read partially, though thoroughly professionally, as follows:

Abstract. What mode of knowledge production is possible and adequate in the postmodern world? The ethnography is a principal research method for studying culture, our own and others', yet the status of the ethnography as a window on to the real has been rendered problematic (see Clifford and Marcus 1986; Clifford 1988; Marcus and Fischer 1986; [R.] Brown 1987; Clough 1986; [de] Certeau 1988). As sociologists, how do we rethink the ethnography, our primary story-telling device, in a world where the real is no longer self-evident, where the social fact may be more properly understood as an artifact, and where the description of cultural life is made problematic by the very mode of producing such a description? One of the key problems facing sociology and cultural study, more specifically, is to take up the historical, theoretical, and methodological challenges of our own changing cultural landscape and to grapple with issues related to the narrative structuring, fictive composition, and historical provisionality of claims to true knowledge. These issues have everything to do with how theories are inscribed socially and institutionally and are aggravated by "the often deluded sense of the state of theory produced by the narrow framing of the social terrain in which we do our intellectual work [and by] the uncanny ways in which traditionally male academic practices can return to haunt us even as we try to disavow them" (Nelson 1987: 155). This paper offers a meditation on the limits and possibilities of sociological method within our present, an historical conjuncture which, of necessity and desire, must question the boundaries separating the truth from delusion, the fact from the artifact, the visible from the invisible, science from literature, the ghost from the empirical, and the mode of producing knowledge from the product that mode creates.

In other words, fiction is getting pretty close to sociology. Social reality seems made-up and real at the same time. Lots of people claim to know this now; some claim to have known it all along. But what do we know, really, beyond this abstract collective cognitive familiarity with the making, the making-up, of social facts? There are thus good reasons to be suspicious of the abstract: the authoritative tone of the words, the materiality of its signification; the misleading staging of identifications—"we, as sociologists"; the emphasis on ethnography by someone who is not sure she really is an ethnographer; the imperial gestures of global academic relief—"the postmodern world, our present." I could fix these and fix nothing of what is inadequate in the perfectly respectable statement concerning the made-up and the making of social scientific stories, a concern that ought to have some urgency for sociologists, whose discipline, in one perhaps mythic rendering of it, mandates a curiosity about sociological modes of curiosity.

There is a certain degree of repetition here. It began with a question, *what method have you adopted for your research?* Or, more precisely, how can a fiction be data? What is this about ghosts and haunting? Why do you call it sociology? It began with a question demanding to know the implications of understanding the ethnography within an epistemology of the truth as partial, as an artifact of the complex social rituals, bound historically to modernity and its uncertain aftermath, that produce an understanding, a truth, the real. It became clear that they wanted to know—that they were drawn in despite their normal modes of curiosity—what it meant to understand the real as an effect (as something produced) and as an *affective relation* between analyst and analyzed, between I and it or them or you. They wanted to know how the real could be a powerful fiction that we do not experience as fictional, but as true. And they were concerned about the implications of understanding social relations as made-up *and* real because entrance into this place blurs the institutional, disciplinary, and political boundaries that separate the real from the fictive without in any way diminishing the powerful self-evidency of real fictions.

Some took comfort in the idea of discourse, relieved that "the fact that every object is constituted as an object of discourse has *nothing to do* with whether there is a world external to thought, or with the realism/idealism opposition" (Laclau and Mouffe 1985: 108). Some even turned the classification of discourse into its own social science (Ibarra and Kitsuse 1993). But something was missing. Ghosts in the house, skeletons in the closet, unseen forces broadcasting, large white men in uniforms with guns, invisible hands across the globe, polar bears in the zoo, contracts and property and markets and profits and the color line (see Williams 1991: 202–14; Gordon 1993). How can we tell the *difference* between the symbolic, the imaginary, and the real, they insisted? How can we *tell* the difference between one story and another's? It will all hinge, as we shall see, on that double modality of telling—to recount and to distinguish. But I was still struggling with acknowledging that sociology and its world of self-confident facts did not always seem more real than its haunting remainders, that I the analyst was negotiating with my so-called object of analysis to produce a true story. (The honest truth is that at that point any story would have done.) Perhaps my method was a mess. But, as I said all along, my interest in fictions was other than a strictly professional one.

There is a certain degree of repetition here. Why did they want to know the difference between all these things? Why was their desire to know so tenacious? I was thus struck by the answer Luce Irigaray gave to this question when asked by those judging her doctoral thesis defense. The question, *what method have you adopted for this research?* Her answer, "A delicate question. For isn't it the method, the path to knowledge, that has always also led us away, led us astray, by fraud and artifice" (Irigaray 1985: 150).

A detour has already begun. The question seems less than delicate; hard, actually. This is a hard question to answer and to be asked continually. It is a persistent question. One asked within a certain tone of voice, an almost imperceptible sigh of relief that the one asking is not the one answering; the sound also of a powerful demand to know, a distanced usually firm utterance capturing in its delivery the authority of the interrogator. I was a little nervous about my answer since I knew that Irigaray was later fired from her job for what appears to have been an improper defense of an institutional territory. Or how about Sabina Spielrein, whom I started to worry about too? Here was a woman who believed in the "prophetic powers of [her] unconscious" (S 39) and who thought, despite all the historical odds against such a thought, that schizophrenia, her burden, meant not "isolation from the world and the impossibility of being understood, but rather, a way of understanding the world and of expressing oneself" (S 146). Her method was inextricably linked to her unstable and "ill" condition and to everything that happened to her in the process of being cured or analyzed. Led away from schizophrenia and toward being a psychoanalyst, going somewhere else, she was also led astray. And into all that nasty trouble with Freud and Jung, both of whose actions involved elements of artifice and fraud: Jung lying in his letters to Freud and Sabina's mother about the nature of his involvement with her and about the quality of her work; Freud using Spielrein's relationship with Jung as a moral cover for his theoretical disagreements and professional rivalry with Jung, making the break from "Dear Friend" to "Dear Doctor" on Sabina's time.

Sabina Spielrein transferred from one field, madness, into another, psychoanalysis, and the story of that fieldwork traces the institutional markings of heterosexual desire within an intellectual enterprise, within the institution of psychoanalysis itself. It also traces the making of a ghost. Spielrein's fieldwork, dealing with the spirits and the real famous men who haunted her, was a risky business. She moved into the shadows of psychoanalysis and she never made it to the Weimar Conference. Of her paper on the death drive written ten years before his own "seminal" study was published, Freud had this to say: "her destructive drive is not much to my liking, because I believe it is personally conditioned. She seems abnormally ambivalent" (S 146). Jung, after having written to Spielrein to compliment her study on its "extraordinarily intelligent and . . . excellent ideas," wrote to Freud: "One must say: *desinat in piscem mulier formosa superne* [what at top is a lovely woman ends below in a fish]. . . . She has . . . fallen flat in this paper because it is not thorough enough. . . . Besides that her paper is heavily over-weighted with her own complexes" (S 183). As we shall see, those ever-present complex conditions will stalk psychoanalysis and Freud, in particular, like the "rising" of "renegade ghosts" (T. Davis 1978).

Something is missing its mark. A detour has already begun. *What method have you adopted for this research? A delicate question. For isn't it the method, the path to knowledge, that has always also led us away . . . by fraud and artifice?* The question of method may be a matter of fraud and artifice, but they wanted to know how to tell the difference between one story and another, and in order to try to provide some clues it will be necessary to speak of ghosts and hauntings and crazy women and territorial dislocations. It will be necessary to take a detour.

A sentence about the duplicity of method is pursuing a rigorous abstract promising to demonstrate the fabulations of powerful claims to knowledge, promising to give *evidence* of the factual's always encroaching other and its claims on truthful knowledge. Irigaray continues, "It was . . . necessary to note the way in which the method is never as simple as it purports to be" (Irigaray 1985: 150). What I am trying to write about, to evoke for you, is not only how the method "is never as simple as it purports to be," but also how focusing on the question of method at the metadiscursive level allows us to pass quietly over the least methodical places in our work as analysts, as intellectuals, the places where our discourse is unauthorized by virtue of its unruliness. The detour takes us away from abstract questions of method, from bloodless professionalized questions, toward the materiality of institutional storytelling, with all its uncanny repetitions. The detour takes us away from abstract questions of method into what lies outside the metadiscursive talk about method, which is, well, us, our involvement, or at least our unruliness and sometimes our rudeness. Theodor Adorno once said that "the traumatic is the abstract" (1968: 80) and as usual he understood the counterintuitive truth of switching the normal poles of negative and positive thinking. The detour picks up, then, where abstractions leave off. It picks up at the point where all those vectors of power pulsing through the analytic scene converge in our desire to know and to stay awhile, there, where in normal social science the method usually cleans up all traces of this unruliness, later after the fact.

Let me therefore write a different abstract. In what fields does field-work occur? "How precisely, is a garrulous, overdetermined . . . en-counter shot through with power relations and personal cross-purposes circumscribed as an adequate version of a more or less discrete 'other world' composed by an individual author?" (Clifford 1988: 25). Pre-cisely how will we evoke the path to knowledge, with all its detours, within an institution like the First World Academy that is "shot through with power relations and personal cross-purposes" and yet so effectively disavows the "strategically repressed marks of the so-called private" (Spivak 1987: 15)? Along circuitous paths, we enter into and exit out of our accounts, which are also shot through willy-nilly with power relations and personal cross-purposes. There is no free space here; everybody pays. And so we will need to invent other forms of cu-riosity to engage those haunting moments that take us down the path of the helplessly repetitive, of the fictional pretense, of the contradictory, of the ghostly, in order to capture back all that must be circumscribed in order to produce the "adequate" version. Sometimes this will involve the so-called private, sometimes not, even though I am clearly flaunting the impropriety of the autobiographical gesture here in Spielrein's name, even though her story differs markedly from my own. Perhaps the key methodological question is not *what method have you adopted for this research?* But what paths have been disavowed, left behind, covered over and remain unseen? In what fields does fieldwork occur?

The Psychoanalytic Field

> About 'and/or of psychoanalysis.' . . . It seems to me that this elaboration is surely not possible so long as psychoanalysis remains within its own field.
> LUCE IRIGARAY, *This Sex Which Is Not One*[7]

I was on my way to a conference with an abstract and a promise but then I got distracted by a photograph and had to take a detour into psychoanalysis in order to follow the traces of a ghost, a woman who never made it to the conference that she had planned to attend.

Sabina Spielrein transferred from one field, madness, into another, psychoanalysis, and so we will go to psychoanalysis because that is where Sabina Spielrein lives and because that is where the human sciences have been most willing to entertain ghostly matters. Why the detour? It is really very simple. The focus within psychoanalysis on desire, power, fantasy, and memory helps me to understand why I am haunted by a woman ghost; why the memory of her absence in a photo (which is both a real memory and an analytic staging) makes me attentive to the systematic exclusions produced by the assumptions and practices of a normalized social science. These normal methods foreclose the recognition of the exclusions and the sacrifices required to tell a story as the singularly real one. As we will see, Freud will disappoint, but at least he "problematizes any statement of method that would begin, putatively, 'I choose because . . .'" (Spivak 1985: 257). The difficulty of articulating what produces stories such as Spielrein's (a story overcharged by being *in* psychoanalysis) leads me to where storytelling is at least problematized. In order to write about invisibilities and hauntings—a dead woman was not at a conference she was supposed to attend—requires attention to what is not seen, but is nonetheless powerfully real; requires attention to what appears dead, but is nonetheless powerfully alive; requires attention to what appears to be in the past, but is nonetheless powerfully present; requires attention to just who the subject of analysis is. To the extent that psychoanalysis is concerned with exploring and transforming scenes in which these binary oppositions (visible/invisible, real/imaginary, dead/alive, past/present) are experienced as both fluid and maddening, it may have some lessons for those of us also undertaking analysis that we think is of a different kind.[8]

Transference

> I see absolutely no difference between transference to the doctor and every other sort of transference: in giving one's own personality, one takes on the personality of the Other, whom one loves.
> *A Secret Symmetry: Sabina Spielrein between Jung and Freud*[9]

Within the analytic scene stories are accomplished or enacted within a field of intersubjectivity that psychoanalysis calls the transference-countertransference. The transference-countertransference is a chaotic field of energy in which, by virtue of the compelling force of that field, memories are remembered and forgotten, desires are forged and re-forged, and a story is the affective consequence of the dynamics of speaking and listening within a dyadic relation.

> It's a question of transferring not only old desires but also, continuously, what comes up in the real, what the patient imagines has existed. This is not the precise meaning dictionaries of psychoanalysis give to the word transference which describes, rather, a 'process' of fixation on the person of the analyst. But the word draws its own myth in its wake, and carries psychoanalysis back to its anchorage, to the very place it refuses to take into consideration. Transference onto the psychoanalyst; the transfer(ence) of populations; the crossing of streams, adrift, at the mercy of the waves of the river. (Clément 1987: 75)

It is the recognition of the transference, a demand "that insists on being recognized as *real*" (Rose 1986: 42) that throws into crisis what had previously been taken to be the real crisis (i.e., the "original" reason for the analysis). As Freud notes, "There is a complete change of scene; it is as though some piece of make-believe had been stopped by the sudden irruption of reality" (quoted in Rose 1986: 42–43; Freud 1914: 162). *It's a question of transferring not only old desires but also, continuously, what comes up in the real, what the patient imagines has existed.* A young Russian woman is suffering from a schizophrenic disturbance or severe hysteria. She enters as an object into analysis, as a subject to be transformed. Something happens in that field that paperback books call a love affair between the doctor and the patient, and that psychoanalytic books call a transference-countertransference. In either case, a reality is imagined and enacted. She is cured of her "original" illness but now suffers from unrequited love, or suffers from the real impact of being the ghostly object of the psychoanalyst's desire. She becomes an analyst too, writes a diary and about death. Her lover-doctor writes about "Her" as the devil within his soul, gives this a name (the anima) for science's sake, and later forgets about her when he writes a very long essay on transference, but remembers that the transference has something to do with alchemy and transformations (Jung 1954). For his part, Freud will insist on the different positions patient and analyst must occupy in order for these transferential affairs to remain on track: the patient always resisting, acting out rather than actively remembering, the analyst always productive in his distanced scientific involvement.

But the analyst and the patient are not as different as all that, and so an acknowledgment of the transferential relations in any analytic encounter suggests that our field is often not what we thought it was, that the reality the analyst tests is subject to and is the subject of reversals, displacements, and overdeterminations.

> Academically, the term "field" refers simply to some relatively circumscribed and abstract area of study. However, that particular sense gives no indication of how scholars operationally relate to their field; that is, *how* they study it. When we add the term "research" [or work, as in fieldwork] . . . this adds a locative property. [It tells us that a researcher is in a field or fields.] . . . The field researcher understands that his field—whatever its substance—is continuous with other fields and bound up with them in various ways. (Schatzman and Strauss 1973: 1–2)

If the fields that are bound up with and overdetermine any analytic encounter are not just other academic fields, or the sociohistorical in the abstract, but the field of transformation that draws us in and sometimes away, then the "real story" is always a negotiated interruption of that seemingly two-party system of analyst and analysand. Traversing fields, the story must emerge out of the field of forces that *really* attract and distract the storyteller, out of the encounter with the oftentimes barely visible presence of the several other parties or things moving in and out of the analytic scene, out of a kind of haunting.

But also out of a "will to heal": "What is at stake, then, in this passage, is help—recourse and relief. To become an analyst, one must have had the ideal at least once, in this form: *the will to heal*" (Clément 1987: 75). This might account for Bettelheim's evaluation of Spielrein's cure. "The most significant event in Spielrein's young life was that whatever happened during her treatment by Jung at the Burgholzli . . . call it treatment, seduction, transference, love, mutual daydreams, delusions or whatever . . . it cured her. True, Spielrein paid a very high price in unhappiness, confusion, and disillusion for the particular way in which she got cured, but then . . ." (S xxxviii). It is more than expensive. There are real limits to the psychoanalytic transference and its curing rituals.

But then, "for women it is of particular importance that we find a language which allows us to recognise our part in intolerable structures—but in a way which renders us neither the pure victims nor the sole agents of our distress" (Rose 1986: 14). Many of us, including especially feminists, have wanted and needed an "unequivocal accusation of the real" (ibid.: 12), an empirical safety net, access to what really happened, to challenge the powerful mechanisms that structure our exclusions, pains, and pleasures. Maybe this is because there has been no room within the academic institution for staging the kinds of rememberings the (psycho)analytical situation at least allows, for analytically inhabiting a really shifting reality. But there, too, the hope was that in opening up those "strategically repressed" markings again, a transferring, a transformation, would occur. And this repetition the (psycho)analysis strives to accomplish by situating a story of the present as a complex staging of a past remembered and forgotten. But this past is barely the origin of the story. A memory is never simply repeated within analysis because there was never a memory as a thing to remember in the first place. The repetition is always a repetition-as-displacement. The transference creates a "complete change of scene," a memory of the present.

Psychoanalysis recognized the importance of transference, "from one stage to the next, from one wish to the next," but it could not turn that recognition with all its consequences for the analytic relation into an institutional practice, into *the transfer(ence) of populations; the crossing of streams, adrift, at the mercy of the waves of the river* (Clément 1987: 74–75). Because of this failure, among other things, women's stories remained the seductive object of an analysis of secret symmetries based on a "model privileging symmetry as the possible condition for mastery in the non-recognition of the other" (Irigaray 1985: 128). Sabina Spielrein saw *absolutely no difference between transference to the doctor and every other sort of transference,* giving over to what one loves a recognition of the complicated love relation between oneself and another. This love is not mystical or a mystification; it is the intimacy of a contact with another, often asymmetrical, usually fragile and fraught with the strains of mastery. It is a prerequisite to sensuous knowledge.

The Unconscious

> In setting itself the task of making the discourse of the unconscious speak through consciousness, psychoanalysis is advancing in the direction of that fundamental region in which the relations of representation . . . come into play. Whereas all the human sciences advance towards the unconscious only with their back to it, waiting for it to unveil itself as fast as conscious-

ness is analyzed, as it were backwards, psychoanalysis, on the other hand, points directly towards it, with a deliberate purpose—not towards that which must be rendered gradually more explicit by the progressive illumination of the implicit, but towards what is there and yet is hidden, towards what exists with the mute solidity of a thing, of a text closed in upon itself, or of a blank space in a visible text. . . . [P]sychoanalysis moves towards the moment . . . at which the contents of consciousness articulate themselves, or rather stand gaping.

MICHEL FOUCAULT, *The Order of Things*[10]

The unconscious draws us, as social analysts, into another *region* or field where things are *there and yet hidden,* where things *stand gaping,* where the question of how we present a world, our own or another's, becomes a question of the limits of representation. We enter a kind of disturbance zone where things are not always what they seem, where they are animated by invisible forces whose modes of operation work according to their own logics. The world of the unconscious is far away from that of the contemporary social scientist whose scientific covenant is precisely to ward off the mythological, the place where things stand gaping—even if Michel Foucault identified a certain common field for psychoanalysis and social anthropology, a promise, more accurately, of "the possibility of a discourse that could move from one to the other, . . . the double articulation of the history of individuals upon the unconscious of culture, and of the historicity of those cultures upon the unconscious of individuals" (1973: 379).

The unconscious means everything to psychoanalysis and so it is worth looking at Freud's justification for it. He did not have to begin the way he did. He could have just said that the unconscious is *not* a commonsensical concept or a logical result of careful steps taken to advance previously held views about repression. He could have just said that it is not like anything we have ever seen before. But he did not. To justify the concept of the unconscious, Freud begins with the dialectic of self and other, with identification and otherness, with our experiences of similitude and dissimilarity in people and things: "By the medium of consciousness each one of us becomes aware only of his own states of mind" (Freud 1915: 119).[11] We know other people possess consciousness because we identify with them in order that they may be "intelligible to us": "Without any special reflection we impute to everyone else our own constitution and therefore also our consciousness, and . . . this identification is a necessary condition of understanding in us" (Ucs 119). This identification with others, our sense of intelligible connection, "was formerly extended . . . to other human beings, to animals, plants, inanimate matter and to the world at large." We no longer presume that plants and animals possess a correspondence with us we call consciousness and we "relegate to mysticism the assumption of its existence in inanimate matter" and in "*the world at large*" (Ucs 119, emphasis added).

This identification with the consciousness of others is uncertain, Freud says, because it relies only on an inference that it is like our own. This uncertainty turns back upon us as we leave our former state in which we could conceive of an intelligible, if not also enchanted, connection to the world at large. If we upend that uncertainty, that inferential moment, onto ourselves, "we must say that all the acts and manifestations which I notice in myself and do not know how to link up with the rest of my mental life must be judged as if they belonged to someone else and are to be explained by the . . . life ascribed to that person" (Ucs 120). Here, Freud is very close to suggesting that the unconscious is inconceivable outside of the worldly relations that structure the encounter between myself and another and that bring the encounter inside as my own otherness I cannot explain without knowing something of the life world from which the other came.

That is not what he wants to say, though. Thus "this method of inference, applied to oneself in spite of inner opposition, does not lead to the discovery of an unconscious, but leads logically to the assumption of another, second consciousness which is united in myself with the consciousness I know" (Ucs 120). The problem with this view is clear to Freud: "a consciousness of which its own possessor knows nothing is something very different from that of another person" (Ucs 120). Freud moves quickly from things I notice in myself and do not know how to link up with the rest of my life to things "having characteristics and peculiarities which seem alien to us, or even incredible" (Ucs 121) to a something of which I know "nothing." But this is the Freudian unconscious he is inventing, the self-contained closed system, inaccessible to worldly consciousness, accessible only to a certain kind of analysis competent in treating its symptoms.

But Freud cannot quite get away from the possibility that the unconscious derives its characteristic force from its role as the place where all the others out there in the world and their life come inside me and unhinge my sense of self as they make me what I am, as they live within me: "We must be prepared . . . to assume the existence not only of a second consciousness in us, but of a third and fourth also, perhaps an infinite series of states of consciousness, each and all unknown to us and to one another" (Ucs 120). What could we understand by these multiplying—into infinity, no less—consciousnesses if not the specter of all those "someone elses" *unknown to us and to one another* taking residence within us, without our full permission, making us who we are yet alien to ourselves, showing up in "incredible" forms? Here in this small moment where Freud is vexed by the possibility of conceiving the unconscious as the life of others and other things within us, the specter of a social unconscious raises its head. The Freudian unconscious is not a social unconscious.[12] But his early conceptualization of the unconscious remains haunted by its origins in the fundamental encounter between self and world, between me and you:

> The psychoanalytic assumption of the unconscious . . . appears to us a further development of that primitive animism which caused our own consciousness to be reflected in all around us, and, on the other hand, it seems to be an extension of the corrections begun by Kant . . . [who] warned us not to overlook the fact that our perception is subjectively conditioned and must not be regarded as identical with the phenomena perceived but never really discerned. (Ucs 121)[13]

Freud will not entirely resolve the ambivalence surrounding the unconscious and its social origins until, oddly enough, he turns his attention to civilized society in decline. At that point, the theory of the drives will eliminate the possibility of elaborating an idea crucial to psychoanalysis and to a social psychoanalysis, namely, "that all reality undergoes modification upon entering the unconscious" (Adorno 1968: 80). Instead, as Adorno carefully observes, "the psychic is made into an historical event." Freud's initial understanding of the unconscious, tied as it is to otherness and to animism, might have been a more fruitful path. For what does animism represent if not the idea that everything in the world outside yourself is alive, perhaps with designs on you, clearly capable of quietly creeping in or noisily invading, assuredly in the same field as you? Freud's science will try, once and for all, to rid itself of all vestiges of animism by making all the spirits or the hauntings come from the unconscious, from inside the troubled individual, an individual, we might note, who had become increasingly taken with the animation of the commodity world. Freud's mature unconscious replaces the origins of haunting in the worldly contact between self and other, in what Michael Taussig calls the dialectic of "mimesis and alterity" (1993a), with what Adorno calls an "ontological property" (1968: 80). Freud will try to demystify our holdover beliefs in the power of the *world at large*, hoping to convince us that everything that seems to be coming at us from the outside is really coming from this now shrunken inside, tormented by its own immortality. Maybe Freud's unconscious is a brilliant description of "the subjective conditions of objective irrationality" (Adorno 1967: 68). Maybe the separation of society and psyche is the consciousness of a modern capitalist society "whose unity resides not in being unified" (ibid.: 69). But it is not enough. And Freud almost knows this too since uncanny experiences are where the unconscious rejoins its animistic and social roots, where we are reminded that what lies between society and psyche is hardly an inert empty space.

The Wolf

I sat down to the work I had earlier planned on doing, that is, reading his [Jung's] paper. After only a few lines I was completely entranced by him again; it struck me as so silly to have to talk with this brilliant person about such trivialities as his own bad manners, when we had so many really interesting topics of discussion. . . . In the evening I learned I had done my friend an injustice; that very day he had had a little girl and could not leave his wife. This information was understandably both gratifying and painful, yet I had myself well in hand and went back to work. When I looked at myself in the mirror before going to bed, I was taken aback; that couldn't be me, that stony gray face with the uncannily grim, burning black eyes staring out at me: it was a powerful, baleful wolf that lurked there coldly in the depths and would halt at nothing. "What is it that you want?" I asked myself in horror. Then I saw all the lines in the room go crooked; everything became alien and terrifying. "The great chill is coming . . ." (S 19).

Sometime in the evening of an unknown day in September 1910, Sabina Spielrein looked at herself in the mirror and saw a wolf. She had had an up and down day, by turns feeling "happy and foolish," "weary" and angry (S 18–19). September had been like that and she had been writing in her diary regularly. She looked into the mirror and saw a wolf. Everything that differentiates her experience of the uncanny from Freud's rests on what she did next. She spoke to it, asking it what it wanted. And lo and behold, it answered back. "The great chill is coming." Terrified in a familiar room become alien, in that quintessential space of the uncanny, the haunted house, she saw herself animistically, as if herself and yet unknown, a stranger. Whatever her fear—and it must have been great indeed since she believed in spirits—she nonetheless listened to the wolf, knowing it was in some way identified with her. And the funny thing is she went to bed and woke up the next morning feeling "transformed": "The air was cool, and I breathed in the coolness ecstatically" (S 19).

The Uncanny

Freud published "The Uncanny" in the fall of 1919, harking back to "Animism, Magic and the Omnipotence of Thoughts" in *Totem and Taboo* (1913) and prefiguring the elaboration of the compulsion to repeat found in *Beyond the Pleasure Principle* (1920), Spielrein's text. "The Uncanny" is, among other things, an important bridge between Freud's first and second systems or topographies, a resting or wrestling place, depending on your point of view (cf. Hertz 1985), before Freud undertakes the reconsideration of his major theories in *Beyond the Pleasure Principle* (see Laplanche and Pontalis 1973). The details of Freud's reappraisal do not concern me here, although it is fair to say that the concern with ghosts persists and could even be said to be enhanced by Freud's adoption of the notion of the death instinct (see Rickles 1988, 1991). My concern is much more simple. What happens when Freud begins not with neurosis, but with uncanny experiences? What do we learn about haunting?

Quite a good deal descriptively. We learn that uncanny experiences are "qualities of feeling," something like what Raymond Williams called a structure of feeling. Uncanny experiences are haunting experiences. There is something there and you "feel" it strongly. It has a shape, an electric empiricity, but the evidence is barely visible, or highly symbolized. The investigation of these qualities of feelings is, according to Freud, a more properly aesthetic than psychoanalytic topic of inquiry (U 219) since Freud, drawing on Kant, associates aesthetic judgment with a "critical . . . 'primitive' mentality" (Pietz 1993: 139). We learn that uncanny experiences are usually frightening. We learn that "doubts whether an apparently animate being is really alive; or conversely, whether a lifeless object might not be in fact animate" (U 226) arouse uncanny feelings. We learn that all manner of phantom doubles conjure up "archaic" desires for dead things to come alive, a haunting experience, if nonetheless increasingly common in the modern world. We learn that involuntary repetition, recalling a "sense of helplessness experienced in some dream-states . . . surrounds what would otherwise be innocent enough with an uncanny atmosphere, and forces upon us the idea of something fateful and inescapable" (U 237). We learn that the "idea that the world was peopled with the spirits of human beings . . . the belief in the omnipotence of thoughts and the techniques of magic based on that belief . . . the attribution of various persons and things of carefully graded magical powers" (U 240) linger and sometimes touch us, haunting us with the "residues" of what we have lost. We learn that "many people experience the [uncanny] feeling in the highest degree in relation to death and dead bodies, to the return of the dead, and to spirits and ghosts" (U 241). We learn that "we can speak of a living person as uncanny" (U 243). We learn that some people find psychoanalysis itself uncanny since it lays "bare . . . hidden forces" (U 243). We learn that "an uncanny effect is often and easily produced when the distinction between image and reality is effaced, as when something that we have hitherto regarded as imaginary appears before us in reality, or when a symbol takes over the full functions of the thing it symbolizes, and so on" (U 244). We learn that when you are haunted or having an uncanny experience, you feel like there are ghosts in your house (U 225). You are not homesick, nor are you simply in a state of intellectual doubt or uncertainty in the face of a new or foreign reality you have not mastered yet (U 221). Rather, something familiar "and old-established in the mind and which has become alienated from it . . . through the process of repression" (U 241) has transmuted into an unsettling specter. This is important. We are haunted by somethings we have been involved in, even if they appear foreign, alien, far away, doubly other. Finally, we learn—and this is a remarkable admission given his life and work—that Freud himself feels a "special obtuseness in the matter, where extreme delicacy of perception would be more in place. It is long since he has experienced or heard of anything which has given him an uncanny impression." He will try to "translate himself into that state of feeling, by awakening in himself the possibility of experiencing it." But "such difficulties make themselves powerfully felt" (U 220).

Freud divides uncanny experiences into two classes, those that arise from the revival of "repressed infantile complexes, from the castration complex, womb-phantasies, etc." (U 248) and those that arise from the return of "surpassed" "primitive beliefs." ("An uncanny experience occurs either when infantile complexes which have been repressed are once more revived by some impression, or when primitive beliefs which have been surmounted seem once more to be confirmed" [U 249]). The revival of repressed infantile complexes and the return of surpassed primitive beliefs link uncanny experiences to "remote" (in the first case) and "improbable" (in the second case) conditions. Since Freud's enterprise involves the scientific description and explanation of the proximity of the remote (the past that is in the present, the childhood that is in adulthood, the dead that are in the living), the first class of uncanny experiences provides less explanatory trouble for him (and requires far less of his attention in the essay) since he has a handle on infantile complexes. They explain all manner of unsettling occurrences, including Freud's own always tremulous relationship to all the stories in which he traffics, including the seeming persistence of "primitive" beliefs or experiences: "primitive beliefs are most intimately connected with infantile complexes, and are, in fact, based on them" (U 249).

The significance of the "Uncanny" essay here is not so much that Freud says that animism is culture's infantile thought, thereby attempting to absorb these two classes into one, but rather that he admits, and is troubled by, the presence of uncanny experiences that are not reducible to the acting out of an individual's psychic state. Indeed, Freud goes so far as to concede that uncanny experiences based on repressed infantile complexes are far less frequent than the other type:

> Let us take the uncanny associated with the omnipotence of thoughts, with the prompt fulfillment of wishes, with secret injurious powers and with the return of the dead. The condition under which the feeling of uncanniness arises here is unmistakable. We—or our primitive forefathers— once believed that they actually happened. Nowadays we no longer believe in them, we have *surmounted* these modes of thoughts; but we do not feel quite sure of our new beliefs, and the old ones still exist within us ready to seize upon any confirmation. As soon as something *actually happens* in our lives which seems to confirm the old, discarded beliefs we get a feeling of the uncanny; it is as though we were making a judgment something like this: 'So, after all, it is *true* that one can kill a person by the mere wish!' or, 'So the dead *do* live on and appear on the scene of their former activities!' and so on. (U 247–48)

There is an elaborate set of qualifications and distinctions Freud makes as he figures out how to deal with a set of uncanny experiences he cannot quite assimilate to repressed childhood wishes.[14] Among the most important is his concern that we understand that psychic life is not subject to the same "reality-testing" as real life. The unconscious has its own rules and regulations, and its procedures are not to be evaluated with reference to the outside real world or to conscious beliefs about what comprises it: "Where the uncanny comes from infantile complexes the question of material reality does not arise; its place is taken by psychical reality. What is involved is an actual repression of some content of thought and a return of this repressed content, not a cessation of *belief in the reality* of such a content. We might say that in the one case what had been repressed is a particular ideational content, and in the other the belief in its (material) reality" (U 249). This is a difficult passage, but important because the distinction Freud is making is designed to ensure that being haunted remains either a question of repression, the sine qua non of psychic life, or "purely an affair of 'reality-testing.'" Thus,

> anyone who has completely and finally rid himself of animistic beliefs will be insensible to this [animistic] type of the uncanny. The most remarkable coincidences of wish and fulfillment, the most mysterious repetition of similar experiences in a particular place or on a particular date, the most deceptive sighs and suspicious noises—none of these things will disconcert him or raise the kind of fear which can be described as . . . 'uncanny'. The whole thing is purely an affair of 'reality-testing', a question of the material reality of the phenomena. (U 248)

Having admitted a form of haunting that does not track itself back to the individual's personal psychic life, Freud is ready to minimize its significance before the discussion even begins. Where psychoanalysis, as a mode of thought or analysis, considers itself capable of identifying the visible and disquieting symptoms of repression and bringing their origins and nature to light, "reality-testing" simply refutes the reality of haunting by treating it as matter of lingering superstition. *But it is precisely the experience of being haunted in the "world of common reality," the unexpected arrival of ghosts or wolves or eerie photographs, that troubles or even ruins our ability to distinguish reality and fiction, magic and science, savage and civilized, self and other, and in those ways gives to reality a different coloring.* The "reality-testing" that we might want to perform in the face of hauntings must first of all admit those hauntings as real.

I was sitting alone in my wagon-lit *compartment when a more than usually violent jolt of the train swung back the door of the adjoining washing-cabinet, and an elderly gentleman in a dressing-gown and a traveling cap came in. I assumed that in leaving the washing-cabinet, which lay between the two compartments, he had taken the wrong direction and come into my compartment by mistake. Jumping up with the intention of putting him right, I at once realized to my dismay that the intruder was nothing but my own reflection in the looking-glass on the open door. I can still recollect that I thoroughly disliked his appearance. Instead, therefore, of being frightened by . . . [my] 'double' . . . I simply failed to recognize . . . [it] as such. Is it not possible, though, that [my] dislike of [it] was a vestigial trace of the archaic reaction which feels the 'double' to be something uncanny?* (U 248).

Freud is on the train alone in his compartment. The door is flung open and an elderly gentleman enters. It is a mistake. He is an intruder. Freud jumps up to correct the old man and to send him where he belongs, elsewhere. When he does, he sees that the old man "was nothing but" himself reflected in the mirror. Freud was not afraid, he just "thoroughly" disliked the appearance.

The uncanny is drawing Freud away from himself. He looks in the mirror and sees an elderly man, an appearance distasteful to him. He is not himself, he is strange, a stranger to himself. Freud does not believe in ghosts, but he cannot quite get it out of his mind that he might be having an "archaic" reaction, that the vestiges of an old animism have stalked him to the train. There is no expectation that Freud could turn his attention to the colonialism that partially underwrites his distaste for the specter of primitive thinking inhabiting his civilized mind, much less his train compartment. But we might have expected less denial of what is uncanny in this situation. What is unsettling Freud in the train is not the animism of dead souls per se, but his own self become strange. Freud's haunting experience consists of his looking into a mirror and seeing an alienating figure that turns out to be him too. What Freud calls the archaic here is the recognition of himself as another, as a stranger, the arrival of the person from elsewhere, from the world outside himself, from what we call the social.

Freud might have called the primitive or the archaic the social and thereby have supplemented the Marxist notion of estrangement. The social is ultimately what the uncanny is about: being haunted in the *world of common reality*. To be haunted is not a contest between animism and a discrediting reality test, nor a contest between the unconscious and the conscious faculties. It is an enchanted encounter in a disenchanted world between familiarity and strangeness. The uncanny is the return, in psychoanalytic terms, of what the concept of the unconscious represses: the reality of being haunted by worldly contacts. This is why Spielrein's uncanny experience is so significant by contrast to Freud's. It does not return to that clawing narcissism Freud consistently misattributes to animism as a mode of apprehending the totality of the world (see *Totem and Taboo*) and then to its lingering remains. And indeed, to the extent that "primitive" animism "assumed the existence of a unified causal field for personal actions and physical events, thereby positing reality as subject to animate powers whose purposes could be divined and influenced" (Pietz 1993: 137–38), it has a complex and expanded notion of causality that is exactly the opposite of narcissism's tendency to reduce the magic of social encounters to the realm of the self.[15] There is a small opening in Spielrein's experience of selfsameness and frightening otherness and it is all because, despite her fear, she talks to the wolf, listens to its answer, and believes in the transformative power of the encounter. It is just a small opening, but very critical nonetheless.

"The Uncanny" is a bridge text into the decade of Freud's most advanced social thinking. Throughout the 1920s and into his last works of the 1930s, in *Beyond the Pleasure Principle* (1920), *Group Psychology and the Analysis of the Ego* (1921), "Dreams and Telepathy" (1922), *The Future of an Illusion* (1927), *Civilization and Its Discontents* (1930), and *Moses and Monotheism* (1937–39), Freud is deeply concerned, haunted you might say, by society and its institutions. Yet their force in the life of the individual is consistently overwhelmed, if not disavowed, by his discovery of the drives and by his archetypal histories. Having repudiated Jung's unconscious and its archetypes, it is surprising indeed that Freud brings them back into history itself. But this is the path he takes, joining haunting to drives, to predetermined family romances, and to a prehistoric past. This affiliation is a kind of haunting memory. Freud forgets about Spielrein's role and the nature of her role in all his thinking about repetition, death, and the decline of civilization.

The layers of institutional memory and amnesia run deep in psychoanalysis:

Can we make a story out of it? . . . For example, could we say that the theory of repetition Freud worked out in March 1919 followed close upon—
was a consequence of—his realization that he was once again caught in a
certain relationship to Tausk [a colleague and follower]? Could we add that
Freud was bound to perceive that relation as uncanny—not quite literary,
but no longer quite real, either, the workings of the compulsion glimpsed
"through" an awareness of something-being-repeated? Could we go on to
suggest that it was this experience of a repetitive triangular relationship
that underwrites his analysis of "The Sandman" in May? That is, that the
glimpse of his relationship to Tausk has the same "documentary" status
vis-a-vis Freud's retelling of "The Sandman." (Hertz 1985: 117–18)

Hertz's explanation of Freud's insight about the uncanniness of involuntary repetition itself is intriguing given the existence of the Spielrein/
Jung/Freud triangle some ten years earlier. Hertz does not mention this
triangle, but it provides more evidence for his case as well as some
twists since Spielrein was the first to present completed work on the
death instinct. There are two moments key to Hertz's analysis, the first
in 1912 when Lou Andreas-Salomé arrived in Vienna and a relationship developed between Salomé, Tausk, and Freud, characterized by the
usual rivalries. Sabina Spielrein was present at the Wednesday meetings
of the Psychoanalytic Society in Vienna when Salomé arrived; she had
been in Vienna since October 1911 and remained there until March
1912, when she moved to Berlin. She "spoke up for the first time" in
the first week of November 1911, "intelligently" and "methodically,"
according to Freud's letter to Jung of November 12, 1911 (McGuire
1988: 458). What's more, she presented her paper on the death instinct
("Die Destruktion als Ursache des Werdens") on November 29, 1911, as
Freud also reported to Jung in his letter of November 30, 1911 (ibid.:
469). Freud had not yet decided that he didn't understand it (1920: 55
n1). Quite the contrary, and he noted that its delivery was "followed by
an illuminating discussion." Spielrein was still a "little girl" in Freud's
eyes and still primarily a medium for Jung's ideas: "I have hit upon a
few objections to your . . . method of dealing with mythology, and I
brought them up in the discussion with the little girl. I must say she is
rather nice and I am beginning to understand" (McGuire 1988: 469).

The second scene of Hertz's story is winter 1918–19. The drama of
the relationship between Spielrein and Jung was long over, although
Spielrein was still corresponding with Jung as late as 1918, while Freud
had ceased his contact with Jung in 1914. But Spielrein was still partici-
pating in the Psychoanalytic Society meetings during 1918–19; she con-

tinued to do so until she returned to Russia in 1923. Helene Deutsch, the female member of the second Trausk/Freud triangle, "had a faint recollection of her" (S viii).

Freud forgot about her. Perhaps if he had pursued the clues about primitivism he would have gotten further. That is just speculation. I was on my way someplace and got distracted and had to follow the traces of a ghost. Increasingly, though, I am wondering about what psychoanalysis has lost, not only about what it has repressed, or marginalized as we say now. "Freud should not be reproached for having neglected the concrete social dimension, but for being all too untroubled by the social origin of this abstractness, the rigidity of the unconscious, which he registers with the undeviating objectivity of a natural scientist" (Adorno 1968: 80). Perhaps he was too troubled by those social origins, a trouble that manifested itself in a deep pessimism regarding the possibility of a will to heal the social itself, fastening him into sublimating civilizations and scientific cures.

I really do not know for sure. I do know that after all he takes us through, Freud leaves us with an extraordinary restriction of the haunted field. After having dragged the human sciences into all these ghostly affairs, Freud's science arrives to explain away everything that is important and to leave us with adults who never surmount their individual childhoods or adults whose haunting experiences reflect their incorrect and childish belief in the modes of thought of their "primitive" ancestors. After getting so close to so much, he forgets his own important lessons about the transferential field and about the fundamental insight the discovery of the unconscious inaugurated: "we do not know those things we think we do" (Mitchell and Rose 1982: 4). Freud gets so close to dealing with the social reality of haunting only to give up the ghost and everything social that comes in its wake.

Freud barely had the ghost to lose, but he was close. The willingness to follow ghosts, neither to memorialize nor to slay, but to follow where they lead, in the present, head turned backwards and forwards at the same time. To be haunted in the name of a will to heal is to allow the ghost to help you imagine what was lost that never even existed, really. That is its utopian grace: to encourage a steely sorrow laced with delight for what we lost that we never had; to long for the insight of that moment in which we recognize, as in Benjamin's profane illumination, that it could have been and can be otherwise. I think Freud was afraid of what he saw. Sometimes this is necessary in the face of ghosts.

But he gave it up too quickly. If you let it, the ghost can lead you toward what has been missing, which is sometimes everything.

Talking to the Ghost

> To exorcise not in order to chase away the ghosts, but this time to grant them the right . . . to . . . a hospitable memory . . . out of a concern for justice.
>
> JACQUES DERRIDA, *Specters of Marx*[16]

We may have gotten only so far as to ponder the paradox of providing a hospitable memory for a ghost. It is no simple task to be graciously hospitable when our home is not familiar, but is haunted and disturbed. It could require an effort to which our manners are not yet accustomed. It could require a different sort of receptiveness and welcome. And out of a "will to heal," or *out of a concern for justice*? Well, yes, but that leaves everything of the precise nature of the hospitality to be decided.

Perhaps, then, we should be grateful for such a story. A young Russian girl, *the first child of intelligent, well-educated, well-to-do Jewish parents, her grandfather and great-grandfather . . . highly respected rabbis,* is suffering from a *schizophrenic disturbance or severe hysteria.* In 1904, her *deeply concerned parents* take her to Zurich *to be treated at the world-famous Burgholzli mental hospital.* A patient of Jung's, by 1905, she has enrolled at the University of Zurich to study medicine, receiving her *doctor's degree in 1911 on the basis of a dissertation entitled "The Psychological Content of a Case of Schizophrenia". . . . The former schizophrenic patient had by then become a student of schizophrenia, a doctor treating mental disturbances, an original thinker who developed ideas that later became of greatest significance in the Freudian system* (S xvi). A young woman patient falls in love with her doctor. A doctor falls in love with his young woman patient. The history of psychoanalysis *is changed.* Perhaps we should be grateful for such a story, a story at least acknowledging that in the retelling of an untold story an institution is "changed" by a love affair involving a great man and a young woman. But what if this is just a ghost story marking the itinerary of one woman's haunting by a ghost, a kind of made-up story? It is what the story leads to that is important. When a ghost is haunting a story about intellectual storytelling, what is important is not to be afraid.

Dear Sabina, I'm uneasy about using your story, or the story of the places you were between, as a pretext for speaking about methodology and other matters, about needing or seeming to need a dead woman to enliven matters, to make them have some material force. *Subjects repose in the archives, always inconsolable, never having the right to speak. They are, of course, spoken about—rumours of this reach them, but the materiality of their contents is forgotten* (Robin 1980: 234). Is this why you have come back to haunt me, because rumors of your recovery have reached you? I found you by accident in a book that treats your diary and letters as evidence of your "decisive influence" on Jung and on the development of his system, your contributions, "of greatest significance [to] the Freudian system," and the "startling new light [your life throws] on important aspects of the Freud-Jung correspondence" (S xvi).

But I have not really told the story of your "decisive influence" and significant contributions, or what happened to you when you returned to Rostov-on-Don in 1923 to write, teach, and raise your daughters. Psychoanalysis was banned in the Soviet Union in 1936, the home you founded for children was closed, and you disappeared from the psychoanalytic literature. Your three brothers, all professors and scientists, died within a span of four years, between 1935 and 1937; and your eldest daughter, Renate, unfortunately returned from Moscow to Rostov, where she had been studying the violin, on June 22, 1941. Finally, you and your daughters died on November 21, 1941, when Rostov was occupied by the Germans and *all the Jews in the city were taken to the synagogue and shot* (S xi). I could not write that story, not because it cannot be recounted, but because you led me beyond yourself, to think about the implications of your absence in the photograph and your willingness to talk to the wolf. I admit that I may have gotten only so far as to insist on our need to reckon with hauntings and to ponder the paradox of providing a hospitable memory for ghosts *out of a concern for justice.*

Perhaps this is not nearly enough. But I was on my way to a conference with an abstract and a promise and then I got distracted by a photograph and had to take a detour to follow the traces of a woman ghost. And it is true, now at the end of the story, all that remains is an abstract that could not be realized and the markings of a detour. Why the detour? Because it would not have been quite the story I wanted to tell if I had just told you that sociology needs a way of grappling with what it represses, haunting, and psychoanalysis needs a way of grappling with what it represses, society. No, that wouldn't have been the story at all. And so we are left to insist on our need to reckon with haunting as a prerequisite for sensuous knowledge and to ponder the paradox of providing a hospitable memory for ghosts *out of a concern for justice.*

EL MUNDO

carrying the weight of the world on your shoulders

3

the other door, it's floods of tears
with consolation enclosed

To confront those who become *desaparecido* (disappeared) under the
auspices of state-sponsored terror in Argentina, within what Michael
Taussig (1992) calls the Nervous System, or, as we will see in chapter 4,
to confront those who were lost on their way to North America in the
flow of a juridically enforced international trade in human property, is
to contemplate ghosts and haunting at the level of the making and unmaking of world historical events.[1] Yet if there is one point to be
learned from the investigation of ghostly matters, it is that you cannot
encounter this kind of disappearance as a grand historical fact, as a
mass of data adding up to an event, marking itself in straight empty
time, settling the ground for a future cleansed of its spirit. In these matters, you can only experience a haunting, confirming in such an experience the nature of the thing itself: a disappearance is real only when it is
apparitional. A disappearance is real only when it is apparitional because the ghost or the apparition is the principal form by which something lost or invisible or seemingly not there makes itself known or apparent to us. The ghost makes itself known to us through haunting and
pulls us affectively into the structure of feeling of a reality we come to
experience as a recognition. Haunting recognition is a special way of
knowing what has happened or is happening.

Thus far, I have considered three characteristic features of haunting.
We have seen that the ghost imports a charged strangeness into the
place or sphere it is haunting, thus unsettling the propriety and property lines that delimit a zone of activity or knowledge. I have also emphasized that the ghost is primarily a symptom of what is missing. It
gives notice not only to itself but also to what it represents. What it rep-

63

resents is usually a loss, sometimes of life, sometimes of a path not taken. From a certain vantage point the ghost also simultaneously represents a future possibility, a hope. Finally, I have suggested that the ghost is alive, so to speak. We are in relation to it and it has designs on us such that we must reckon with it graciously, attempting to offer it a hospitable memory *out of a concern for justice*. Out of a concern for justice would be the only reason one would bother.

To look for lessons about haunting when there are thousands of ghosts; when entire societies become haunted by terrible deeds that are systematically occurring and are simultaneously denied by every public organ of governance and communication; when the whole purpose of the verbal denial is to ensure that everyone knows just enough to scare normalization into a state of nervous exhaustion; when there are guileless ghosts and malevolent ghosts living in tight quarters; when the whole situation cries out for clearly distinguishing between truth and lies, between what is known and what is unknown, between the real and the unthinkable and yet that is what is precisely impossible; when people you know or love are there one minute and gone the next; when familiar words and things transmute into the most sinister of weapons and meanings; when an ordinary building you pass every day harbors the facade separating the scream of its terroristic activities from the hushed talk of fearful conversations; when the whole of life has become so enmeshed in the traffic of the dead and the living dead . . . To broach, much less settle on, a firm understanding of this social reality can make you feel like you are carrying the weight of the world on your shoulders. It simply cannot be carried with any delicacy, a strict requirement in these circumstances. Changing shape more readily than the scholarly analyst might like, all the bits and pieces—the screams and cries, the silences, the density of the nation's history, the ideological justifications, the geopolitical forces, the long-standing creative capacity for domestic terror, the cultural pathways of the tango and the pampas, the debts, the international economies of money and national pride, the courageous political resistance, and so on—do not quite add up. They can be isolated and laid bare, and they can be put to the political task of exposure, but it seems as if in that very act the ghosts return, demanding a different kind of knowledge, a different kind of acknowledgment.

My purpose is not to malign the political injunction to speak truth to power where the truth arrives, bearing the positive facticity of all those bits and pieces, in a social scientific language designed to unmask and demystify. (Although, one must admit that there are very good reasons to lie to power even if this is not usually what is meant when the distinction between truth and power is repudiated.) Rather, my purpose is to encourage us to think that the very way in which we discover things or learn about others or grapple with history is intimately tied to the very things themselves, to their variable modes of operation, and thus to how we would change them.

It is here that the ghost story meets up with Walter Benjamin's materialist historiography, a historiography compatible with the sociological task of writing histories of the present:

> Materialistic historiography . . . is based on a constructive [as opposed to an additive] principle. Thinking involves not only the flow of thoughts, but their arrest as well. Where thinking suddenly stops in a configuration pregnant with tensions, it gives that configuration a shock, by which it crystallizes into a monad. A historical materialist approaches a historical subject only where he encounters it as a monad. In this structure he recognizes . . . a revolutionary chance in the fight for the oppressed past. He takes cognizance of it in order to blast a specific era out of the homogeneous course of history—blasting a specific life out of the era or a specific work out of the lifework. As a result of this method the lifework is preserved in this work and at the same time canceled; in the lifework, the era; and in the era, the entire course of history. (Benjamin 1969: 262–63)

This is a different type of social constructionism than most social scientists are familiar with, drawing a good deal of its inspiration from modernist montage techniques, requiring not only attention to the thing thought, but also attention to the thinker's mode of engagement (*the flow* and *arrest* of thoughts). *The historical materialist approaches a historical subject only where he encounters it as a monad,* encounters what I have been calling the ghost. All of a sudden your thinking is stopped, shocked, as it were, into a configuration or conjuncture that crystallizes the social gist of a dramatic or mundane event. The monad or the ghost presents itself as a sign to the thinker that there is a *chance in the fight for the oppressed past,* by which I take Benjamin to mean that the past is alive enough in the present, in the now, to warrant such an approach. Benjamin goes even further, calling on us to protect the dead from the dangers of the present as if they were proximate enough for such loving embrace, a point to which we will return. This oppressed past is neither linear, a point in a sequential procession of time, nor an autonomous alternative past. In a sense, it is whatever organized violence has repressed and in the process formed into a past, a history, remaining nonetheless alive and accessible to encounter. Fighting for this past appears to be a paradoxical gesture, but it is Benjamin's way of figuring the historical materialist's relationship to what seems dead, but is nonetheless alive, operating in the present, even if obliquely, even if barely visible. Upon recognition, the oppressed past or the ghostly will shock us into recognizing its animating force. Indeed, to fight for an oppressed past is to make this past come alive as the lever for the work of the present: obliterating the sources and conditions that link the violence of what seems finished with the present, ending this history and setting in place a different future. Benjamin's insight here is to recognize the reciprocal relationship between the type of thinking the analyst employs, ready for the shock and the moment of understanding, and the animating role of the life or the era or the events the analyst confronts.

Encountering a ghost or approaching a subject in this way is never quite as easy as Benjamin might be taken to suggest. It takes some effort to recognize the ghost and to reconstruct the world it conjures up. This may account for Benjamin's use of the notion of blasting, a method of dialectics that reconstructs a lifework by following the scrambled trail the ghost leaves, picking up its pieces, setting them down elsewhere. Blasting might be conceived as entering through a different door, the door of the uncanny, the door of the fragment, the door of the shocking parallel. Entering one place, another often emerges in juxtaposition, along the lines of a defamiliarization coalescing into a moment of connection, a configuration. Through this door a certain kind of search is established, one that often leads along an associative path of correspondences that invigorates Benjamin's montage-based constructivism. This path of correspondences is not like the causality associated with social science or related modes that share its basic epistemology: it blasts through the rational, linearly temporal, and discrete spatiality of our conventional notions of cause and effect, past and present, conscious and unconscious.

There is a certain routineness to shocking associations in Argentina. For example, you are studying the work of an author who is very interested in the similarities and differences between individual and social madness. The title of a book of her short stories, *Open Door*, turns out to be the name of "the most traditional, least threatening lunatic asylum in Argentina" (Valenzuela 1988a: viii). However, as soon as you think you have simply come across an interesting little fact to share, or just smile at, you find yourself at the El Banco detention camp where a "system called 'open doors' was started, whereby the doors of the cells were opened while the prisoners remained inside chained to a wall" (Amnesty International 1980: 8). In and of themselves, these correlations do not provoke the tensions to which Benjamin is referring and of which hauntings are made. They can be collected, but they will lie like the debris of a system barely thinkable and yet abounding in excessive significations. Benjamin's materialist historiography depends fundamentally on animation, on being able to demonstrate to others the moment in which an open door comes alive and stops us in our tracks, provoking a different kind of encounter and recognition. And for that, the quickening experience of haunting is essential.

It is through the door of Luisa Valenzuela's surreal or magically realist fiction that I enter, at the risk of offending those who would prefer less ambiguity in the face of state-sponsored terror, but in order to further an understanding of ghostly matters. Luisa Valenzuela is an Argentine writer, the author of several novels and short story collections all exploring the social and psychosexual dimensions of repression and desire. Like several other women writers from the Southern Cone, she is particularly concerned not only with the mentality of the torturer, but also with the intimate bonds between military captor and the usually female captive, the bonds of political and sexual repression.[2] Willing to entertain the idea that a certain kind of wicked sorcery has dominated Argentine life, Valenzuela has also made it her task to understand the sensitive issue of middle-class quiescence and complicity during the years of terror, during the "dirty war," a war never officially declared, but nonetheless undertaken. *Como en la Guerra* (As in War), translated as *He Who Searches* for reasons we shall see, is a 1977 novella first published in English in 1979. It is not a *testimonio* or a naturalist novel.[3] It is allegorical, fragmented, narratively incoherent, and difficult to comprehend in any straightforward way that would easily answer the questions all readers ask: who speaks, what happens, where does it happen, how, what does it mean? It offers its opinions on various theoretical questions concerning the nature of subjectivity, the project of psychoanalysis, the dimensions of political and sexual repression, and the form of revolution. Luisa Valenzuela gets into the story and comments on its developments; characters change shape and form; the duration of time and space expands and contracts. Valenzuela's mode is ironic, full of black humor and complicated puns, yet serious. One might describe her as a writer who understands the difference between storytellers who claim ownership and possession of the words they speak and storytellers who mediate between ritual and writing, who speak seriously yet with a certain abandon.

He Who Searches is divided into five times, places, or fields—Page zero, The Discovery, The Loss, The Journey, and The Encounter—that constitute a mapping of an exploration and the strategic maneuvers of a war. The plot goes something like this:

Page zero. A man is being interrogated. They keep asking him about an unnamed "her" and about what he was looking for when he visited her apartment regularly in Barcelona. He is being interrogated and tortured. He is in great pain. He thinks "There have been better times" and shouts "'I don't know a thing!'" (V 6). A trigger explodes.

The Discovery. The protagonist, AZ, is an Argentine living in Barcelona; he is a professor of semiotics and a psychoanalyst familiar with the teachings of Jacques Lacan.[4] His work, which he does nightly in sundry disguises and masquerades, involves analyzing a patient, variously a woman, a prostitute, a witch, a "She." She, who has no name, is in political exile from Argentina perhaps—this is not clear—because she has been betrayed by her lover, the revolutionary Alfredo Navoni, whose dreams she tells/dreams as if they were her own.[5] Her twin sister, whom she calls "she-she," has "vanished during the day and no one ever saw her in the Pasaje des Escudellers" (V 56). According to the professor, She does not know she is being analyzed and cannot know this so he visits her in disguises, a transvestitism of sorts. He initially desires to know: What does she want? Who is she? He who masquerades in his weekly nocturnal visits to her wants her to reveal the self behind the mask. He wants to know her real name. She, who has no name and knows everything, laughs and thinks of murdering him because it is dangerous to be the object of desire and the object of a search, the question of his desire. His visits are both analytic and sexual encounters, and they both keep getting the two confused. Her neighbors complain, calling her a bitch/witch because she has organized the prostitutes into a union and they are demanding social security and an eight-hour day. The neighbors are scared of her and think that she "eats . . . men's most vital parts" (V 33). There is a wife, Beatriz, who warns AZ about going out in the night, worries that the other woman has "swallowed her husband alive," but begins to get involved in his case.

The Loss. AZ loses his patient, but retains the tape recorder that has broken down when Bea tries to transcribe She's words, in a hallucinatory episode involving an empty room and some photographs. *As if restored to life on the third day, he came out knowing* (V 92). He has to "change levels in order to continue his search" and so he begins to both lose and search for himself. One part of the analysis is over.

The Journey. He leaves Spain and travels to Mexico, where he undergoes a purification ritual with indigenous women who give him mushrooms for dreaming. He speaks a name, María Sabina, but that may be more from the mushrooms than anything else. (María Sabina was a holy woman, living in Oaxaca, Mexico, who shared her knowledge of Mazatec sacred mushroom healing ceremonies with outsiders in 1955. She was born in 1894 and died in 1985, having first eaten psilocybin mushrooms to overcome hunger.) Magic and dream time, mythic memories, and political surreality confront him as he meets revolutionaries in a jungle and hears two important tales, one about the defeat of the guerrillas in Tucumán and another, a Mystery, about a young comrade named Fatty.

The Encounter. He continues to travel southward and arrives in a Latin American city. He sees people waiting in lines that stretch endlessly throughout the city. At times, the police kick people to the ground, police with "good Argentine boots" (V 128). He meets an old woman who asks what he is searching for. He has learned that to "consume stories like swallowing swords is not a heroic deed" and so he keeps on going, ignoring the vendors selling flags inscribed with the words "Holy and Miracle." "His task is to arrive" (V 131). "Suddenly a hand grabs him by the arms and pulls him down. His body hits the ground just as he hears the chatter of a machine gun. Someone puts a helmet on his head, a rifle in his hand, and he experiences an inexplicable puff of happiness because he feels that he finally belongs" (V 131–32). Thrust into battle, he takes the charges and the instructions the mudwoman gives him and blows up the designated target. "The walls of the fortress burst like a great husk and the gleaming heart of the fruit emerges" (V 134).

It is worth withholding the judgment that Valenzuela's novel too simply aestheticizes or psychologizes a reality best understood as brutally realistic. Not unlike Walter Benjamin, Luisa Valenzuela employs a different kind of materialism where a great deal of what can be known is tied to the search for knowing it. Indeed, Valenzuela's writing seems centrally concerned with the hinges that open and close what is apparent and what is disappeared; what can be seen and what is in the shadows; what can be said and what is whispering inaudibly; what is true and what is a lie; what is rational and what is magical; what is real and what is surreal; what is conscious and what is unconscious. There are no

bridge between binaries

doubt practical considerations that lead Valenzuela to write such a fragmented, allegorical, and hard-to-understand-what-is-happening narrative. These practical considerations include censorship, exile, and the
threat of becoming the very thing you are writing about, that is, disappeared.[6] When the goal is to effectively express or represent the ghosts
(and not only the dead) that haunt state-sponsored systems of disappearance, other considerations come into play: the difficulty of representing what seems unrepresentable, if not unthinkable, a difficulty that
tosses the writer between paralyzing silence and dead, cold language;
the nature of disappearance itself and its peculiar dialectic of certainty
and doubt; the political importance of transcoding, if not transforming, the concern with the one who searches into a concern for what
the search will yield; the recognition of the impossibility of carrying the
world on your shoulders without a certain degree of magic and help.
Some of this assistance comes from knowing that the various stories of
disappearance, ranging from the fictional to the official document, form
a type of constructive principle themselves such that they lie like
palimpsests upon each other, helping us along in the process by which
Benjamin's monad or our ghost creates its apparitional impact.

In Luisa Valenzuela's story, a man becomes haunted by a woman
who is barely there. He is searching for her, for knowledge, for himself.
She is haunted by something else it takes him a long time to figure out.
The search is everything to him. What does he find when he goes looking for the woman who has become an apparition? The knot of the
ghostly and the real. And so now, with our constructivist principle in
mind, let us follow the path Valenzuela establishes from Page zero to
The Discovery, The Loss, The Journey, and The Encounter.

Page zero

> Mrs. A.Z., (case number 1127), Argentine citizen, lawyer, was
> kidnapped on Saturday 20 November 1976 at 11 a.m. . . . . She
> was submitted to the usual torture (blows, the *picana*) as well
> as other treatment such as the one known as "burial": "When
> people were brought here they were put in ditches which had
> been previously dug, and buried up to the neck, sometimes for
> four days or more. . . . They were kept without food or water,
> exposed to the elements. When they were dug out they were
> covered with insect bites; they had been buried naked. From
> there they were taken straight to the torture chambers."
> SIMPSON AND BENNETT, *The Disappeared and the Mothers of the Plaza*[7]

[handwritten margin note:] revised or altered but original haunts

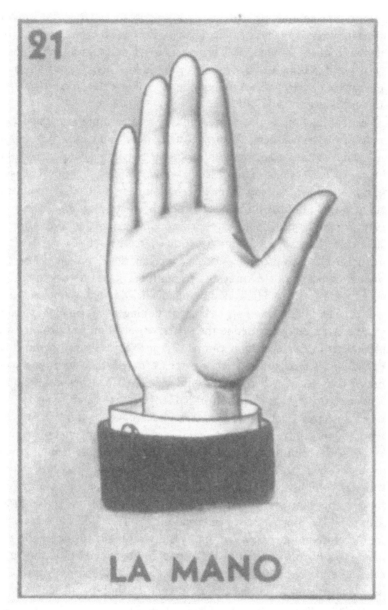

LA MANO

an enormous hand approaches his face, about to explode

Despite the shadow that surrounds disappearance, *He Who Searches* opens in two brief pages by placing us in what has become its most paradigmatic mise-en-scène.[8] "'I wasn't there. I don't know anything, I swear I had nothing to do with her'. . . . 'Talk'. . . . an enormous hand approaches his face, about to explode. . . . pain. . . . IMGOINGTOPULL-THETRIGGERNOW" (V 5–6).

Illegal abduction by the police, military and paramilitary squads, detention in secret centers, torture, usually death and improper burial, and denial by the authorities—these are the horrifying characteristics of the organized system of repression known as disappearance. Disappearance is a widespread form of repression, used in many countries and in varied political situations. Although the term *disappearance* initially arose to describe political repression in Guatemala "after 1966, in Chile since late 1973, and in Argentina after March 1976 . . . [t]he practice itself . . . is probably not such a recent development" (Amnesty International 1981: 1). Amnesty International traces its origins to the chief of the German High Command, Field Marshal Wilhelm Keitel, whose 1941 Night and Fog Decree pertaining to Germany's western occupied territories resulted in the arrest, deportation to Germany, and internment in concentration camps of approximately seven thousand individuals. The Night and Fog Decree "ordered that, with the exception of those cases where guilt could be established beyond a doubt, everyone arrested for suspicion of 'endangering German security' was to be transferred [secretly] to Germany under 'cover of night'" (Amnesty International 1981: 2). Secret arrest, transportation under cover of darkness, the refusal to give information "'as to [the prisoners'] whereabouts or their fate,'" and the belief that "deterring" resistance could be best accomplished by people vanishing "without leaving a trace" are the elements that prefigure the system of repression known as disappearance (Keitel in Amnesty International 1981: 2). Disappearance is not therefore unique to Argentina. It is a worldwide phenomenon that may have a history antedating this name. In the context of Latin America, Argentina remains a significant case not only because disappearance was practiced there with a systematic vigor paralleled only by Guatemala, but also because it produced an important model of collective resistance to state terror through disappearance in the actions and philosophies of the Mothers of the Plaza de Mayo.

During the military government of 1976–83, it is estimated that thirty thousand people disappeared. It does not entirely matter whether forty-five thousand or nine thousand disappeared.[9] Thirty thousand *desaparecidos* is the symbolic number to which the equally powerful retort *Nunca Más* (Never Again) is directed. Most were young—approximately 80 percent of those disappeared were between the ages of sixteen and thirty-five—and most were workers and students (Argentine National Commission on the Disappeared 1986: 284–385).[10] Some disappeared before 1976 and fewer disappeared after 1979; the height of the so-called Dirty War took place between 1976 and 1978.

The long history of military privilege, military dictatorship, and the reliance on the sacred salvation of military order in Argentina created a veritable tradition of repression. There were six coups and twenty-one years of military dictatorship between 1930, when the first military coup in Argentina's post-Independence (1816) history occurred, and the overthrow of Isabel Perón in 1976. Juan Perón's 1946 to 1951 administration was the only civilian government to last its full term. He too was removed from office in 1955 and did not return from exile until 1973. The immediate "precedent for the junta's repressive measures" was the 1966 coup led by General Juan Carlos Onganía, who deposed the elected civilian government of President Arturo Umberto Illia. Onganía outlawed political parties, imprisoned union leaders, and eliminated the universities' internal governance structures and the student associations. He assumed office with a promise to "combat 'ideological infiltration, subversion and chaos'" (Andersen 1993: 52), bequeathing "to the junta that took power in 1976 [under the direction of General Jorge Videla, Admiral Emilio Eduardo Massera, and Brigadier Ramón Agosti] the military's role in preserving the moral and ideological health of the nation as well as the concept of the enemy as internal" (Bouvard 1994: 20).

Thirty thousand. All of them tortured, most of them killed, their bodies burned, thrown into the sea, into the River Plate, or into the jungles of Tucumán by the air force and navy; or buried by the army in *Non nombre* (identity unknown) graves. The River Plate, named after a hope, silver, the birthplace of Argentina as a nation. The River Plate, there where on the "first, deceptively peaceful, day of the military takeover" on March 23, 1976, "several hundred lower-ranking union officials [were] arrested and taken to vessels moored out in the River" and shot (Simpson and Bennett 1985: 34). That same river into which the air force and navy would later dump the bodies of their victims. "Only the Army buried people in graveyards," obviously believing military rule would "last for ever." Virtually every cemetery had its quota of *Non nombre* graves. Getting rid of corpses was a problem for a country that denied there were any corpses to bury. *There is no question of asking the director why there is such a difference between the one plot and the other; the subject is not one which he or his staff want to talk about. It is as though they feel, with a superstiousness which belies their smart suits and obvious education, that harm can come from discussing so unlucky a subject* (ibid.: 32).

As a result of meticulous and often courageous investigation by Amnesty International, the Mothers of the Plaza de Mayo, the Argentine National Commission on the Disappeared (CONADEP), and the journalists and scholars who draw upon their efforts, we now know a good deal about disappearance. The commission alone compiled fifty thousand pages of documentation: fifty thousand pages of gruesome data, designed to dismantle the dialectic of certainty and doubt that so characterizes disappearance. Fifty thousand pages that attempt to communicate a violence virtually unimaginable to most of us in the United States. Fifty thousand pages that attempt to reconstruct, case by case, the individuals disappeared, the special person each was: conjuring up your neighbor, brother, sister, mother, daughter, friend from within a mass of data of violation, pain, and political surgery. Fifty thousand pages designed to bring back to life the person in torture where only the signs of the social body's purported decay and subversion exist. Fifty thousand pages and hardly a word of it gotten from the torturers. Despite the judicial trials and the commission's investigations, the torturers have not spoken, except perhaps to themselves or each other. CONADEP condemns their silence and the truth it hides, the immunity it flaunts. Cast for understandable moral and ethical reasons as a monster lacking in basic human capacities, the torturer is almost a category of missing person elaborately etched in the available reports and analyses. It would be beyond the current parameters of political mandate and moral tolerance to expect it to be otherwise, but we must nonetheless acknowledge that something of the nature of disappearance is thus lost to our understanding. So too something of what ties the torturer to the ordinary citizen who shuts his or her eyes to the presence and persistence of systematic torture is then not understood.[11]

Stopping torture and terror from happening or preventing them from happening again by notifying the public of what they do to others and by implication what they could do to oneself is one reason Amnesty International suggests that "'disappearances' is a misnomer. . . . Many prisoners who have 'disappeared' may well, at worst, have ceased to be. None, however, is lost or vanished. Living or dead, each is in a very real place as a result of a real series of decisions taken and implemented by real people. *Someone* does know and, more importantly, is responsible" (1981: 1). We will return to think more about why disappearance is not a misnomer after all, but here it suffices to note the good reason Amnesty International has for arguing thus. No one has vanished in an abstract metaphysical sense: real actions are taken by identifiable agents toward real people in real places. Particularly in the context of coercive secrecy, an emphasis on making visible and palpable the "invisible" pain of being detained and tortured becomes an important means of linking knowledge to oppositional and remedial action (see Scarry 1985: 51). Humanitarian and political urgency, then, leads to an emphasis on both the "body in pain" (Scarry 1985) and on what we might call the social architecture of the scene of torture.

Combined with the passionate eloquence of an analyst like Elaine Scarry, the pages of detail contained in official reports and human rights documents convey something of what disappearance means when it is viewed from these perspectives.[12] The details include the following.

Illegal abduction. Illegal abduction was violent, frightening, and a world-shattering interruption of one's normal life. It was also what Michael Taussig (1993b) has called a public secret, something known but unspoken and unacknowledged. Covert and clandestine, the illegal abduction was at the same time planned and coordinated with local police and implemented to make sure others knew what was happening. The public secret of disappearance simultaneously announced terror's power and normalized the impossibility of living in a constant state of fear. Illegal abduction was also a medium of economic appropriation: houses, household goods, and money stolen from the abducted were a significant resource base for military and paramilitary activities, war booty.

Detention centers. Secret and unofficial detention centers were where "'disappearance' began" (CONADEP 56) and where the disappeared lived (barely) in deplorable conditions on sickening food, the key operations site for their housing, interrogation, torture, and death. Approximately 340 detention centers, housed in civilian buildings, military buildings, police stations, and common prisons, were found throughout the country. Their ironic names, the layout of bed, toilet, torture room, and guard quarters, have been reconstructed and mapped by investigators and surviving witnesses. Survivors, in particular, have demonstrated an extraordinary ability to remember, establishing patterns by recollecting "the change of guard, the noise of planes and trains, and usual torturing times" (ibid.: 58) and by retracing the number of steps and turns taken to move from bed to door, from door to toilet, from hallway to torture room, from inside to outside. Survivors have described the social architecture of the detention centers where they were constantly blindfolded through a corporeal memory whose nonvisual senses were sharpened "as a means of clinging to reality and life" (ibid.). In a telling form of remembering, "on many of the inspections of the SDCs [secret detention centers] carried out by the Commission, witnesses would put on a scarf or bandage, or simply shut their eyes tight, in order to relive that time of terror and be able to remember the ordeal in detail" (ibid.).

Normalization of excess. Terror and torture create their own world, complete with a cartography of systematic and physically violent subordination. As the National Commission on the Disappeared states, "The cases highlighted in the report were not due to any 'excesses,' because no such thing existed, if by 'excess' we mean isolated incidents which transgress a norm. The system of repression itself, and its planning and execution, was the greatest 'excess'—transgression was common and widespread. The dreadful 'excesses' themselves were the norm" (ibid.: 10). Brought blindfolded and beaten into a self-enclosed world closed off from any contact with relatives, friends, or lawyers, detainees lost their names and were assigned a number that had its own place within the general bureaucratic apparatus of green cards, coding schemes, and ordinary errors and mishaps. A number that became the person.

> *The psychological torture of the "hood" was as bad or worse than the physical, although the two cannot be compared since whereas the latter attempts to reach the limits of pain, the hood causes despair, anxiety and madness. . . .*
>
> *With the hood on, I became fully aware of my complete lack of contact with the outside world. There was nothing to protect you, you were completely alone. That feeling of vulnerability, isolation and fear is very difficult to describe. The mere inability to see gradually undermines your morale, diminishing your resistance. . . .*

The "hood" became unbearable, so much so that one Wednesday, trans-
fer day, I shouted for them to have me transferred: "Me . . . me . . . 571."
The hood had achieved its aim, I was no longer Lisandro Raúl Cubas, I
was a number. (File No. 6974). (ibid.: 57)[13]

With little sense of location and recognizable temporality, and in a
context where domestic objects and familiar names and activities were
transformed into their sinister and defamiliarizing counterparts ("My
first *Señor* choked in my throat and I had to spit it out. . . . I say . . .
first . . . because it can't be the same word I knew. It's not the word I
used when I said, 'Señor, could you please tell me the time?' or 'Señor
Perez, could you wait a while.' . . . It's not the same *Señor* of 'Señor
Gonzalo Martínez and his wife are very pleased to invite you'" [Part-
noy 1986: 98, 97]), life as a *desaparecido* was characterized by the un-
predictable regularity of torture, interrogation, kindness, brutality, small
resistances, dramatic repressions.

Interrogation. Interrogation and torture are not two discrete sets of
acts, but together constitute a routine of terror. But it is also the case, as
Elaine Scarry points out, that the interrogation or the putative information to be gained therein is not the driving motivation for the abduction
or the torture: "The idea that the need for information is the motive for
the physical cruelty arises from the tone and form of the questioning
rather than from its content: the questions, no matter how contemptuously irrelevant their content, are announced, delivered, *as though* they
motivated the cruelty, *as if* the answers to them were crucial" (Scarry
1985: 28–29). Indeed, testimonies suggest that the questions asked during interrogation were often incomprehensible and primarily designed
to break down perceptual boundaries and to convert all past and present knowledge and activity into that dangerous subversion the torturer
was trying to eliminate.

The Interrogation Room. Noon time.
   "Are you going to tell us who your wife wrote this for?"
   His eyes infected, he tries to read from the old notebook that still has
the smell of his home.
   "She wrote it remembering the Naposta stream." When he talks his
tongue aches from the wounds.
   "Don't lie to us."
   "Sir, I'm telling you the truth. She wrote the poem about that stream
near our house."
   "If you keep on telling lies, we'll take you to the machine."

"Sir, I'm not lying. She wrote it when they channeled the stream underground."

"Bullshit, I know that poem was written to honor some fucking guerrilla. Get the electric prod ready." (Partnoy 1986: 106)

Torture. The perverse meeting of weapon and body part, torture was
a ubiquitous feature of disappearance, undertaken with extraordinary
vigor and scientific precision, reflected to some extent in the clarity with
which witnesses recount what happened to them and to others. In the
torturers' vigilant and hysterical attempts to unearth and cast out subversion, that barely human object they saw as mortally endangering
their world, they created a corollary form of dehumanization and ob-
jectification, thereby establishing for themselves the "fiction of [their]
absolute power" (Scarry 1985: 27). The primary mechanism for the
maintenance of this life-threatening fiction was the attempt to keep
prisoners in a constant state of imminent death: "to just stop short of
taking life while inspiring the acute mental fear and inflicting much of
the physical agony of death" (Taussig 1987: 39). Prisoners were forced
to witness and often participate in the torture of family, friends, or
other prisoners and were compelled to receive medical "treatment"
from doctors whose sole job was to sustain life only so that it could
withstand more torture. Perhaps the most telling feature of life in this
"death-space" (Taussig 1987: 4; Timerman 1981) was the reminder,
constant and loud, that you were disappeared, lost to your world, without any hope of retrieval.

> The most vivid and terrifying memory I have of all that time was of always
> living with death. I felt it was impossible to think. I desperately tried to
> summon up a thought in order to convince myself I wasn't dead. That I
> wasn't mad. At the same time, I wished with all my heart that they would
> kill me as soon as possible. . . .
> The normal attitude of the torturers and guards towards us was to
> consider us less than slaves. We were objects. And useless, troublesome
> objects at that. They would say: "You're dirt." "Since we 'disappeared'
> you, you're nothing. Anyway, nobody remembers you." "You don't
> exist." "If anyone were looking for you (which they aren't), do you imag-
> ine they'd look for you here?" "We are everything for you." "We are jus-
> tice." "We are God.". . . Repeated endlessly. By all of them. All the time.
> (CONADEP 23, 25)

*Since we disappeared you, you're nothing. Anyway, nobody remem-
bers you. You don't exist.* A terrifying constituent feature of disappearance is that the *desaparecidos* have disappeared and so too all public

and official knowledge of them. There is shadowy knowledge, to be sure, and indeed disappearance terrorizes a nation's population to a large extent through the uncertainty that such a publicized secret harbors, but the state and its various representatives claim to know nothing. Or only that your child has gone abroad, or that your husband is having a secret affair, or that your guerrilla sister must be hiding out underground. Of course, there were the official pronouncements. The denials. "There are no political prisoners in Argentina except for a few persons who may have been detained under government emergency legislation. . . . There are no prisoners being held merely for being political or because they do not share the ideas held by the government," declared General Roberto Viola in 1978 (Bouvard 1994: 34). And the brazen declarations. "As from 22 April 1976, it is forbidden to report, comment on, or make reference to subjects related to subversive incidents, the appearance of bodies and the deaths of subversive elements and/or members of the armed and security forces, unless these are announced by a high official source. This includes kidnappings and disappearances" (Simpson and Bennett 1985: 41).

Recovering knowledge of the disappeared and making public what has happened to them is thus a crucial political activity that human rights organizations carry out. The pressing humanitarian needs that drive this recovery require a mode of address considered credible and legitimate by governments, media, and international agencies. Such an address must minimize the ambiguity, complicity, imagination, and surreality that necessarily characterize the theater of terror. It is obliged to communicate an unambiguous, unequivocal reality of pain and violence at the level of the ordinary individual body. Clearly defined moral boundaries, disclosure as truth, visible evidence of injury, accessible language, verifiable intent, impartiality, objectivity, authenticated witnesses, and so on are the means by which investigators make sense of and rationally communicate a patterned but irrational terror.

However, if there is one thing that those who have returned to tell their tales can report it is that "we are . . . blind to the way that terror makes mockery of sense-making" (Taussig 1987: 132). It makes a mockery of sense-making not because terror is senseless but, on the contrary, because it is itself so involved with knowledge-making. Spiraling between unbelievable facts and potent fictions, fantastic realities and violent fantasies, the *knowledge* of disappearance cannot but be bound up with the bewitching and brutal breaks and armature of disappearance itself. And a key aspect of state-sponsored disappearance is precisely the elaborate suppression and elimination of what conventionally constitutes the proof of someone's whereabouts. The disappeared have lost all social and political identity: no bureaucratic records, no funerals, no memorials, no bodies, nobody. "All societies live by fictions taken as real. What distinguishes cultures of terror is that the epistemological, ontological, and otherwise philosophical problem of representation—reality and illusion, certainty and doubt—becomes infinitely more than a 'merely' philosophical problem of epistemology, hermeneutics, and deconstruction. It becomes a high-powered medium of domination" (ibid.: 121). Uruguayan Marcelo Vignar captures well the vocabulary of this medium:

> All torn and twisted and broken, with so much of the brokenness concentrated around this notion of knowledge, of *knowing*: "You can't possibly know what it was like." "We didn't know, we didn't realize." The torturer's "I know everything about you." The victim's "I don't even know what I said, what I did." (Weschler 1990: 171)

Knowledge is also a medium of resistance, as the invaluable work the human rights reports accomplish attests. But despite the charts, maps, tables, file numbers, cases, despite all the detail set out with the social scientific precision of establishing the way it was/is, we are left with the impression that a crucial aspect of what we need to know in order to understand disappearance is missing from the human rights reports and official documents (even if "a single one of these testimonies would in itself be enough to permit the moral condemnation which the Commission has expressed" [CONADEP 10] and is enough to make you feel as if you really don't want to know any more). Because while torture always accompanies disappearance, and death almost always is its consequence, disappearance is not just a euphemism for torture and death. The power of the tremulous and complex relationship of subjectivity and subjection is not adequately framed as torture or homicide.[14] Even with the very significant knowledge that terror makes epistemological doubt itself a form of domination, we must nonetheless repeat the questions, as if we were not so certain. What is disappearance? How do we investigate and know it? How do we prevent it from happening? To the elaboration of these questions, which will turn on the ghostly elements missing from the human rights reports and the official documents, is where we now proceed.

an enormous hand approaches his face, about to explode. And it is thus with that hand that Luisa Valenzuela invites us into an image of danger, to that hand approaching all present tense and yet a memory of what has or will befall AZ, or what has happened to many. (Mano [hand] was the name of a right-wing group reportedly made up of off-duty police, who, as early as 1970, abducted students and leftist trade unionists. "Most of these victims simply vanished without trace, and the few to reappear spoke of torture" [Rock 1985: 355].) That enormous hand approaching AZ's face is only the beginning, not simply the way it was but the point of entry into the search for that which has disappeared, but has seized hold of us. Luisa Valenzuela begins her book where the official documents can go no further. Perhaps fiction can more easily establish an unreality principle the better to understand certain elements of what Jean Franco so aptly terms the "violence of modernization" in the complicated neoimperialism that characterizes Latin America. It is certainly the case that literature and a literary intelligentsia have played an important role historically in criticizing the violence of modernization in Latin America, a legacy Luisa Valenzuela both inherits and transforms.[15] Valenzuela gets us further than the reports not only because the medium she employs is more suited to the task but also because she uses it to capture the haunting elements of disappearance, the way it is "a kind of ghost dance . . . around the dead of a war that began with the conquest and goes on today" (Franco 1986: 7).

AZ is not only or just a victim of torture and murder by the state. Deliberately, Luisa Valenzuela will not provide such a rationalistic explanation for his death. She writes to *"add to the confusion and complicate this story that the less enlightened claim to see clearly. But if he had had access to certain information, his torture in the end, and perhaps even his death, would have given him a reason for being and* that *is intolerable: the cause that justifies the ends, the rational explanation creeping in in the middle of all the irrationality"* (V 66). The refusal of the rationalistic explanation is very important, as we will also see in chapter 4. At the end of *He Who Searches,* in The Encounter, AZ is still heading toward "the motive" (V 127) that never arrives. That he deserved the torture (and the death?) that opens the novel on Page zero is unacceptable to Valenzuela because it is the reasoning of the state. " 'He must have done something' " (Bouvard 1994: 43). "There's a civil war going on, we've got to stop the communists." "National security requires discipline and sacrifice." These were the refrains of justification

that made ordinary citizens "accomplices to the impunity of the government" (Bouvard 1994: 43). AZ's whole search will be about ceasing
to become a quiet accomplice. AZ becomes a *desaparecido,* not a homicide victim. He is a messenger from the other side.

The hand approaches; the state is about to strike. But "suddenly the
hand that is approaching dissolves and we are inside it, we enter a universe formed by its life-line, its heart-line. . . . The hand is the vehicle
and it is not easy to be transported by it to the bottom of things and
enter a diffuse world" (V 5). Luisa Valenzuela asks us to take that hand
and enter its world, a world where we will be touched and altered, for
good or ill, by the search for the disappeared. Luisa Valenzuela is looking for the disappeared. She is looking for a way to search for the disappeared. She also knows that the disappeared are looking for each other.
And, most significantly, she is looking for how to identify the effects of
disappearance on what is visible and tolerable. *an enormous hand approaches his face, about to explode.*

The Discovery

Events Beside the Point

AZ is a lousy analyst, despite his multimethodological identity as an
interpreter. As an ethnographer, AZ diligently makes his field notes,
recording the things in She's head and carrying that blasted tape
recorder he thinks no one notices around with him all the time. As an
amateur psychoanalyst, AZ delivers silly diagnostic pronouncements to
She like, "One must always take the phallus into account as the signi-
fier *par excellence*" (V 16). And as a "humble" semiotician who seems
to hold a university position, he knows she talks in code, but he can't
seem to read the signs in front of his face. AZ has a research project
that is also a love affair. He has decided to study her unconscious as if
she were a crazy woman, and he collects her childhood memories and
has his wife transcribe them for posterity. All in secret, he thinks, in the
voice of the royal we and with "our own methods of analysis . . . we
ask you to kindly respect" (V 9). He wants to know everything about
her, "except that she could know nothing of me" (V 11). Despite the
elaborate disguises he dons on his visits to her room in the Pasaje des
Escudellers, despite his desire to get the truth out of her ("She must
have no secrets from me, that's my price" [V 15]), and despite his "view

LA SIRENA

what goes unsaid, that which is implied and omitted and censured and suggested, acquires the importance of a scream

to effective therapeutic action" (V 13), he is a timid and moderate man. *I'm a timid man of moderate habits and very few needs. And here you have the timid man of moderatehabitsandveryfewneeds living a double life, not because one life is hidden from the other though there is some of that, but because what he calls his life, the daily routine that takes him to his classroom at the university and makes him study and awakens his interest, has been cut in two. On the one hand there is the man who goes along, who does and undoes, and on the other hand a very different man who mulls over his memories and lives vicariously by digging and scratching around to put himself in somebody else's skin. That of another woman, to cap it all* (V 45).

AZ is a lousy analyst, whether as ethnographer, psychoanalyst, or semiotician. All the interpretive sciences do not help him one bit. His parodic commitment to the "sake of science" (V 41) would be utterly comical if there weren't a grain of truth and a consequential result to this amorous commitment. *Everything around her cries out Argentina, Argentina, and no matter what guise she assumes, or what accent, I smell it immediately* (V 14). Yet he cannot comprehend most of what she says or writes, and he is foolish enough to think that his various disguises fool her: "She didn't know that I was giving her therapy. . . . She didn't know who I was. . . . She didn't know that I was one and the same person every time I saw her" (V 11). He even thinks of leaving his conventional bourgeois marriage to Beatriz (who eventually becomes Bea and then B, a letter just like him), but in the meantime he thoroughly underestimates his wife's insight about him—that he is dangerously innocent and not very good at taking the temperature of others (V 28). She, with no name, is barely there, despite her multiple identities and potent presence. She is variously a writer, a prostitute, a witch to her neighbors because she has organized the prostitutes into a union and "bewitched those girls into believing they're somebody" (V 33), a disenchanted revolutionary in exile, a woman already long disappeared. She is also less than an ideal heroine. In fact, everything about her is meant to point up the dangers of misplaced idealizations, especially ideals of women and nations and clean body politics and innocent knowledge. She is associated with the uncanny, with unsettled things confounding explanation. Who can understand the cryptic and haunting words she speaks in code? And she has a wolf face—*Many times I arrive right on her heels and find her cool and collected, her clothes changed, a wig in place, her face made up and lights on that made her look like . . . a wolf* (V 26)—a provocative reminder of that singular moment of animation when Sabina Spielrein saw the wolf in the mirror and spoke to it.

Despite her hallucinatory appearance and words, she knows much more than AZ thinks, including that he disguises himself ("I see him arriving in different disguises and pretend not to recognize him" [V 25]), including that he has a tremulous fear inside of him, and not just a moderate timidity. She is even considering murdering him, after which, in a hilarious revenge fantasy, "I can study him, find out what he's up to, what he's like inside, what he wants. at last a man for me alone, at last a dream come true" (V 24). She's trying to hide everything of importance from him, so she will give him *pleasure* but no information. She has a story, though: *because I didn't dare put the bomb in the right place?* (V 37). And she has a need, *The need to escape was enormous, to escape from herself, to get out of her badly wounded skin, to forget the love of Alfredo Navoni not knowing if he was the traitor who finally turned them in to the police* (V 57). She has a life that can never be told to a third party. *She had her universe then and a lover enrolled in the guerrilla forces who went underground and forgot her. . . . She was careful not to speak of Navoni, of her sister the guerrilla leader, of Adela or Michael. If AZ had known these details he might have interpreted the symbols, deciphered the meaning of her companions in the jail in Formosa (Argentina). He might have interpreted her hatred of her mythical sister, her double, and might even have drawn conclusions* (V 51, 66). And in a moment of "indefinable suspicion," she believes he is from Army Intelligence or Interpol or the CIA (V 43), but she also suspects that what she hides does not concern him. *What she really wants to hide is of no importance to him, it could only interest him if there were some remote possibility of his joining the cause* (V 51). She is *afraid of being only a ghost in the memory of certain gentlemen who find it pleasant to busy themselves with me but can't bear my presence for long* (V 50), which may partially be the result of her capacity to dream other people's dreams, as she does with those of Alfredo Navoni. Her twin sister "she-she" has disappeared. "She vanished during the day and no one ever saw her in the Pasaje des Escudellers in the street of the same name or in the Plaza Real which might have pleased her with palm trees that reminded her of her South America" (V 56). Or is it She who has disappeared? *used to fight for the same cause and even found a way to have hope. Not later, no, trapped as they had been, tortured and humiliated. . . . Losing sight of her sister, of the group* (V 57). Images return to her "as if sketched under threat" (V 52). She is compelled to forget a "past too painful to be true" (V 57). But she is also *the guardian of the monsters that he worshipped* (V 59).

He's trying to hurry the transference along, "we said to ourselves impatiently. The sick woman can't be left a prey to her affects" (V 10). His scientific spirit is ardent and ever so stupid. She laughs and tells him, I remember all this for you, doctor, a prophetic spell cast by a specter if ever there was one. He's trying to get her to remember everything for him. Of course, this makes him blind to the fact that the transference is never a two-party affair: what she will remember for him will lead him to what he's missing that can kill him. She's trying to hide what does not interest him. This is her blindness to the fact that the transference is never a two-party affair: she will generate in him, if not an interest, then a dangerous curiosity, about the cause into which he will fall looking for her. They are disappearing people. A charged scene of study, AZ and She go on for quite some time (half the book) in this dance of secrets and disclosures and stumbling desires, eating tamales and talking to themselves. It is a setup and he does not have much of a chance. If she was already *desaparecido* when he encountered her, by the end of The Discovery she will be gone from his sights entirely and it will be a long time in the story before he gets close to the social world she keeps, and even then he will understand much less than we might hope for. He who searches is he who misses what he is missing, an error that almost always establishes the conditions for a haunting. The ghostly woman will have an impact on him well beyond his hopes for a stimulating analytic experience and a well-received publication. And it is precisely her ghostliness that launches the search that will, ineluctably, change him. *What goes unsaid, that which is implied and omitted and censured and suggested, acquires the importance of a scream* (Valenzuela 1986: 10).

What, then, do we discover in The Discovery? *She's a valid subject for study . . . so I must concentrate on my work and not . . . be distracted by prior events beside the point* (V 51). AZ is almost a caricature of the rational and neutral scholar as he insists on detachment from "prior events beside the point," events that are happening in the spooky social world, events that are happening to him. The analyst of signs is having a hard time seeing what is significant, including that he himself is, despite his stated preferences and his endless chatter about methods, acting like he is in Argentina. Living in a dual and surreal reality where a fragile veneer of normalcy and stability simultaneously cloaks and reveals the nervous workings of a system of terror such that one can witness an event without seemingly ever hearing or seeing it, AZ is already there and not there where She is. Living a ghostly existence. But he is not yet searching for himself, he is only trying to analyze the unconscious of an Argentine woman whom he has met and who alleviates the boredom of his job and marriage. It is no surprise that he can't read the political symbols and signs when he is so focused on her individual unconscious and on her personal childhood traumas. Nothing of what haunts her or of what her haunting existence means can be broached when the past and the present, the public and the private have been so artificially segregated, when so much energy must be expended to remain alert to "my work" and not be distracted by what seems "beside the point." Even if we admit that the human rights reports and the official documents describe individuals who have no psychic lives that significantly influence their experience of disappearance (and there is evidence that Luisa Valenzuela is concerned that we understand that political activists, revolutionaries, and those who are disappeared possess an unconscious that is not simply the repository of traumatic political memories), the obverse evacuation of the political from the unconscious is certainly not a solution. And thus Luisa Valenzuela makes sure that we see that AZ's detachment is malfunctioning. He is so transparently bound up with the most conventional of heterosexual male fantasies and desires that his analytic distance is laughable.

The detachment is not working. AZ really does know this, even as he insists on operating under the name of a scientific ideal hardly anybody ever practices. *I regret not having someone . . . capable of checking my work. At times I panic and think with horror that I'm using her as a mirror, putting on masks in order to see myself better, expecting her to send back my real image. I must know. I want to know. . . . It's hard to untie this knot* (V 51). But his connection to She is sexual, personal, narcissistic, and ultimately foolish. (Foolish because, as AZ will learn, it is a grave mistake to try to become the one you are studying as if in a reversal of detachment you can become immersed in the world of another without consequence.) AZ is not, then, as obtuse as he might seem. He is alert to the emotional, subjective, and unreasonable relations between analyst and analysand; indeed, he hopes to cultivate them by hurrying the transference along.

The notion of transference is a signal contribution of psychoanalysis to our understanding of the impact of the to-be-known upon the knower. Transference registers the powerful way in which the forces structuring and crisscrossing the encounter between an analyst and the things or people she studies affectively transfer or carry analyst and knowledge from one place to another. But as I suggested earlier, the transference is never solely motivated by nor its results limited to the libidinal field of individual desires, investments, and attachments. AZ is involved, all right, but he is also stuck in a Freudian (or sometimes Lacanian) terrain of confidences, concealments, and exposures, ferreting out the secrets he believes reside and originate in She's body and head, hoping to discover the very enigma of femininity, there in the world of dreams and wishes and unconscious symptoms.

Valenzuela confers considerable power on transference in the general sense to expose the falsity of detachment, to dislocate the analyst's secure footing so that when the analyst stumbles the view from the fall provides new awareness, and to make the analytic scene something other than what we think it is. The transference, which AZ is always inviting and trying to manipulate, becomes his undoing, not simply because he is invested and involved and interested, as we inevitably all are, but because he believes he controls his not-working detachment, as if simply knowing about transference and discussing it were all there was to it. *I must have passed on the word fear to her. I believe it was before she spoke to me of murderers or mentioned their names* (V 46). But Valenzuela is clear that AZ is being prepared to be dispatched right into the real world he has been running away from and that he thinks is her "beside the point." Alas, the very real, if also fantastic, world of state terror, the nervous system that will take hold of AZ, is more powerful than he is. And so, whatever other authority and power the analyst may possess—to silence the one studied, to treat analysis as if it were an interrogation, to tell one's own story in the name of another, and so on—it is not equivalent to the power the state exercises or the violence it administers. This is why understanding that there are always more than two parties at a transference is so crucial. It is precisely the third party—the hand of the state and the *universe formed by its lifeline*—that is making this Discovery what it is: she hiding everything to do with it, unsuccessfully; he smelling it and acting like he's in

Argentina, but sticking to the pleasures of a loving discovery of a woman's unconscious, abysmally.

The unconscious world of psychoanalysis is a rich one indeed, and the seduction of its narratives, drives, and processes, not to mention its intellectual prestige, has led many scholars to find in it all the world they need (see Clément 1987). It seems unnecessary to belabor the point that the psychoanalytic connection AZ establishes and promotes, the one he believes he can orchestrate, is a very circumscribed way of em-pathically understanding another's conscious or unconscious life world. The deeply privatized associations AZ's psychoanalysis cultivates cause him to miss the public and social significance of the ghostly woman he is so intent on making his own. The psychoanalysis AZ practices knows less about secrets than it thinks. Indeed, it denies the overwhelming public secret that is disappearance itself as it reproduces its very logic of knowing and not knowing. AZ does not yet grasp that She bears the ghost of the state, that its hand has entered into his enclosed universe, that it is more powerful than he is, and that he cannot control it with the analytic tools at his disposal.

Psychoanalytic Implications

Valenzuela's ironic lambasting of psychoanalysis, and the prominent place it occupies in her novel about disappearance, is designed to show that the separation of psyche and society is clearly wrong-headed any-where and certainly ludicrous in Argentina. But she also suggests that we can be aware of the fallaciousness of the separation while still re-maining impervious to some of its deeper implications. The Argentine Psychoanalytic Association (APA) was founded in 1942, nineteen years after the translation of Freud's complete works into Spanish. As Nancy Caro Hollander notes in her extremely important and original study of psychoanalysis in Argentina, "By the 1980s, Argentina's psycho-analytic community was the fourth largest in the world, led only by those of the United States, France, and Germany. It is said that in Buenos Aires, where a third of the country's 26 million people reside, there are more psychoanalysts per capita than anywhere else in the world" (1990: 889). Indeed, as Valenzuela has commented, "There is a fashionable area of Buenos Aires that has so many psychologists and psychiatrists, it is known as 'Villa Freud.' The bars there are named 'Freud' and 'Sigmund.' The most popular comic strip character in Argentina is a ducklike bird named Clemente who undergoes psychoanalysis" (Katz 1983: 62).

Psychoanalysis has long held a prestigious place in the cosmopolitan culture of the Argentine metropolitan capital, a culture forged by large-scale immigration of European peoples, ideas, and class politics beginning in the nineteenth century.[16] From the founding of the Argentine Psychoanalytic Association in the 1940s through the turbulent years of the 1960s, psychoanalysis had an "extraordinary impact" on the capital's culture. Psychoanalysts gave public lectures, taught courses for students and the general public, traveled, and presented papers. They "spoke on the radio, wrote columns for newspapers, and published monographs and books, all dedicated to the dissemination of psychoanalysis within the population at large" (Hollander 1990: 897). The middle class, in particular, responded enthusiastically, making psychoanalysis remarkably popular and making psychoanalysts by the mid 1950s "among the port city's most prestigious professionals" (ibid.: 898). While middle-class consumption of psychoanalysis might have "functioned as a less expensive tactic than acquisition of material goods in the frenetic impulse to acquire the accoutrements of upward mobility and status" (ibid.: 897), psychoanalysis also appealed to many liberal and left activists and students, particularly after Perón's loss of power in 1955, the subsequent rise of the right, and the military coup of 1966. Psychoanalysis "permeated the intense discussions among middle-class students and intellectuals who frequented the film clubs, philosophical societies, and literary groups that multiplied during this period" as it provided a source of answers to a range of existential, philosophical, and social questions (ibid.: 898). Cheaper than medical school, whose large-scale research projects had been defunded by the state, and safer than the social sciences, which had been subject to severe political persecution because of their "progressive political orientation and emphasis on community research," psychoanalysis provided a home of sorts for the left-liberal intelligentsia (ibid.).

The history of psychoanalysis in Argentina highlights the contradictory role played by the middle class, the professional middle class, and the intelligentsia in Argentine political life. On the one hand, psychoanalysis was a source of critical thought and radical opposition to exploitation, oppression, and political repression. Psychoanalysts attempted to synthesize Marxism and psychoanalysis, to forge links to worker and union movements, and to develop a popular and nonelite institutional and clinical practice. On the other, more official, hand, psychoanalysis promoted a cautious and conservative professionalism. It focused on developing technique, it insisted on the principle and practice of analytic and professional neutrality, it cultivated a depoliti-cized understanding of trauma, and it provided a kind of social sedative as it assuaged the anxieties of the middle class reclining on its couches. This struggle over the political parameters of psychoanalysis marks its origins and development in Argentina.

The founders of the Argentine Psychoanalytic Association—Angel Garma, Celes Ernesto Carcamo, Arnaldo Rascovsky, Enrique Pichon Riviere, Marie Langer, many of whom had studied in Europe—sought to establish psychoanalysis in Argentina as both a social and a psycho-analytic theoretical practice.[17] They believed, as many have before and since them, that Marxism's analysis of the contradictions and injuries of capitalism could be integrated with a psychoanalytic understanding of subjectivity and psychic repression and that a full theory of revolu-tion and liberation could be established (see Adorno [1950] 1969, 1967, 1968; Brenkman 1987; Deleuze and Guattari 1983; Fanon 1967; Fromm 1962; Jacoby 1975, 1983; Lichtman 1982; Marcuse 1955, 1969; Mitchell 1974; Reich 1970, 1972; Rubin 1975; Rustin 1991; Turkle 1992; Žižek 1989). Yet, as Hollander points out, the early years of the development of the APA were heavily focused on building a "highly professional training institute and society," an energetic success that nonetheless spelled crisis for the APA (Hollander 1990: 895). If during the 1950s prestige and cultural radicalism more or less coex-isted, after the coup of 1966, the General Strike of 1969, and the 1969 (Rome) and 1971 (Vienna) International Psychoanalytic Congresses, a political conflict of major proportions, partially generationally defined, erupted. At both the 1969 and the 1971 international meetings, the general political climate of student and worker dissent was, not surpris-ingly, palpably evident. At the 1971 congress in Vienna, however, Marie Langer delivered

a highly controversial paper entitled "Psychoanalysis and/or Social Revo-lution." Langer asserted the inevitability of radical transformation of con-temporary society and urged her colleagues to use their psychoanalytic knowledge to facilitate rather than to oppose the process of change. She admonished her audience not to follow in the footsteps of the analysts who had left Cuba following the revolution or those who were departing from Chile on the heels of the election of Salvador Allende. "This time," she declared, "we will renounce neither Marx nor Freud." (ibid.: 903–4)

Langer's paper brought the critique of the APA to a head and in October 1971 the two dissident groups Plataforma and Documento formally left the APA, splitting the organization and the Argentine psychoanalytic community.[18]

The conflict, now more than twenty years old and renewed in the context of increasing public protest to military rule, revolved around the link between social and individual repression and the APA's refusal to engage social and political questions as a fundamental mandate. Two general issues framed the contentious and fractious debate. First, do individual psychic or psychological symptoms and processes have social determinants, or do they remain fundamentally immune to social life and social violence? Should psychoanalysis diagnose and treat the relationship between social reality and the individual unconscious, or should psychoanalysis focus exclusively on the individual's unconsciously derived symptoms of familial experience? The radical psychoanalysts argued for the fundamental imbrication of public and private life, rejecting a view of trauma as individualized or infantile, while the APA upheld the separation. Determining the role of social determinants in psychic life had serious consequences for the meaning of basic psychoanalytic concepts, particularly in the context of political repression and, after 1976, widespread disappearance and state terror. The dissidents asked questions like these: How could "free association," the technique of unstructured talk crucial to both the appearance of the unconscious and the ritual of cure, occur in the analytic setting when free association was not possible in society? How could an analyst tell when psychic resistance begins and when the concealment of painful or incriminating or unspeakable realities is being necessarily and consciously pursued? How could an analyst understand a patient's singular unconscious when the state itself is a major agent of repression? How could an analyst understand the complicated sense of fear and loss that crawls under the skin of people living in a state of state-produced terror? How could an analyst believe in, much less manage, a dyadic transference that eliminates all the "social and political content of patients' thoughts and feelings" (ibid.: 906)? Wouldn't those analysts be "guilty of conscious or unconscious repression or an inability to deal with their own countertransference reactions to threatening material which touched their lives as well as those of their patients" (ibid.)?

These questions formed their most charged articulations around the question of analytic and political neutrality, around whose lives were touched. However the majority or even a minority of psychoanalysts actually responded to the challenging questions posed to them, the official response of the APA was to insist on the viability and necessity of neutrality. The entire integrity of the profession, they believed, was threatened by subordinating value-neutral standards of analysis and professional conduct to social and political criteria and aims. By contrast, the opposition argued that neutrality was an "impossible professional ideal" (ibid.) that incorrectly presumed that science is free of ideology and that the psychoanalyst is somehow different from the other members of society who are bound to class, culture, and gendered embodiments. For the dissidents, this implausible nonpartisanship actually constituted a form of denial that was, whether intended or not, a highly mystified politicized choice under the circumstances. Accusations of complicity and collaboration flew hard and fast. Indeed, some went further and suggested that "*only* [political] repression could account for a lack of affect on the part of either patient or analyst regarding the experience of living in the midst of state terror" (ibid.: 906–7, emphasis added). In the place of desocialized psychoanalytic concepts and in the place of a fraudulent professional impartiality, the radical psychoanalysts "demanded a psychoanalysis bound to an ethic of engagement in the struggle against a repressive society," a psychoanalysis whose methodology would not be put in the service of "adapting to the status quo," but rather would "contribute to the alteration of existing psychological and social realities" (ibid.: 905, 903).

These were not, strictly speaking, theoretical issues. The radical psychoanalysts took their critique to the heart of the APA's organizational structure, accusing it of elitism in training and client services. The radical psychoanalysts sought to "democratize psychoanalytic training," and they formed the Organization of Mental Health Workers, "which for the first time eliminated the long-standing differences between medical and nonmedical members of the mental health community by offering psychoanalytic training and supervision to psychologists and social workers who had not been able to enter the medically controlled APA" (ibid.: 907). A number of psychoanalysts abandoned psychoanalysis altogether to become labor activists, and those who did not attempted to cross heavily guarded class lines to offer their services to the unions and working-class people.

The coup of 1976 significantly and severely altered the conditions under which the institution of psychoanalysis and all psychoanalysts operated. The activities of the political psychoanalysts made them open targets (Marx and Freud were the greatest enemies of Western Christian civilization, thought the armed forces), and as they came to be viewed as a ruinous threat to military order and national security, they were forced into exile, arrested, tortured, disappeared, and killed. Military rule made overt dissent and organizing, as well as publication of any material mentioning the armed forces or disappearance or anything at all deemed critical by the censors, illegal and impossible. Thus the radical analysts shifted their attention to the challenges of treating people who were suffering from political trauma. They began to deal with the difficulty of analyzing disappearance and terror through talk when talk of disappearance was legally prohibited; the difficulty of confronting the layers of fear, of the terror itself and of speaking of it; the difficulty of not knowing whether at any moment the analysis might be abruptly interrupted by police or soldiers or paramilitary personnel dragging someone away, leaving the one remaining in doubt about who informed; the difficulty of dealing with and resolving the mourning process of those whose loved ones had disappeared.[19] And what of the other analysts, the ones who surely would have condemned the violation of human rights and the police or state interference with patient confidentiality? As their colleagues were being persecuted and as the state refined its use of psycho-symbolic-therapeutic techniques for an ever more calculated and precise terror, they clung to the necessity of the formal neutrality of the institution and their scientific interest, believing with a different kind of valence and urgency than before that the survival of their own institution depended upon it.

The question of survival is not to be treated lightly, and casting stones from a distance does not advance our understanding of the quiet, unmotivated complicity of those who shut their eyes, go about their daily routines, and find every means available to not know, to shelter themselves from what is happening all around them. After all, a very powerful institution was engaged in a sustained and violent campaign to create a society of deaf and mute "sleepwalkers" (Galeano 1978: 307). I will come back at the end of this chapter to discuss the crucial problem of middle-class quiescence in the face of national crises. But there was no excuse for the refusal of the International Psychoanalytic Association (IPA) to name Argentina when, in 1981, it issued a statement opposing "'the violation of human rights which has occurred in certain geographical areas'" (Derrida 1991: 208). At a 1981 meeting of French and Latin American psychoanalysts held in Paris, Jacques Derrida delivered the opening address. The IPA's statement and the specific violence in Argentina hidden by the abstraction "certain geographical areas" provide the occasion for Derrida's discussion of what he calls "geopsychoanalysis":

> What I shall from now on call the Latin America of psychoanalysis is the only area in the world where there is a coexistence, whether actively adversarial or not, between a strong psychoanalytic institution on the one hand and a society on the other (civil society or State) that engages in torture on a scale and of a kind far surpassing the crude traditional forms familiar everywhere. . . . The kinds of torture to which I refer sometimes appropriate . . . psycho-symbolic techniques, thereby involving the citizen-psychoanalyst, as such, as an active participant either on one side or the other, or perhaps even on both sides at once, of these abuses. In any case, the medium of psychoanalysis is in consequence traversed by the violence in question, and this, whether directly or indirectly, inevitably leaves
> its mark on all its intra-institutional relationships, all its clinical practice, and all its dealings with civil society or with the State. This is an area, then, where no relationship of the psychoanalytic sphere to itself can be conceived of that does not bear traces of internal and external violence of this kind. In short, the psychoanalytic medium no longer enjoys any simple interiority. We are obliged to acknowledge that this pattern—a dense psychoanalytic colonization and a strong psychoanalytic culture coupled with the highest possible intensity of modern military and police violence—is at once *without equivalent* and *exemplary* in character. (1991: 228–29)

The implication and involvement of psychoanalysis with state terror is exemplary in Argentina. Luisa Valenzuela knows this. It is one reason she shares with the radical psychoanalysts a vehement critique of institutionally sanctioned detachment and of the disassociation of scholar and citizen it implies. It is also one reason why most of her writing, even more than the work in question here, evokes and describes the presence of what Derrida has called "the agency of psychoanalysis," describes its presence in detention, in the relationship between torturer and victim, in the experience of exile, in the everyday rituals of Argentines trying to go about their business amid widespread state terror. But my examples of the agency of psychoanalysis are not primarily designed to call for a "properly psychoanalytic reflection upon human rights, upon what the meaning of 'right' might be in a world where psychoanalysis is a contemporary reality" (ibid.: 216), although Valenzuela herself might welcome such an innovation. Neither, however, are the examples designed to simply replace psychoanalysis with a rational sociology. The discovery of determinant social forces and politics by psychoanalysis is not the enlightenment AZ achieves.

Valenzuela exposes the absurdity of a scientific practice (whether it is psychoanalysis, semiology, or anthropology) without social and political reference. And she is simply brilliant at conveying that absurdity; those who have read her book can attest to her very pointed black humor. The folly of the scientific pretension, however, is not only methodologically derived. It is a function of the very nature of a society that has long been engaged in a deadly struggle to define itself and whose official means have more often than not involved fantastic forms of state-sponsored terror that have had an inevitable impact on the very fabric of the society itself. Argentina is a country where the dead are just nameless bodies, entirely disposable in an effort to cleanse and disinfect the body politic, and also a country where the dead are venerated to the point of obsession. Argentina is a country where bodies are dumped without burial into the river or sea and also a country where the rich and powerful are buried in their own opulent city, the Recoleta cemetery, "one of the most popular [tourist] attractions in Argentina" (Barnes 1978: 2). Argentina is a country where people are disappeared for seemingly having fallen into "enemy" hands and where a whole people was impassioned over the theft and disappearance of Eva Perón's dead body and where a former Argentine president was murdered in an attempt to make him tell where this body had been hidden (ibid.: 176). Argentina is a country where "it's a relief to see people arrive these days, confirming the fact that they're still alive. [And] . . . also a relief, unfortunate, but a relief, to find out they're dead . . . [because] the other possibility is the most intolerable one" (Valenzuela 1983: 127). Such a society and the actions, feelings, and beliefs of its people can be explained, diagnosed, and analyzed; indeed, a "deep rationality lurks behind appearances" (Galeano 1978: 306). But something crucial to its very modus operandi—the arbitrariness, the paralyzing blanket of fear, the macabre fascinations, the abundant absence of explanation, in short, the fundamental haunting quality of it—is lost when a rationalism of human behavior and social system is presumed to be the definitive measure of its disposition and spirit. And so too something crucial to what is needed to motivate the fight against it and succeed is missing.

Luisa Valenzuela opens a necessary door—not the only one and not a self-sufficient one, but necessary nonetheless—when she shows us that AZ is missing what he is missing. What is missing could have been filled in with the kind of psychoanalytic Marxism the radical psychoanalysts valiantly advocated; it represents a long and honored tradition of critical analysis and political struggle. There is no doubt Valenzuela shares with the radical psychoanalysts their passion for social justice. But the psychoanalytic Marxism or the Marxist psychoanalysis she envisions would require a social psychoanalysis *and* a Marxism capable of treating haunting as an objective force. Beyond "comparing procedures" and "positing analogies of situation" (Jameson 1995: 84), however fruitful, it would require a new form, along the lines of the nonadditive interdisciplinarity Roland Barthes called for. The efforts to create a psychoanalytic Marxism or a Marxist psychoanalysis have thus far, however, attempted to patch together two distinct modes of analysis and healing, two distinct worlds, all the while allowing neither to be essentially altered by the union and leaving the crucial question of mediation to be answered by the most mechanical of solutions. The merger, bound to previously existing priorities of training and belief and to often incommensurate vocabularies, always seems to produce disappointment. The more-psychoanalytic-than-Marxist never quite accept that the subject is a superstructural effect or that the psychic world could really be trumped by the social world. Their hearts are really with Freud and his texts and the richly aesthetic experience of ambivalence and complication. The more-Marxist-than-psychoanalytic never quite accept the autonomy of the psychic world and distrust a politics that relies on psychological explanation. Their hearts are really with Marx and his texts and the demanding task of tracing the flow of capital and the struggles of oppressed social groups. Heart and force, individual and class, repetition and revolution, drives and networks—the marriage never quite succeeds.

Disappearance is an exemplary instance in which the boundaries of rational and irrational, fact and fiction, subjectivity and objectivity, person and system, force and effect, conscious and unconscious, knowing and not knowing are constitutively unstable. Nothing characterizes a terroristic society where the state, in the name of a patriarchal, nationalistic, Christian capitalism, is disappearing people more than haunting does. Haunting, however, is precisely what prevents rational detachment, prevents your willful control, prevents the disaggregation of class struggle and your feelings, motivations, blind spots, craziness, and desires. A haunted society is full of ghosts, and the ghost always carries the message—albeit not in the form of the academic treatise, or the clinical case study, or the polemical broadside, or the mind-numbing factual report—that the gap between personal and social, public and private, objective and subjective is misleading in the first place. That is to say, it is leading you elsewhere, it is making you see things you did not see before, it is making an impact on you; your relation to things that seemed separate or invisible is changing. This is not to say that the gap or the reification is not an enormously powerful real experience. Nor is it to say that haunting somehow transcends the actually existing social relations in which we live, think, and think up new concepts and visions of life. Quite the contrary. But these questions remain: what effectively describes the gap as an organized and elaborate symptom, and what describes the moment when we understand that it is, in fact, misleading us?

This is Valenzuela's concern and her focus: what does a haunted society do to the analyst who is searching to discover certain mysteries or mystifications of life? The ghostly matter of it haunts the analyst. AZ does not understand what is about to happen to him, which is that he will not be able to control the contact he makes with She. He has a drive to understand and to enter her world, but this world of hers (which is his too, only he refuses to acknowledge it) is dangerous. This is partly why the politics toward which he is indirectly moving is not a solution but a condition of his search and its resolution. Haunting is not reason: it is being carried away and into the forces that are more powerful than you . . . at the moment. At the moment because the balance of forces is always there to be restruck, prosaically and dramatically. This is why Valenzuela's story of the searcher is more than anything else a narration of the story of contact. The narration of the story of contact is a kind of reverse colonization (and in this story, as we shall see, AZ will literally have to retrace the steps of the initial conquest of Latin America). The end point of Valenzuela's story is the Encounter, which, in inverse fashion, precedes the failed Discovery, the crucial Journey, and the inevitable Loss of contact and self. AZ discovers She, and before he realizes just how the ghost has a determinant agency on the one who searches, he loses her and some of his old self.

gap in knowledge & desire to know more

ghost as a transformation

The Loss

EL VALIENTE

I could recognize her anywhere even though it's a blurred, rather nondescript photo

A *thousand surprises because today everything has returned to nor-mal. . . . Nothing overemphasized, everything moderate. . . . Everything nicely weighed again and under control* (V 68). Everything is normal but not for very long, you can be assured. AZ is at home reading the paper when a news story catches his eye. *It all began in the afternoon in a bar on the Calle des Escudellers* when a young "banderillero" was sit-ting in the bar and a boasting match ensued among the men of two cou-ples having drinks there. To win the match, which had gotten wilder and wilder, the banderillero broke a beer bottle and slashed his left wrist, exclaiming, "'There!'" (V 70). Rushed to the hospital half un-conscious, the banderillero "got out of bed, subdued the physician and his assistants, took to his heels, and vanished" when he heard that the doctor was going to call the police (V 70). Having returned to his room to seek first aid, the banderillero was eventually caught by the police, released, and then arrested again for fighting in another bar. AZ's "red blood" starts to rush and *by the grace and favor of an unfolding of the paper, I recognize her in the sketch that illustrates the page, I could rec-ognize her anywhere even though it's a blurred, rather nondescript photo* (V 72). Not just anywhere but in the Calle des Escudellers, which keeps repeating like a bad dream, the street where She lives, the street where her sister has disappeared. Apparently Calle des Escudellers is the very surreal every street and the only street the Argentines traverse. Moreover, AZ does not just recall a familiar face; he sees *the work of her hand* even though, properly speaking, she was not the one who broke the bottle and cut the banderillero's veins (V 74).

And AZ then knows that "she is inside me" (V 72). *every little inter-nal part of my body duplicates her and conforms to her, each and every I-particle has her name despite the strange contingency that makes her unnamed* (V 72). AZ's moderate, normal, underemphasized analytic stance is starting to unravel. *Even if she were duly measured and tabu-lated and vivisected and recorded, classified, printed, it wouldn't help at all* (V 67). He begins to understand that "I have remained blind in that strange way that means: my eyes no longer serve to help me find her, my eyes do not take me to her door. they now see the life of other people, they have been blinded because of their sheer confor-mity" (V 73). Her reality seems doubtful to him now, and the "false concepts" of an "empirical mirror" no longer inspire him to gestures of scientific grandeur, but seem deprived "of so many gifts, of wisdom, both superficial and profound" (V 75). "Losing her," he grasps hold of her shadow, a shadow that "forces me to turn a corner," that "permits me to *see*" (V 76). There is not much left of his normal self, and he pursues her shadow, climbing "steep stairs," walking "down long corridors," and going "around angles," and "I don't find her" (V 76). AZ is "running in search of her and coming up against those all too real zones where I know she isn't" (V 80). *and I felt so learned, believing she could be studied and studying her. . . . and I thought I was magnanimous in wanting to defend her against her own self* (V 80, 90).

AZ recognizes She in a photograph in the newspaper and as if in a miracle, he hears what has been silent to him before, the hidden "machine guns" and *her cries, the stones have been clawed in a desperate attempt to cling to something, here she had a spasm, convulsions. she turned down this winding street, she stopped under this arch-way, and despite the darkness managed to project shadows of pain and fear. . . . he takes her by the hand* (V 75, 80–81). He is at a door knocking. There is no response from the other side. *then an explosion. in my head* (V 82). She was here, in this darkened room, he smells it. And then he spies them, the other photographs: *the images of her are cruelly attached to the wall with pins. . . . each photo of her offers me a different face and all of them are for me; the fourth up from the bottom smiles at me, the first to the right has her back to me, there's one with eyes that say no* (V 83). He thinks of saying her name but he doesn't want to and "anyway I don't know it" (V 83). AZ is afraid. Afraid of "falling apart," afraid of "becoming one with her in this room," afraid of "exploding and spattering all four walls" (V 83). Little by little he melts and "weeps" and discovers "everything that I've been losing little by little in life because of fear" (V 85). He hears voices that "reduce me to nobodyness, that leave me by myself so they can talk among themselves and come to a complete understanding" (V 85). And he does indeed "receive" her, but "she tears me apart" and "I finally appreciate what it means to penetrate someone" (V 85).

Sleeping and waking, thirsting and drinking, shuddering and trembling, AZ is sinking and losing himself in the whirling experience of vanishing and regaining consciousness. AZ, dark, alone, and naked: "they are breaking me inside little by little, demolishing my scanty defenses. at times they cut with a sharp scalpel, at times they claw me apart with a hand and tear off pieces of flesh" (V 90). They? The invisible fathers. *adopt an invisible father, the placards say. . . . adopting an invisible father means running unsuspected risks, becoming unlimited,*

losing one's footing even inside one's own bed and no longer knowing
what it means to feel secure. in our city there are seventeen sons of
adopted fathers and one can recognize them clearly. . . . they are . . . the
fearful ones . . . they drag themselves along the unbroken walls. . . . af-
terward they move ahead a few steps more, one can see how sickly and
sterile they are, and they drag their heavy boots that aren't heavy, what
weighs on them is nameless, impossible to forget (V 89). AZ knows
that he "shall never . . . adopt a father" (V 90). He makes a decision: "I
don't think I'll let them win this game in which my life and hers are at
stake. I'll search for her along the road they took when they dragged
her away, she'll reappear for me if I follow the trackless paths they used
to carry her off" (V 87). But is it too late?

The Animating Photograph

AZ, "red blood" pumping, perceives She in a newspaper photograph
illustrating an entertaining human interest/crime story that took place
in an uncanny street. AZ also comes face to face with a wall of photographs, stuck with pins, in a darkened room where he hears voices.
The photographs seem to be there for him. Is it She AZ sees in the
photographs, or is it the *work of her hand*? AZ's analytic stance comes
unglued as ordinary photographs turn the world upside down. (Susan
Sontag says that photographs "fiddle with the scale of the world"
[1977: 4].)

Photographs furnish a type of evidence. Their declarative verisimilitude convinces us of what we already know or surmise, or proves the
existence of something we have doubted, but suspected. The quality
and intensity of that evidential "ah yes!" photographs produce depend
not only on the specific image in question, but also on the social context
of their appearance. What are the photographs AZ sees certifying?
They provide the evidence that a disappearance is real only when it is
apparitional, only when the missing or the lost or the not there shines
through, there where it might not have been expected, there in that moment of affective recognition that is distinctive to haunting. We return,
then, to the question of the photograph's relationship to haunting and
to the ghost story. The photograph is involved in the ghostly matter of
things and not surprisingly, since the wavering quality of haunting
often hinges on what sign or image raises the ghost and what it means
to our conscious visible attention. The photograph's relationship to
haunting is never simple. When photographs appear in contexts of

haunting, they become part of the contest between familiarity and strangeness, between hurting and healing, that the ghost is registering. The photograph is involved in the ghostly matter of state-sponsored disappearance.

On June 28, 1966, President Arturo Umberto Illia was in his office in the Casa Rosada, having spent the night there with a group of young Radical men preparing for the coup that would end his thirty-two-month government. The president was *signing photographs as mementos for the young men who had kept him company during the last night of his presidency* (Simpson and Bennett 1985: 46). As General Alsogaray of the First Army Corps swept the photos off the desk and onto the floor, indifferent to them, he announced that he represented the armed forces and had come to receive Illia's resignation. The president was reputed to have said, " 'The armed forces . . . are represented by me. You are making use of a force which should be at the disposal of the Constitution and the law. You cannot invoke a representation which is not yours' " (ibid.). But you can indeed invoke, uphold, and use representations that do not belong to you, making them yours, as the general well knew. He had had experience in this regard.

From the first use of the surveillance photograph by the Paris police in the arrest of the Communards in June 1871 to the ubiquity of the photo identification card we display on demand, photography has proved to be a propitious tool by which modern states can survey and control their populations. During military rule and as part of the system of disappearance, the Argentine armed forces and their paramilitary auxiliary not surprisingly used photographs for surveillance. But this was not the only application. Photographs were also employed, along with other props and weapons of which they inevitably became a part, during torture and interrogation. Two principal types of photographs were deployed in interrogation and torture. The military always photographed the bodies of the assassinated, and they routinely confiscated family photographs when they abducted people and ransacked their homes. Both of these types of photographs literally become "memento mori" in the context of disappearance (Sontag 1977: 15). If the family photograph already evokes the ghostly traces of dispersed relatives—because it "memorialize[s] . . . [and] restates symbolically . . . the imperiled continuity and vanishing extendedness of family life" (ibid.: 9)—its use in torture gives dispersion, if not also the security of kinship, a highly sinister charge. Waving the family photograph in front of your face, the torturer may shout or speak quietly, intimidating you to nervous exhaustion: "We have them too." "They don't care about you anymore." "Nobody loves you anymore." "You are nobody." "We own your memories." "You are part of our family now."

To disappear is to exist in a world where dispossession and unreality rule. The photograph has an enormous power to "give people an imaginary possession of" an "unreal" past or present. This photographic power is harnessed in torture, where past and present do not have the same boundaries they have in normal life and where the torturer attempts to make the *desaparecido* own and own up to the subversiveness it is the military's purpose to eliminate. The photograph of the "dead subversive" serves this purpose because although "the picture may distort . . . there is always a presumption that something exists, or did exist, [or will exist] which is like what's in the picture" (ibid.: 5). The always lingering documentary quality of the photograph becomes a potent weapon in this perilous construction of reality. "Who is that? What's her name?" "We know you know. Come on, talk now." "Your comrades have killed each other." "We're winning the war. You and your kind are doomed." "You think we're joking, here's the proof." "This is your face, this is your fate." *each photo of her offers me a different face and all of them are for me; the fourth up from the bottom smiles at me, the first to the right has her back to me, there's one with eyes that say no.*

But the torturer rarely rises above the rank of colonel. The generals and admirals and commanders try not to get their hands dirty, and they certainly do not take the pictures. (Who does take these pictures? I wonder about that. Do they get to take pictures instead of torturing and killing? Or does the shooting feel comparable? Does taking the photographs limit the photographer's experience of death, war, and transporting people into the netherworld of disappearance or convert it into a manageable still image? Do they take pride in their work?) This is military rule, after all. There are procedures to be followed, ranks to be respected, and paperwork to be completed. The armed forces had not only to perform, but also to provide evidence of meritorious conduct, through appropriate channels, and in that quintessential representational form of bureaucratic rationality, the memo. And so the photograph of the "dead subversive" was taken not only for the *desaparecido,* it was taken for one's superiors. Not only taken, but included "in the monthly resumés," the memos the colonels "dispatched to the

First Army Corps and to the President of the Republic" (Amnesty International 1980: 17–18) to show that the job was being done well and to give them copy for the morning newspaper.

"An object that tells of loss, destruction, disappearance . . . does not speak of itself. Tells of others" (Jasper Johns in Sontag 1977: 199). The newspaper photograph that disturbs AZ does not only speak of itself, of the boasting banderillero and his exploits. It tells of others, or, rather, it conjures up a missing woman and the signs (the street, the police) of her mysterious yet organized disappearance. It is not much to go on, but nonetheless, in an important moment of unsettling solicitation, AZ sees both She and the *work of her hand* in a new way. The encounter with the photograph is the inaugural moment of AZ's ability to see what he had been missing before. The photograph of the disappeared or the photograph that summons the missing presence of a *desaparecido* always registers the double edge of haunting: the singularity of the loss of my previously held securities and supports, the particular trouble the ghost is making for me; and the sociality of those abstract but compelling forces flashing now (and then) in the light of day, the organized trouble the system is experiencing.

Roland Barthes's small book on photography, *Camera Lucida* (1981), might help us to understand AZ's experience with the photograph and the haunting it inaugurates. Who better than Barthes, who "wanted to learn at all costs" what the photographic essence consisted of, who "'scientifically' alone and disarmed" found it in a photograph of his mother as a child, found it there as his own haunted past became a *shared* hallucination (3, 7)? Barthes begins uneasily, feeling torn between languages: "one expressive, the other critical; and at the heart of this critical language, between several discourses, those of sociology, of semiology, and of psychoanalysis" (8). He gets fed up with all of them and the reductions their paradigms enforce. Barthes makes a critical analytic decision, one bound to raise red flags for suspecting sociologists: he resolves "to start my inquiry with no more than a few photographs, the ones I was sure existed *for me*" (8). Barthes hopes to confound the stalemate between "science and subjectivity" by inventing "a new science for each object" (8)!

Barthes's wish to invent a new science notwithstanding, his crucial discovery is attained through an experience (or an experiment) that normally makes science nervous. *In this glum desert, suddenly a specific photograph reaches me; it animates me, and I animate it. So that is how*

I must name the attraction which makes it exist: an animation. *The photograph itself is in no way animated . . . but it animates me: this is what creates every adventure* (20). The decisive insight of Barthes's meditation on photography and of the methodological turn he makes upon its discovery is the pivotal role of animation. Barthes grasps that the photograph's capacity to make meaning meaningful, to convey the existence of something profoundly or vividly or eloquently so that it matters to the viewer, is bound to its power to attract, "to animate me," to draw me in, sometimes besides myself. Barthes is looking for the essence of the photograph—he has spent many years studying sign systems, their grammatologies, and their ideological effects. He finds the irreducible essence of the photograph in its affective power. He has found what he is looking for: "it was thereby what I wanted, what I ought to reduce the Photograph *to*" (21). But he doesn't want to reduce the affective "intentionality" of the photograph. He wants to keep it with him (to "retain" it), and he wants to deliver its magnetism and its enticements to us. "But could I retain an affective intentionality, a view of the object which was immediately steeped in desire, repulsion, nostalgia, euphoria?" (21). On the basis of his experiential inquiry into the photographs he "was sure existed *for me*," Barthes devises a distinction of elements that helps foreground the way in which the photograph's incitements or its animism works and that enables us to better understand how photographs participate in haunting.

Barthes names the element of the photograph that "transforms 'reality' without doubling it, without making it vacillate," the element without "duality . . . indirection . . . disturbance," the *studium* (41). The *studium* creates an interest, "one that is even stirred sometimes, but in regard to [it] my emotion requires the rational intermediary of an ethical and political culture" (26). The *studium* does not refer to the detached study of a photograph, but rather to a kind of participation in the cultural, historical, and politically transparent information of the photograph, "without special acuity" (26). It is usually the most obvious tableaux of the photograph—the recognizable and culturally comprehensible signs of a family, a disaster, a revolution, an atrocity, a loving moment, a dignified portrait. Because it appeals to our cultured habits, the *studium* generates "*polite* interest" and educates and communicates with civility (27). It may shout, but it does not wound (41).

The *punctum* is what "breaks" or "punctuates" the *studium*. In Barthes's view, it is not so much something that one looks for as what "rises from the scene, shoots out of it like an arrow, and pierces me" (26). The *punctum* is "that accident which pricks me (but also bruises me, is poignant to me)" (27). The *punctum* is a "wound," or a "prick," the punctuation mark of an affectively moving episode. It is the "off-center detail" that draws one in and around the polite cultural engagement with the historically interesting or the politically poised *studium*, that causes me to "*give myself up*" (43). It creates a compelling astonishment with reality—"*that-has-been*"—and with truth—"*there-she-is!*" (113). "Whether or not it is triggered, it is an addition: it is what I add to the photograph and *what is nonetheless already there*" (55). For Barthes, the *punctum* is the detail that arouses the still image from its flat immobility and from which the moving world beyond the four corners of the image emerges for us: it is the medium by which the photograph and its reference come alive. The *punctum*, then, is not simply my individual aesthetic experience; it is what brings to life the life external to the photo, what Barthes calls the "dynamics" of the "blind field" (57). An example from him might help:

> Here is Queen Victoria photographed in 1863 by George W. Wilson; she is on horseback, her skirt suitably draping the entire animal (this is the historical interest, the *studium*); but beside her, attracting my eyes, a kilted groom holds the horse's bridle: this is the *punctum;* for even if I do not know just what the social status of this Scotsman may be (servant? equerry?), I can see his function clearly: to supervise the horse's behavior: what if the horse suddenly began to rear? What would happen to the queen's skirt, *i.e., to her majesty?* The *punctum* fantastically "brings out" the Victorian nature (what else can one call it?) of the photograph, it endows this photograph with a blind field. (57)

The blind field and its fundamental imbrication in the visible field is what we are aiming to comprehend. The blind field is what the ghost's arrival signals. The blind field is never named as such in the photograph. How could it be? It is precisely what is pressing in from the other side of the fullness of the image displayed within the frame; the *punctum* only ever evokes it and the necessity of finding it. Yet the blind field is present, and when we catch a glimpse of its endowments in the paradoxical experience of seeing what appears to be not there we know that a haunting is occurring. If you are looking for the blind field, you first have to make your way to it, open to its particular mode of address. If you are not looking for it, it can take you to it without your permission.

For the searcher of essences, what significance should we make of the punctuating photograph? The *punctum* is what haunts. It is the detail, the little but heavily freighted thing that sparks the moment of arresting animation, that enlivens the world of ghosts.[20] The enchanting detail cannot be predicted in advance or calculated for methodological rigor. It is without doubt, and despite Barthes's desire to create a science of it, a highly particularized, if also fully social, phenomenon. Luisa Valenzuela does not tell us what triggered AZ's recognition of the *work of her hand*. Was it the look on the banderillero's face? Was it something in the background she does not identify? Was it the writing on the beer bottle? Was it the askew apron the waiter was wearing as he stood to the side of the table? Was it the angle of the shadow AZ's coffee cup made on the unfolding newspaper? The evidence for the ghostly matter is what *I add to the photograph and what is nonetheless already there.* Yet much hinges on the relative balance of forces between what I add and what is nonetheless already there. We have seen that the photograph's very power to haunt—the animating force we do not want to reduce—can be used by the state to intimidate, to wage war against the imagination, to control the balance of certainty and doubt, reality and unreality that disappearance manipulates. The photograph, then, takes its place in this contest of haunting.

Into such a contest is exactly where the Mothers of the Plaza de Mayo entered, photographs pinned to their hearts. The Mothers were middle-aged women, mostly housewives with no political experience, who met while searching for their children in the various waiting rooms of the Interior Ministry.[21] They made their public appearance, the first and for a long time the only (illegal) public protest against the regime, in the shadow of the security police in April 1977 when fourteen women walked quietly in a circle around the Plaza de Mayo. (The Plaza de Mayo is the center of state authority in Argentina. The presidential palace faces it, as do government offices, major banks, and the cathedral.) This was to be the start of their weekly Thursday demonstrations and the crucial organization they formed first to find their disappeared children and then later to demand the end of military authority and economic repression and to fight for a radical transformation of Argentine society. The women wore "'flat shoes so we could make a run for it if they came after us'" and left their handbags at home (María del Rosario in Fisher 1989: 28). The Mothers donned white shawls (the *pañuelo*) embroidered initially with the names of their own disappeared children and the dates they disappeared, and later in 1984 embroidered with their new slogan, *Aparición con vida,* or Bring them back alive. They also carried posters with enlarged photographs of their children on them or wore the photographs attached to their clothing with pins. Their own children at first, but by the time of the trials after the democratic election of Alfonsín, the Mothers had moved well beyond the unique photograph of my child that I long for to handing out photocopies of faces, eyes, and mouths (see Bouvard 1994: 159). *The photograph is in no way animated . . . but it animates me and others.*

For the Mothers, the photographs were a spirit guide to the *desaparecidos* and to disappearance as an organized system of repression. The photographs—"token[s] of absence" and potent evidence of what is harrowingly present—constituted a repertoire of counterimages, part of a movement to punctuate the silence, to break the *studium*-like quality of disappearance, to "lay claim to another reality" (Sontag 1977: 16). Repossessing what has been taken away "as if by a diabolical magic act," the photographs abrade: "*This face is mine . . . and I have a right to find it*" (Agosin 1989: 94). The Mothers transformed the docile portrait or, in the case of the photocopies, the disembodied mechanical reproduction of a bodily organ into a public *punctum*. The prickly detail that triggers the presence of the blind field, these photographs gave specific reference: They have been here once. They should be here now. Where are they? And they personified the missing person, the figure around which the banal and the singular power of the state to repress converged. The Mothers' photographs express a "longing to inhabit . . . neither oneiric . . . nor empirical . . . it is fantasmatic, deriving from a kind of second sight which seems to bear me forward to a utopian time, or to carry me back to somewhere in myself" (Barthes 1981: 40). This second sight, which transports longing between the somewhere in myself that is right here in the middle of all the terror and the utopian elsewhere that I imagine for my future, is what embracing the ghostly image can sometimes bestow. The longing to inhabit carries me forward and back, from force to hand to face, and "it is as if *I were certain* of having been there or of going there" (ibid.).

The Mothers came out of the shadows carrying that most modern of image-making devices in order to precisely name the terror and repression otherwise simply known as the *Proceso* (the Process of National Reorganization) and to end it. Systematic disappearance of people is a method of control that requires a calculation that can easily go wrong.

Everyone must know just enough to be terrified, but not enough either to have a clear sense of what is going on or to acquire the proof that is usually required by legal tribunals or other governments for sanction. The architects of the Dirty War were well aware of this and were, for a time, successful in avoiding the mistakes made in Chile and Uruguay. (In Chile, public mass assassinations were too public; in Uruguay the political prisoners were able to organize.) "No one was demonstrating in the capitals of the Western world about Argentina as they had four years earlier [1973] about Chile. No foreign government had broken off diplomatic relations with the Videla regime, as they had with that of General Pinochet. It was generally known that unpleasant things were happening in Argentina, but since it was impossible to say precisely what the nature of those things was, protest and complaint were difficult to focus" (Simpson and Bennett 1985: 152). The Mothers used the photographs to represent just this knowing and not knowing that is characteristic of disappearance, its terror and its political power. In this context, the photographs had hardly to be melodramatic, but they did need to conjure the ghosts and the haunting quality of disappearance. The photographs did this not only because they captured the essence of the lost loved face and voice but also because of their public display, itself already an instance of an oppositional political imaginary at work, an act of sedition.

The power of the Mothers' photographs was not the moral condemnation the portrait of atrocity commands. After the coup had ended and the Alfonsín government started exhuming bodies prominently displayed in the daily newspapers, the Mothers were especially sensitive to oversaturation of images of suffering. "'When Alfonsín took power the sensationalist press began the "show." People were saturated with horror and they didn't want to know any more about it, because horror has its limits. That was the intention'" (Graciela de Jeger in Fisher 1989: 129). The Mothers had other intentions. They wanted to force a national confrontation with irrevocable wounds and grief; by this time in their development as an organization, they had a full blown political agenda for the fundamental restructuring of Argentine society that first and foremost required accountability and punishment for those responsible for disappearance. But they also wanted us to understand something very important about disappearance. The photograph attests "that the object has been real, the photograph surreptitiously induces belief that it is alive. . . . Photography's inimitable feature . . . is that someone has seen the referent *in flesh and blood,* or again *in person"* (Barthes 1981: 79). More than this surreptitious belief, the Mothers would insist that disappearance is a state of being. *Aparición con vida.* And thus we come not only to what AZ learns through loss, but also to the heart of the Mothers' second sight.

Aparicíon con vida

The military government thought the mothers were crazy—*las locas,* they called them. (*"'This is a matter of no concern to us. These women are mad.'*—Official of the Office of the President of the Argentine Republic, questioned about the campaign on behalf of the disappeared, June 1977" [Simpson and Bennett 1985: 152].) Initially, they also thought the women were laughable:

> After their success in stamping out all organized resistance of working-class and political organizations, the military dismissed as laughable the suggestion that a group of women could pose any threat to their position. In reality the sudden appearance of the Mothers in Plaza de Mayo had provoked serious difficulties in the seemingly impenetrable repressive apparatus of military rule. They had failed to anticipate that the trail of deceptions they had laid in government offices, police stations and military headquarters would be the setting for the first real challenge to their rule.
>
> They were also surprised by the nature of the challenge. The military had acquired much of their moral authority by promoting themselves as the only ones capable of defending the values of Christianity and the family in the face of a threat from 'Marxist subversives.' They found themselves confronted by the very image which, in a vision they shared with the church, personified the stability and order of family life. They did not know how to react to the silent accusing presence of Mothers in the square. . . . They tried using force to break up the meetings, made arrests, issued threats, believing that this would be enough to frighten them off, but every week the Mothers came back in greater numbers. (Fisher 1989: 60)

That the Mothers of the Plaza de Mayo created a powerful political movement by appropriating and transforming conventional and Christian notions of motherhood has been well documented. The transformation of relatively apolitical middle-aged mothers into the inheritors and guardians of "their" children's political aspirations for social justice was a trenchant refutation of the usual conservatism of motherhood. And indeed, the social maternity and radical right-to-life philosophy their political strategies and actions reflected was a model for women organizing against state repression throughout Latin and Central America. Motherhood was without doubt the originating identity that drove the Mothers and that continued to sustain their always dangerous political work. But the truly unique contribution of the Mothers was their extraordinary understanding of haunting and its crucial place in a society fraught with state-sponsored disappearance.

The Mothers are the ones who understood, better than Amnesty International or CONADEP or the radical psychoanalysts and all the rest, what it meant to be *connected* to the disappeared, connected viscerally, connected through kinship, connected through a shared social experience. They understood this connection not because they were mothers per se, but because they made, as AZ begins to make, a special contact with loss and with what was missing but overwhelmingly present. The maintenance and cultivation of the connection to the disappeared, the responsibility the Mothers took for them, their attempt to communicate with them and to locate them, showing their faces, eyes, and mouths in public, and the Mothers' extraordinary absence of fear of trafficking in and with the haunting remains of state terror enabled them to assert that disappearance is not torture, death, or homicide.

Disappearance is a complex system of repression, a thing in itself. With less noise than expected, it removes people—including and significantly those it never tortures or kills—from their familiar world, with all its small joys and pains, and transports them to an unfamiliar place where certain principles of social reality are absent. The disappeared, then, are not dead terrorists or dead children. They are people who have disappeared through enforced absence and fearful silence. When the disappeared make their presence known outside their own netherworld of darkened rooms, mournful moans, terrifying agony, and stolen moments of tenderness and solidarity with their fellow *desaparecidos,* they must perforce appear as ghosts. Even when the dead return to the world of living, they are always ghostly, they are alive with the force that has prompted their return.

It would certainly be reasonable to consider "the disappeared" the dead since the probability of death was very high. Why then did the Mothers, those who searched for the disappeared, insist that disappearance, not death, is the salient and crucial condition? Because they wanted to know what happened to the missing ones; they wanted us to know; they wanted those responsible to account for their actions; they wanted to talk with the missing; they wanted the disappeared returned.

Death exists in the past tense, disappearance in the present. In 1978 a delegation of Mothers was in Rome. Standing in a receiving line, hoping to speak to the pope, "Hebe de Bonafini thrust pictures of their children into his hands, crying out, 'Please help the *disappeared*!' He allowed the pictures to slip through his hands onto the floor and kept walking. Hebe cried out once again, 'Do something for the *disappeared*!'" (Bouvard 1994: 88). Help the disappeared. Do something for them. Tell us where they are . . . because they are somewhere.

Where are the disappeared? The disappeared are in another world, a world some Mothers were taken to also. This is, surely, one of the reasons the Mothers knew that disappearance was not death. Disappearance was all around them, they smelled it, they sensed it, they felt its bewitching compulsion: it was always threatening to envelop them. The disappeared have gone through *the other door, its floods of tears with consolation enclosed*. The precise power of disappearance as a system of terror and repression is the other door, being thrust across a menacing threshold and into a somewhere whose whereabouts and coordinates are unknown and threatening. The other door and *its floods of tears* are what haunt the population into trembling silence. The other door is what must be conjured otherwise. Not death. To insist that disappearance is not death but its own state of being *consolation enclosed*—because it exists and is living with us, doing things to us, scaring us, driving us from our homes into exile, making us inconsolably lonely, or crazy, or unable to see what is right in front of our faces, or because it is goading us to fight—is to pinpoint its haunting quality. To withstand and to defy its haunting power requires speaking to it directly, not paralyzed with fear, out of a concern for justice. *How we can talk with them?* (Agosin 1990: 37).

There is no contradiction between the probability or even the fact that most disappeared had been killed and the Mothers' demand, *Aparición con vida*. Bring them back alive. This is an extraordinary demand and one that was not entirely popular in 1984 when a civilian government was restored to power and the national mood favored forgetting and moving on. Although the junta initially denied all disappearances, they passed two laws in 1979 that defined the disappeared as dead: the presumption of death law and a law granting economic reparations to the families of the deceased. The presumption of death law applied to those who went missing between 1974 and 1979; its purpose was to turn the disappeared into the "'presumed dead' so that the Mothers would stop pressing their cases" (Bouvard 1994: 139). Upon taking office, Alfonsín revised these laws, but their basic features remained the same, including the proviso that the state could "request a declaration of death against the wishes of the family" so that "a judge could then declare a person dead without any attempt to investigate the circumstances of the *disappearance*" (ibid.). By 1984, when mass exhumations of *Non nombre* graves were a daily feature of Argentine life, the Mothers began to receive letters from the government instructing them to collect the remains of their children. Or they received boxes of bones accompanied by letters like the following one that Beatriz de Rubinstein got about her daughter Patricia, who had disappeared in February 1977:

> Mar del Plata, November 1984
> Dear Madam,
> As a culmination to your endless search for your daughter Patricia, we have decided to send you what's left of her, which, without any doubt, will satisfy your anxiety to meet her again earlier than was foreseen by God.
> This decision was taken as a result of a long investigation into your daughter's activities with the armed guerrillas and, just in case you don't know, we will give you a synthesis of the crimes that she committed, together with her husband.
> —TREASON.
> —AIDING AND ABETTING THE ACTIVITIES OF THE ENEMY.
> —COLLABORATING ACTIVELY WITH THE MONTONERO MURDERERS.
> As a consequence of all the above we condemned her to death.
> May God, our Father, have mercy on her soul.
> Legion Condor—Squadron 33—Mar Del Plata (Fisher 1989: 140).

Aparición con vida. The Mothers were vigorously opposed to the presumption of death, to posthumous homage, and to economic reparations.

> But the truth is, we know they've killed them. *Aparición con vida* means that although the majority of them are dead, no one has taken responsibility for their deaths. (Carmen de Guede in Fisher 1989: 127)

> We already know that thousands of *desaparecidos* were secretly murdered and buried. The exhumations don't tell us anything we don't already know. . . . With the exhumations they want to eradicate the problem of the disappearances, because then there are no more *desaparecidos,* only dead people. . . . They have returned people who disappeared . . . saying they'd died in "*enfrentamientos*" [armed confrontations, the military explanation for the appearance of dead bodies]. If you accept this, in your desperation

to have the remains of your loved one, you lose all your rights. We don't want the names of the victims. We know who they are. . . . They have to explain what they don't want to explain. This is the meaning of *aparición con vida*. (Graciela de Jeger in Fisher 1989: 128–29)

The bones don't interest us. What are we going to do with the bones? (Beatriz de Rubinstein in Fisher 1989: 129)

A bag of bones tells us nothing about disappearance. A bag of bones is not justice. A bag of bones is knowledge without acknowledgment, the "sacramental transformation" of information into publicly sanctioned truth (Weschler 1990: 4). A bag of bones only aims to eradicate "any meaning that death might have in society," aims to eliminate "historical memory" and public memorials in a context where death is a supreme instance of national sovereignty (Franco 1986: 12). The Mothers insisted on keeping the disappeared alive because they opposed the false reconciliation that national-sponsored grieving for the dead and for burying the "terrible" past promised. The Mothers insisted on *Aparición con vida* because they sought not to bury and forget the dead, but rather a "dynamic reintegration of the dead and disappeared into contemporaneity" (ibid.: 14). Argentina put the generals on trial, which was unusual, but little came of it except restrictions on filing complaints for crimes committed during military rule (*Punto final*) and *Obediencia Debida* (the Law of Due Obedience), which upheld the immunity of military subordinates for actions taken under order.[23] *Aparición con vida* meant ending the conditions that produced disappearance, the only way to provide a hospitable memory for the *desaparecidos*. *Aparición con vida* meant that these conditions had not ended.[24] *Aparición con vida* meant that the haunting ground remained and that the reckoning with the ghosts had yet to take place. In 1987 the Mothers raised the slogan AGAINST MILITARY CIVIL AUTHORITARIANISM (Bouvard 1994: 169).

Disappearance is not only about death. Disappearance is a thing in itself, a state of being repressed. To counter it and its particular mode of operation requires contact with and work on what it is. As we shall see in a moment, disappearance is a state-sponsored procedure for producing ghosts to harrowingly haunt a population into submission.

AZ loses the woman but gains the ghost. We already know that the ghost has a compelling effect on the person who is searching. AZ stops studying and starts to look for her because the visibility of a subject is tied to the mode of its disappearance. He passed through the other door. But Luisa Valenzuela won't let him die. Not yet, she says:

> He then had to change levels in order to continue his search, because in this level she had already been found in a certain form. . . . A few of us sighed with relief, but most people noticed nothing different in the city when a door, a room with a rickety divan, some pin-ups on the wall, and a dark window with bars disappeared. AZ's hell left us forever and almost no one realized it. . . . Luckily he had water, otherwise we would have found him dead right there and without a gesture of rebellion. Found dead where? That there was created only for him and then his corpse, after being shut up for three days, would have emerged in the middle of the Ramblas and within reach of everyone. All those who didn't know, who didn't see: the fortunate ones. (V 92)

AZ entered the other door, and, thrust into the imperious dialectic of visibility and invisibility, learning and unlearning, acknowledgment and denial, thrust into the normalized unreality of the other side, he takes a journey. *He returns to his Latin America and for the first time recognizes it* (V 93).

The Journey

> They were traveling from south to north, while he was going from north to south. . . . The northern hemisphere is perhaps not the one that suits him best. He places himself head down and begins to descend toward the negative pole that is his not so much by choice as by birth. When they say north (to say cold) we say south (south and shadow), and suddenly he is terrified by the loneliness of a continent whose internal liquids turn the other way round.
>
> HE KNOWS THAT HE MUST GO BACK
>   he feels that the search for her may be only an excuse to bring him back to where he belongs. But there is still a long way to go, much to learn. Above all, learning how to recognize the gifts that are offered him, not letting them slip through his fingers by disdaining them a bit on the one hand and squeezing them a little on the other.
>   Here take the gift of a little book of stories
>   radiant thickness
>   bad writing
>   bad writ
>   ba
>   a
>   of America, and onward (V 120, 106–7)

Here I am: traveling the Moebius strip through America

AZ is traveling from north to south, retracing the steps of the original European discovery of the Americas, from Spain to Mexico to Argentina, the southernmost point of Latin America, mostly remembered in our time for bordering on the great states of North American–inspired terror: Chile, Uruguay, and Paraguay. Bad writing or just radiant with the thick magical reality of America and onward, AZ leaves Barcelona and psychoanalysis, having been miraculously resurrected by Luisa Valenzuela. Arriving in Mexico, "very old women receive him (receive *me*). . . . Women who pray with their feet, the world turned upside down" (V 94).

AZ moves "along goat paths," paths he appears to recollect as if in another time he wandered here, the "place where Quetzalcoatl was born" (V 95). Confronting the elements of water, air, and fire in a different dimension, "the hour for his first purification has come and perhaps the women will contrive to make him understand this by speaking nahuatl. Or perhaps they will accomplish this in some more obscure way such as . . . some vague form of hypnosis" (V 96). The smoke in the adobe hut is suffocating, but AZ stays put to complete the purification ritual and emerge cleansed. Journeying up and down the mountainside on a rickety bus poking along "at the pace of a tired man," AZ "arrives at the roof of this world of roofs" (V 100) with a name, María Sabina, on his lips, and on mythical time. *Here I am: traveling the Moebius strip through America because the space where she is to be found is not Euclidean space nor is her time the same time of which we're dimly aware when we see our skin aging* (V 101). María Sabina gives him the mushrooms and "suddenly everything is a maelstrom" (V 102). AZ is rising and sinking, shouting, and catching a glimpse of the misery of others below. "Time seems to stand still" and everything he had known about the sacred and the profane melts as he dances wildly and witnesses his own death. The mushrooms will do that and so he also receives instructions for making candles and a good coffin (V 109).

AZ is a long way now from the world of psychoanalysis and its individualistic curing rituals, or perhaps he has returned to its lost origins in shamanistic healing.[25] It matters little to the one who, having entered the world of myth, is now changing masks and sexes and languages in the "splendor of the moonlight" (V 111). AZ "runs downhill, shakes off the mask, departs in a motor launch, and heads toward the jungle where he knows his brothers are" (V 113). *For the first and last time his lips pronounce her secret name—a whisper. His lips close and he's for-gotten it* (V 114). He will never pronounce her name again.

And the next thing we know AZ is in Chiapas, which is "in fact *also* the Tucumán jungle" (V 114). His journey thus far has brought him to the primal scene of She's disappearance. *He goes through the jungle of Chiapas, how come the words of the others in Tucumán reach him here? He experiences what had been her experiences in the life that she took such great care to hide from him, the life when she was aware of things and fought for a specific cause and felt sure of herself. Periods that she wanted to forget because there were hopes and with the death of hope it was no longer worth the trouble to keep a memory. How did the words of Alfredo Navoni reach him, that man who figures in an-other story, the story she concealed?* (V 114). We will come back in a moment to the important question of how the words of Navoni and the others in Tucumán reach him. But before AZ has the chance to think that question through, and "after so much wandering about and so much effort he finally" meets up with his "brothers" (V 115, 113). He meets up with revolutionaries in the jungle who are "weeping because they are attacked rather than attacking and must keep an all-night vigil for the dead guerrilla in the midst of the jungle. That man was a brother and continues to be one, in the center of the wheel of life that has formed around his death" (V 115).

El Familiar

Tucumán is a semitropical mountainous region with a flat sugarcane-growing plain in the north of the country known for its long history of labor struggles over sugar. In 1962 Mario Roberto Santucho, who had visited Cuba in 1961, issued "Four Hypotheses on Northern Ar-gentina," in which he argued that the sugar industry constituted the center of the regional economy, making its workers the potential prole-tarian vanguard. By the late 1960s, however, many of the sugar mills in Tucumán had closed, primarily because the regime of Juan Carlos On-ganía cut government price supports, and the region became even more impoverished. The tradition of strong labor organizing, the resem-blance Tucumán bore to eastern Cuba, and the expectations raised by Argentine-born Che Guevara's activities in Bolivia led the ERP (Ejército Revolucionario del Pueblo, the People's Revolutionary Army) in June 1974 to launch "its most audacious—and fatal—challenge to the Ar-gentine state" in Tucumán (Andersen 1993: 127).

In November 1974, Isabel Perón declared a state of siege. On February 5, 1975, she signed secret Decree no. 261, which authorized the army to neutralize subversive elements in Tucumán, the "Cradle of Independence and Tomb of Subversion" (J. Taylor 1994: 200). (The junta gave Tucumán this name in part because the Argentine Declaration of Independence was signed there.) Four days later, the army launched Operativo Independencia (Operation Independence) to wage "Holy War" against the ERP. The operation was a ruthless campaign that involved "psychological action" directed by Jorge Conti, who was "reputed to be a ranking member of the Triple A," the Argentine Anti-Communist Alliance. Designed to present the military as the representative of the people, it included "civil actions" directed by the infamous López Rega, another Triple A leader, and indiscriminate abduction, torture, execution, and disappearance. General Vilas's Operativo Independencia actively promoted an image of conventional warfare between two comparable armies. Camped south of San Miguel de Tucumán, the provincial capital, the army told of many battles with the powerful ERP. But five thousand army troops, along with state security police, were "arrayed against" some 120 to 140 ERP guerrillas (Andersen 1993: 125). The army was, in fact, waging a covert urban war, infiltrating the cities of San Miguel de Tucumán and Concepcíon, using the shadow of the mountains to cover their tracks. As Andersen notes, the ongoing rhetoric of a legitimate war in Tucumán served three purposes. It allowed the army to practice methods of terror it would soon deploy in the country at large: the electric prod, live burial, hanging by wire. It provided a "smoke screen," in the words of a lieutenant, for the illegal violence perpetrated by the army. And it legitimated the army's presence and power for its impending takeover.

Throughout the Argentine northwest the tradition of folk legends was very strong. In the province of Santiago del Estero many of the tales had a magical, benevolent twist. . . . But in sugar territory, particularly in Tucumán, where peasants believed in devils and demons, the most important local myth was sinister and threatening. It revolved around the shadowy Perro Familiar (the Family Dog), known to Tucumán's peasants as simply "el Familiar."

It was commonly believed that el Familiar was the son of the Devil and stalked its prey after midnight. When a peasant mysteriously disappeared, sometimes to be found later with his body ripped apart, his co-workers mourned the loss. . . . To explain the phenomenon, they chalked it up to the predations of el Familiar.

There are a number of . . . interpretations for the appearance of el Familiar in the sugar-growing region. . . . Some claimed the work of el Familiar was in fact that of the mill owners and their foremen. . . .

For the peasants of Tucumán the appearance of Vilas and the army in Operativo Independencia was no different than a return of el Familiar (ibid.: 136).

By the end of 1975, Operativo Independencia "had broken the ERP" (Guest 1990: 19). Although right-wing violence had increased dramatically—in the first three months of 1976, 549 murders were attributed to the Triple A death squads (ibid.: 20)—the public justification for the coup, the need to eliminate "left-wing subversion," was a vicious and deadly charade. The so-called Dirty War began after the defeat of the small and largely ineffective ERP. The Dirty War began after the war that didn't quite exist in the forests of Tucumán was over. *Como en la Guerra,* Like in War. The Holy Dirty War, never officially declared, initiated with the defeat of the putative enemy, long in the making, spooky as all, was not any less real for merely being "like" a war. The metaphorical "like" is as real as you can get. *They are weeping.* "Today the province [of Tucumán] possesses the nation's only public Museum of the Subversion . . . where the junta's official memory of its victims has been enshrined . . . and its capital has proven to be the only city in the Republic where it has been impossible to establish discussion groups . . . of the mothers of the disappeared" (J. Taylor 1994: 200).

The Mystery Play

Of course the brothers don't tell AZ all this because they are weeping and are barely there at all in this most powerful of conjuring jungles. Instead, they tell him a story that begins with this admission: "'We're on better terms with ourselves now because finally we understand the struggle. . . . It was different before, though closely related'" (V 116).[26] The story is called "The long night of the thespians." Eight amateur thespians, or comrades, put on a performance of *The Wedding* in the main square of the village where they were staying. But this was no ordinary performance. It started simply with Carlos as the bridegroom, Pedro as the priest, Pancho as the best man, and Fatty, a recent arrival, as the bride. The rest of the cast was cooking pancakes on the stage. Fatty was brought onstage dressed in fancy and colorful saris. She was blindfolded and undressed "so we could cover her body with the lace-pancakes and her face with a veil of salami. We perfumed her with vanilla extract, we put a collar of mazard berries on her, we gave her an artistic bunch of onions to hold, we painted the pancakes covering her breasts with jam." They were following the ritual "strictly." Things went awry when the best man invited the audience to "'come, eat with us,' and we all began to eat Fatty's clothes—in little bites at first, then more and more greedily as the enthusiastic audience joined us onstage and we snorted like hogs, chewing and chewing, and I don't recall when things began to go wrong but suddenly I found something hard between my teeth and I don't know what I could have been thinking of just then but when next we looked for Fatty all that was left of her was bones. And not all of them at that" (V 119). AZ asks, "'So you ate Fatty up?'" The answer: "'Well, if you put it that way. I don't suppose so. There would have been blood, innards, things like that. . . . Something strange took place that night and we never heard of Fatty again. That same night we disappeared" (V 119).

AZ hears a story about how someone can disappear, can be eaten up alive, while playing and having some fun, without anyone really noticing until it is too late. *All that was left of her was bones.* It is also a little parable about the founding of Argentina. In 1534 Charles V of Castile made a land gift and a promise of riches to Pedro de Mendoza, who was expected in return to forestall the Portuguese and to conquer the legendary Indian kingdom of the interior. In 1535 Mendoza left Spain with sixteen ships and sixteen hundred men, "three times the number that accompanied Cortés in the conquest of Mexico some sixteen years previously" (Rock 1985: 10). In 1536 Mendoza arrived at the River Plate and christened his encampment Puerto Nuestra Señora Santa María del Buen Aire. Arriving at the end of the southern summer, the Spaniards had no cereals to plant, and severe food shortages got worse as the Querandí waged war against the Spaniards, attempting to enslave them and steal their food (ibid.). *The founders' teeth chatter from cold and fear [and hunger]. The breeze plays rustling music in the tree-tops, and beyond, on the endless plains, Indians and phantoms silently spy on them* (Galeano 1985: 153). And so they started to eat each other. In the newly christened Argentina, lonely, hungry white men ate their own already dead brothers in silence and secrecy to satisfy the most banal of hungers:

Finally, there was such want and misery that there were neither rats, nor mice, nor snakes to still the great dreadful hunger and unspeakable poverty, and shoes and leather were resorted to for eating and everything else. It happened that three Spaniards stole a horse, and ate it secretly, but when it was known, they were imprisoned and interrogated under the torture. Whereupon, as soon as they admitted their guilt, they were sentenced to death by the gallows, and all three were hanged. Immediately afterwards, at night, three other Spaniards came to the gallows to the three hanging men, and hacked off their thighs and pieces of their flesh, and took them home to still their hunger. A Spaniard also ate his brother, who died in the city of Buenos Aires. (Luis Dominguez in Rock 1985: 11)

The beginning, perhaps, of a culture of terror that secretly eats its own. There is something pathetic in the image of these conquistadors left with nothing but each other to consume, and secretly, surreptitiously, without the benefit of ritual or mythology.[27] But " 'eating people has one danger: the irrepressible belch. It overtakes you suddenly like a mouthful coming up from the guts, and what can you do? put on an innocent face and swallow again while putting out your cheeks.' 'If only that were all there is to it' " (V 120). They were traveling from south to north, while AZ was going from north to south, going along somewhat confused about what is happening in dream time and what is happening in real time, a little irritated about a "grown man" having to accept fairy tales (V 121). AZ has a couple more revelations about incorporating others and the dangers it poses to your insides, but soon he is flying, "flying through other stratospheres" supernaturally, and then of course on a plane to the city "to the south of all souths" (V 122, 124).

The brothers in the jungle tell AZ a very important story. And the telling of this story by self-proclaimed revolutionaries carries its own significance. AZ starts to get to the real political action (and it promises a certain relief: finally, let's get down to business), but instead he is told a Mystery about how someone disappears right before your eyes. Rather than the satisfying clarity of indubitable political analysis, AZ is confounded by myths and dreams and the reversibility of symbols and action. Why? Because the real action involves not only a violent struggle for control over the country's economic and political infrastructure. The real action includes, at its core and indissociably from what we think of as the more sociologically and politically significant battle over capitalism and democracy, a lethal contest for the mastery of people's passions, their thoughts, their dreams and nightmares, and their very capacity to imagine within, against, and beyond the constricting stranglehold of a militarized, patriarchal, Christian, oddly feudal, modern capitalist polity. Such a war, staked as it is on the very essence of what constitutes the fault lines and the lived culture of contemporaneity (our relation to the past and the operating conditions of social life), always occurs at a certain remove from the coldness and emptiness of the big words. Militarized, patriarchal, Christian, capitalist . . . You didn't even need to be a nonbeliever to disappear.

The Real Haunting Business

The organized terror unleashed by the state and the military was designed to destroy not just the organized and overt opposition, but the disposition to opposition, the propensity to resist injury and injustice, and the desire to speak out, or simply to sympathize. The strong, the weak, and even the indifferent were equally targets. " *'First we will kill all the subversives; then we will kill their collaborators; then . . . their sympathizers, then . . . those who remain indifferent; and finally we will kill the timid.'*—General Iberico Saint Jean, Governor of Buenos Aires, May 1976" (Simpson and Bennett 1985: 66). The authoritarian regime could not kill everyone, but the apocalyptic determination to destroy the living, to end the world (how else could we understand the governor's plan to kill everyone except the killers?), created a permanent menace and a collapsing fear that was designed to make "all the Argentineans disappear as persons and as citizens" (the Mothers in Bouvard 1994: 43). Philipe Sollers puts it well: "Who is called on to disappear? A little bit of everyone, and, by extension, those who will dare to ask what became of you. The social fabric is thus held in suspension. . . . Fear, agony, guilt, anxiety, trouble, pervasive malaise: the living become virtually disappeared, potential specters. . . . It is a question of slow poisoning, a delayed psychic bomb. Identity is changed, it becomes hypnotized" (1994: 11). The exercise of state power through disappearance involves controlling the imagination, controlling the meaning of death, involves creating new identities, involves haunting the population into submission to its will. On the ground of the very shape and skin of everyday life itself. To live under the mantle of the omnipresent dread disappearance produces, a fear that "exterminate[s] all social life in the public realm," a fear that eats away at you bite by bite, is to live not "in the light of cold reason, of realistic calculation, of party traditions" (Perelli in Weschler 1990: 89, 213) but in the vestiges of your own shadow, in the gray shades of an everyday life charged with a phantom reality.

Indeed, the military itself saw ghosts everywhere. The Doctrine of National Security (not unique to Argentina by any means) was a program of purification to cleanse the nation of the internal sickness devouring its vital organs and corrupting its mind. The military called this sickness simply subversion, a highly adaptable version of the ever looming International Communist Conspiracy. The definition of subversion was fairly vague, yet flexible. In 1981 the Uruguayan army defined it this way: "actions, violent or not, with ultimate purposes of a political nature, in all fields of human activity within the internal sphere of a state and whose aims are perceived as not convenient for the overall political system" (Weschler 1990: 121). Bad writing certainly, but the most striking and significant aspect of the threat of subversion—the precision in the midst of the vagaries—was just how magical and ghostly it appeared to the military. Listen to General Breno Borges Forte, chief of staff of the Brazilian army: "'The enemy is undefined . . . it adapts to any environment. . . . It disguises itself as a priest, a student or a campesino, as a defender of democracy or an advanced intellectual, as a pious soul or as an extremist protester: it goes into the fields and the schools, the factories and the churches, the universities and the magistracy. . . . It will wear a uniform or civil garb . . . [and] it will . . . deceive'" (ibid.: 122).

What is this enemy if not a conjuring malevolent specter? It is not what it seems to the visible eye. It has extraordinary powers to take familiar shapes and to surreptitiously mess up boundaries and proper protocols. It travels across fields promiscuously. It shimmers through the walls of factories and schools. It emerges uninvited from plots of land growing sugar and wheat. It deceives us, this insinuating all-encompassing force that appears only to some and with such command that it makes all "disconfirmation by empirical contrast impossible" (Perelli in Weschler 1990: 123). The military saw specters, all right, and they were afraid despite all their manly posturing, and it did not matter one bit whether the phantoms they saw were their own malignant and grotesque reflections, because they acted like they saw ghosts and they possessed the power to make their actions matter.

Ghosts and haunting are major weapons wielded by the military in the war to steal and own the people's hands, feet, heads, and hearts. *To eliminate the threatening presence of subversion that the army thought was vexing the nation to hell, the military attempted to replace one set of ghosts with another.* For disappearance is a state-sponsored method for producing ghosts, whose haunting effects trace the borders of a so-ciety's unconscious. It is a form of power, or maleficent magic, that is specifically designed to break down the distinctions between visibility and invisibility, certainty and doubt, life and death that we normally use to sustain an ongoing and more or less dependable existence. Disap-pearance targets haunting itself, targets just that state of being vulnera-ble, and also alert, to the precariousness of social order. The authori-tarian state knows, and with an intentness its sovereignty grants, that people are guided, touched, stirred, moved, reached, troubled, moti-vated, and grieved by things that inhabit them, whether or not these things are sensible or rationally explicable or always visible or arise from an identifiable external source. The authoritarian state acts on this knowledge, demanding blood pacts and honor and courage from the soldiers it deploys to exercise its most pernicious power, the power to haunt. The state ceases to be simply an apparatus or an organization, however qualified by such labels as capitalist or authoritarian, and be-comes a high-powered medium, refereed by hysterical generals, sadistic colonels, and lonely torturers, for exorcising the ghosts it believes are ruining the nation.

From the authoritarian state's point of view, the disappeared cannot remain hidden away, but rather must be discernible enough to scare "a little bit of everyone" into shadows of themselves, into submission. Disappearance is a public secret. Assuming the sovereignty they believe they own and must protect, the military rulers think they can control the ghostly impact of the disappearances they have produced. Because encountering the disappeared or confronting disappearance means col-liding with and touching the bewitching spell of the state. *How come the words of the others in Tucumán reach him here? How did the words of Alfredo Navoni reach him?* Neither the disappeared nor knowledge of them ever appears unaccompanied by ghosts, haunting even those critically motivated accounts of reparation, haunting the revolutionaries, haunting us. A disappearance is real only when it is apparitional.

Disappearance transgresses the distinction between the living and the dead. There are, in effect, two classes of disappeared. First, there are those who have disappeared and who literally return. They may be left standing on a corner, shoes in hand; they may walk out of the detention center and look for the bus. These disappeared can speak for them-selves, haltingly, to be sure, to commissions and judges and newspapers

Roberto as apparition?

and relatives in the language of everyday speech. Second, there are those who have disappeared who reappear only as apparitions. They are not, as I suggested earlier, simply dead and safely ensconced, but are ghostly, animated with a certain kind of life whose future must also be secured. Their faces, eyes, and mouths may be raised high to the sky in the plaza; their bones may arrive in the mail; they may indeed even appear in other guises, such as your patient. These disappeared barely speak for themselves and not in the vernacular. They speak in the language of your dreams. Or you might hear a whisper from around a corner, an inaudible cry emanating from a Ford Falcon. These disappeared speak only the language of haunting. But disappearance transgresses the distinction between the living and the dead and between these two types of *desaparecidos*. Neither of these disappeared ever appear or return or startle alone. The *desaparecido* always bears the ghost of the state whose very power is the defining force of the field of disappearance. The torture, the agony, the terror, the difficult-to-put-into-words experience of being disappeared: the disappeared sustain and convey the traces of the state's power to determine the meaning of life and death. The state creates an identity that remains to haunt those marked by its hand and all the others to whom that hand is extended.

Although the disappeared are only supposed to intimate this menacing state power, the ghost cannot be so completely managed. *Because making contact with the disappeared means encountering the specter of what the state has tried to repress, means encountering it in the affective mode in which haunting traffics.* The disappeared carry the message of the other door, but inside the other door is a flood of tears *and* consolation. What is consolation? What has the state tried to repress? What looming and forbidden desire is this system of repression designed to inhibit and censor? Subversion, opposition, political consciousness, the struggle for social justice, the capacity to imagine otherwise than through the language of the state, the ability to see "what is going on below: hunger, pettiness, misery" and to act on it (V 123). It has many names that I will call simply, and despite the reputation it has acquired of evasive naïveté, the utopian: the apperception of the fundamental difference between the world we have now and the world we could have instead; the desire and drive to create a just and equitable world. The utopian, the most general object of the state's repression, makes its appearance too, lingering among the smoldering remains of a dirty war. *Defeated? Can these things be liquidated by a mere handful of bullets? No* (V 116). The radiant flicker of promise that the ghostly shadow of the disappeared illuminates was what the Mothers grabbed hold of, called living, and tried to keep alive in the wake of their children's deaths and in the wake of the living death the society had become. Their capacity to see in the face of the disappeared, or in a photo of a face, the ghost of the state's brutal authority and simultaneously the ghost of the utopian impulse the state has tried to suppress allowed the Mothers to understand that any successful political response to disappearance had to get on the very ground of haunting.

The Encounter

At times the police beat someone to the ground with their nightsticks, but not too often. By and large a well-placed kick did the trick. Police especially trained in Brazil, experts at handling assailants. And with good Argentine boots.

After a long journey, AZ finally arrives at "his city in the south" (V 125). There are barriers in the street and long lines of people waiting for some vague and unexplained event. "Clean up teams are being formed for the new day of national recovery" (V 126). AZ talks to the people in line and they ask him why he is there. "Because I'm searching. . . . I'm searching for the search," he answers (V 127). AZ is "on the side of

myth toward which all of them are heading: the here-place of ven-
eration, perhaps the motive" (V 128). The motive? For what? For the
people in line? For the police, trained in Brazil with good Argentine
boots, who "at times . . . beat someone to the ground" (V 128)? For
AZ's death? For his search? For the Encounter? AZ hears the words
"Holy and Miracle." He also sees the little flags inscribed with these
words the vendors are selling, like they did on the day when crowds
amassed at the airport to greet Juan Perón on his return to the country:

> On 20 June 1973, the largest crowd ever to assemble in Argentina was
> gathered at Ezeiza airport . . . to greet Juan Perón on his final return to
> the country after 18 years of political exile. It was to prove one of the
> most significant moments in the country's history. . . . The sellers of Party
> favours and of cheap portraits of the general and his dead wife Evita
> did good business. The drums were out in full force too. (Simpson and
> Bennett 1985: 56)

The crowds were composed of three groups who, in fragile coalition,
indicated the ideological complexities of Peronism. One group was the
"working-class . . . who had been won for ever" by Eva Perón, a radio
actress who was once Perón's mistress and then his second wife, who
helped get women the vote, and who engaged in grand public spectacles
of charity. Also present were participants in the Peronist youth and ten-
ant movements and the various rebel groups, including the Tendencia
Revolucionaria. Allied as the Montoneros, they had waged a campaign
of guerrilla warfare that had helped to bring the earlier military dictatorship to an end and Perón back as president. Finally, in addition
to the "big Peronist unions" (ibid.: 57) that Perón had cultivated as a
power base when he was secretary of labor and welfare in the 1943
government, the extreme right factions were there.

   When the Montoneros reached the field, they found that the mostly
military right-wing Peronists had fully occupied the front of the platform from which Perón would address the crowd. After much struggling, the Montoneros forced their way to the front. "As soon as they
did so, a fusillade of shots met them. The right-wing had not, after all,
tried to exclude them: it had arranged an ambush. Several dozen people
on the speaker's platform . . . fired rifles and sub-machine guns into the
densely packed ranks of the Montoneros" (ibid.). Perón was still in
the air and his plane was diverted. The ambush "ruined the effect of his
homecoming . . . but he bore no grudge against the right-wing of
his party for what it had done"; instead, he used the opportunity to ini-

tiate yet another "campaign of persecution against the Revolutionary Tendency" (ibid.). The second Peronist regime was even more corrupt than the first, and Perón's third wife, Isabel Perón, who succeeded him as president after his death in 1974, gave the security forces free rein to terrorize the population and to disappear people in the name of order.

AZ is running and running, and even though "to run after something is to put the machinery of change in motion," who is he now that he knows that "to consume stories like swallowing swords is not a heroic deed, it benefits no one" (V 129)? AZ is "far removed from the waiting crowd because he for his part is moving toward the encounter" (V 130). His "task is to arrive, wherever it may be" (V 131). It is like a graveyard in the streets, crowded with people in line and yet "deserted." Luckily, the cops cannot see him because "they don't see dreams" (V 129). But unhappily, because it is a harbinger of AZ's having become as his beloved She, "he doesn't know that he's gone past the limit and become visible to one and all, just as he never knew that for a few strange days he had been invisible to some" (V 131). Suddenly, a hand grabs him and gives him a rifle and *"he does not know if the search is over now or just beginning"* (V 132). Beginning or ending, this search has already rerouted our conventional notions of the steps, ending here, or so it seems at any rate, with the Encounter. But remember that AZ's search has him "traveling the Moebius strip through America because the space where she is to be found is not Euclidean space nor is her time the same time of which we're dimly aware when we see our skin aging" (V 101). To clarify matters somewhat, Valenzuela declares: in "the beginning is the struggle" (V 132). But AZ does finally get to see She after such a strenuous search. Helicopters are circling and reinforcements are about to arrive and AZ successfully places the dynamite the mudwoman gives him. *The walls of the fortress burst like a great husk and the gleaming heart of the fruit emerges. And he shouts: "It is she!" and the voices, millions of voices also shout, it is she, it is she. . . . And he sees her once again after such a long time, high on a white dais, resplendent, radiating a silent but intense light from within her glass coffin that is like a diamond* (V 134).

Having reached the Encounter, the end of the search, what does AZ find? AZ finds the knot of the ghostly and the real: the police with good Argentine boots, the Holy Day of National Recovery, the beginning of the struggle, and the burst of light that is She. What do we learn about encountering? We learn that in order to understand and to transform state power, to fight even the most coercive, threatening, militarized, and violent state, the story must be told in the mode of haunting. The story of what happens to AZ and to all the others must include this crucial dimension, which is also willy-nilly a mode of experience. Why must the story be told this way?

Because the story, which is very much alive, is happening in and through haunting. We have already seen that disappearance is a state-sponsored method for haunting a population. The power of disappearance to instill tremendous fear and to control, to destroy the life of a people and a society, rests not principally on the cognitive message the state delivers—You will obey or die—but on the way it utters it. Disappearance imposes itself on us where we live: within the already-understood meanings that have been appropriated, worked over, settled into a structure of feeling that oscillates between the banal and the magical. The power of disappearance is the power to control everyday reality, to make the unreal real, to disturb "the essential concepts of our culture" (Barthes 1986: 5) and how we make of them our breathing life world. The power of disappearance is the power to be spoken for, to be vanished as the very condition of your existence. The power of disappearance is to create a deathly consent out of our own stolen hetero-doxy and will to dissent. The fundamental mode by which disappearance does its dirty nervous work is haunting.

But, and this is the very difficult part, haunting is *also* the mode by which the middle class, in particular, needs to encounter something you cannot just ignore, or understand at a distance, or "explain away" by stripping it of all its magical power; something whose seemingly self-evident repugnance you cannot just rhetorically throw in someone's face. Haunting is also the mode by which the middle class needs to en-counter *something you have to try out for yourself, feeling your way deeper and deeper into the heart of darkness until you do* feel *what is at stake, the madness of the passion* (Taussig 1987: 10–11). AZ is not any or every Argentine. He is a representative of the large prosperous mid-dle class, with all its strengths and weaknesses, including its tendency to both conservative and radical romanticism.[28] AZ is a middle-class professional, a university professor and psychoanalyst, who journeys, propelled by a parochial and narcissistic desire to acquire a woman and her feminine essence, into the very heart of what he was always missing yet what was so proximate to him, indeed enveloping him. He has to lose himself to find what he was missing, the blind field of his picture of the world. The middle class plays an important part in Valenzuela's story because its quiescence, its five hands covering its eyes, ears, and mouths, and its desire for order and the good consumer life were crucial for legitimating military rule and the terror it wrought.

The middle class is not the only important actor here, by any means. The role of international banks, U.S.-based corporations, the U.S. foreign policy and security establishment, and, in particular, the assistance and training provided by the U.S. military and its proxies to the Latin American military were obviously significant.[29] By 1976, six hundred Argentine officers had graduated from the U.S. Army School of the Americas in the Panama Canal Zone, set up by John F. Kennedy under the terms of the Alliance for Progress, a program designed, ostensibly, to combat poverty in Latin America. The methods and theory of torture were an important component of the forty-week course, and "students were reportedly hardened to the idea by being tortured themselves" (Simpson and Bennett 1985: 54). The Washington Police Academy, the Academy for Border Control in Texas, and the Special Forces Center in Fort Bragg, North Carolina, also provided training for Argentine and other Central and Latin American officers. But it needs to be said that, as Eduardo Galeano puts it, "it would be unjust not to credit Latin America's ruling classes with a certain creative capacity in this field" (1978: 305). Indeed, many Latin American analysts reject, as an "oversimplification," the view that the doctrine of national security was essentially an American export (Weschler 1990: 119). In addition to the presence of French veterans of Algeria and Indochina and Israeli officers, "the main thing the guests at the School of the Americas and its brother institutions were exposed to . . . was *each other*" (ibid.). "Proud graduates," in keeping with the military's nationalist anti-imperialism, "speculate[d] on an obverse flow of influence, suggesting, for example, that it was the intensely virulent Latin American hybrid of the national security doctrine which subsequently got introjected, with a vengeance, back into U.S. politics, by way of such Latin-America-obsessed characters as Oliver North, 'Chi-Chi' Quintero, Felix Rodriguez, John Hull, and General John Singlaub" (ibid.: 119–20).

Notwithstanding military and elite networks of information and personnel, and hemispheric capital flows—the international culture of warfare states—middle-class consciousness is a potent transnational domestic formation in its own right, one Valenzuela is rightly concerned to identify, and one that raises pointed questions especially for U.S. readers. During military rule, the Argentine middle class as a whole stayed insulated, quiet, and blind to what was all around it, as if behind a shield of glass. And they did not come out until the Mothers forced them and the armed forces' utter failure to win a small real war in the Malvinas/Falkland Islands shamed them. In this they displayed a broader middle-class consciousness engrossed by the personal, the familial, the professional, and the accidental. This is a class consciousness that has an authorizing tendency to personalize and privatize social problems, saving most of its public political energy for natural disasters and various campaigns for order, hygiene, and proper personal behavior. This is a class consciousness that always has something else on its mind: the bills, the errands, the car, the house, the petty tyrannies of administrators, colleagues, relatives—its seemingly absolute advantages and disadvantages. This is a class consciousness that escapes real public civic life because it is tired or busy or what can you do about it anyway? Go fill the car with gas. Your aunt called and did you send her a thank-you note? Answer the phone and by the way I'm going to the wedding this week, what should I wear? I've got to go to work, we'll talk later. It's none of our business. Did you see that woman buying ice cream with her food stamps? The middle class always wants things taken care of, done right, and is always complaining about what it is about to lose, as if the whole world would end if the middle collapses. It fears falling down where the others live and it craves success stories of whatever kind. But it is cowed by the lure of achievement, internalizing an aggressive inferiority it projects remarkably consistently, as it often sits waiting, distracted, while others act in its name. It hates authority and loves authority at the same time, rattling its fists at the *invisible fathers who parade in a martial manner* and reproducing their sons and daughters again and again.[30] In Argentina, the middle class got no respect for its moderation because the military wanted to kill the indifferent and the timid too and they knew that the already scared national center could not stand up to any more fear since their bellies were already filled with it.

Meanwhile the guardianofthefire made monsters out of the flames and cat's eyes out of the coals, and he chose to take part in the game rather than just to talk about it, to be part of the performance rather than a mere spectator, a mere listener (V 121). As she takes AZ, who starts out as a timid and moderate middle-class professional man, on his search, Luisa Valenzuela suggests, or imagines, that haunting can galvanize the middle class, can wrench it from its particular kind of stupor, can shift its investments away from the private world of family and work, can move it away from "explaining away" the forces that run through its veins toward *feeling your way deeper and deeper . . . until you do feel what is at stake.* An encounter of tremulous significance, a profane illumination, is what is required to tear such a veil. Understanding the necessity of the encounter means understanding that you can't run away because the running will exhaust you and besides they have better boots. Understanding the necessity of the encounter means understanding that you can't hide because this power you're hiding from is very adept; indeed, it has perfected the art of infiltrating most hiding places, from under the bed to inside your head. Understanding the necessity of the encounter means understanding that you can't explain the power away because the explanations are cold and this power is hot, pulsing through your blood, and anyway they burn the books. Understanding the necessity of the encounter means understanding that you have to make contact with what is harming you, have to encounter the very heart of it, *the other door its floods of tears with consolation enclosed.* AZ had to unlearn everything that defined the parameters of his investments and desires and motivations, his social field. AZ learned everything that he did because he was haunted, because he took a wrong turn, because he was affected deeply by a woman who wasn't what she seemed, a woman who was a ghost bearing all that he had been avoiding, because he followed the tracks of the ghost.

Haunting is not just talking in your office, or doing a study, or the kind of liberal memory that restricts the official story to "the personal, private anguish of individual[s]" or to the cold decontextualized facts of torture or violence (Marcus 1994: 207). Haunting is "different from moralizing from the sidelines or setting forth the contradictions involved, as if the type of knowledge with which we are concerned were somehow not power and knowledge in one and hence immune to such procedures" (Taussig 1987: 11). Haunting is more magical than that; it is about reliving events in all their vividness, originality, and violence so as to overcome their pulsating and lingering effects. Haunting is an encounter in which you touch the ghost or the ghostly matter of things: the ambiguities, the complexities of power and personhood, the violence and the hope, the looming and receding actualities, the shadows of our selves and our society. When you touch the ghost or the ghostly

4

not only the footprints but the water too and what is down there

Old Kentucky Home

> Where, I wonder . . . is the shadow of the presence from which
> the text has fled?
> TONI MORRISON, "Unspeakable Things Unspoken"[1]

She is coming into their yard uninvited. In a fine dress, brooch at the
neck, those smooth white shoulders holding up a coiffed head ghostly
white against the blurred brown face of the slave woman standing behind her, she is coming into their yard uninvited. At the edge of the picture's frame, a gate separates the big white house from their yard, and
even that big tree that seems to mark a divide and yet shades and
spreads indiscriminately does not prevent her from coming into their
yard uninvited. But nobody flies even though that ax is lying on the
ground in the foreground of the painting right in front of the pretty
young coffee-cream-colored woman fiddling with a piece of green, eyes
averted in the presence of a man who may be sweet-talking her. Everybody seems so still despite the activity. A man is playing the banjo; a
woman is dancing with a small boy, perhaps her child. So still despite
the woman holding a baby and peering out the window looking as if
she has been interrupted from something in the house she needs to do.
Nobody seems to move at all except that woman who is coming into
their yard uninvited. No movement at all except perhaps to create a still
life, to hold still in an image, an imagined scene, of what that white
woman wants and needs to see as she crosses the threshold into the
painting. And even though she is at the far edge of the scene, a scene of
everyday life rendered in mythological detail, it is absolutely essential

137

for her to be there. Not because she represents the "big house"; not even because she "mirrors the curiosity of the white public for whom the picture was painted" (Honour 1989: 217). She has to be there because everything in the image is for her. It is as if everybody stopped what they were doing to pose for her and then allowed her to think that they had forgotten that she had not been invited. Is it only the fact that the yard and the people in it are her property that explains why she wants to go where she has not been invited?

The Failure of the Explanation

> Somewhere between . . . the Actual and the Imaginary . . .
> ghosts might enter . . . without affrighting us. It would be too
> much in keeping with the scene to excite surprise, were we to
> look about us and discover a form, beloved, but gone hence,
> now sitting quietly in a streak of this magic moonshine, with
> an aspect that would make us doubt whether it had returned
> from afar, or had never once stirred from our fireside.
> NATHANIEL HAWTHORNE, *The Scarlet Letter*[2]

"The Modern Medea—The Story of Margaret Garner" (wood engraving of Thomas Satterwhite Noble's painting *Margaret Garner*, 1867, published in *Harper's Weekly*, May 18, 1867)

Somewhere between the Actual and the Imaginary ghosts might enter without affrighting us. Or at least without scaring us so much that we take off running, away from the reckoning, but still without adequate preparation, into the tangle of the historical fault lines that remain. This chapter is about the lingering inheritance of racial slavery, the unfinished project of Reconstruction, and the compulsions and forces that all of us inevitably experience in the face of slavery's having even once existed in our nation. Slavery has ended, but something of it continues to live on, in the social geography of where peoples reside, in the authority of collective wisdom and shared benightedness, in the veins of the contradictory formation we call New World modernity, propelling, as it always has, a something to be done. Such endings that are not over is what haunting is about. This chapter continues my consideration of ghostly matters with Toni Morrison's novel *Beloved*, a work I take to be one of the most significant contributions to the understanding of haunting, a work whose monumental importance goes well beyond, although clearly through the very medium of, its literary achievements.[3] As we will see, the full weight of Morrison's contribution will rest on the exceptional premise of the book. The ghost enters, all fleshy and real, with wants, and a fierce hunger, and she speaks, barely, of course, and in pictures and a coded language. This ghost, Beloved, forces a reckoning: she makes those who have contact with her, who love and need her, confront an event in their past that loiters in the present. But Beloved, the ghost, is haunted too, and therein lies the challenge Morrison poses. *Somewhere between the Actual and the Imaginary ghosts might enter without affrighting us.*

Opening in 1873 and situating itself within the epistemic and political history marked out by W. E. B. Du Bois's Black Reconstruction (see [1935] 1992), *Beloved* retells quietly and extravagantly the chronicle of Margaret Garner, the "slave mother, who killed her child rather than see it taken back to slavery" (Coffin [1876] 1968: 557).[4] Not just the story, but recurrent and varied versions of the account of a slave woman, Sethe, who runs from Kentucky across the frozen Ohio River, giving birth along the way to a daughter named Denver. Arriving just outside Cincinnati, she spends twenty-eight days with her three other children, her mother-in-law, Baby Suggs, and the community before her owners attempt to capture and return her to Sweet Home in Kentucky under the terms of the 1850 Fugitive Slave Act. Faced with this prospect, she attempts to kill all her children and successfully murders one. This one is unnamed, but her headstone bears one affordable word—Beloved. In 1873, when the novel begins, the two boys are long gone, run off by handprints in cakes and a putatively crazy mother. Denver is growing up but has yet to venture out of the yard; Baby Suggs is contemplating colors, ready to die; and Stamp Paid, an underground railroad operator, loyally keeps history alive and the community in communication. Two arrivals set the story in motion. Paul D, one of the men from Sweet Home, makes his way to town and rids the haunted house, "with a table and a loud male voice," of its "claim to local fame" (B 37). And a ghostly young woman walks out of the water and moves into 124 Bluestone Road. Her name is Beloved. A stranger, she arrives with a name and no history she can provide, despite Paul D's persistent request for one. Yet the name she has chosen, which poses a crucial question for us—just who is the beloved?—Sethe and Denver recognize as that of the "already crawling" baby Sethe has killed.

While ghosts are not foreign to the residents of 124 Bluestone Road or their neighbors, they are rarely so visible or demanding as Beloved. Indeed, all of the characters in the novel weave their pleasures, pains, losses, and desires into the embellished crevices of Beloved's words and unspeakable biography. What Beloved cannot or will not say, they fill in with their simultaneously grand and subtle projections; from bits and pieces, fragments and portentous signs, they all make Beloved their beloved. *You are mine You are mine You are mine* (B 217). Yet, what they see or think they see can never quite grasp what Toni Morrison asks us as readers today to comprehend: that Beloved the ghost herself barely possesses a story of loss, which structures the very possibility of enslavement, emancipation, and freedom in which the Reconstructive history of *Beloved* traffics.

And thus Beloved the ghost's double voice speaks not only of Sethe's dead child but also of an unnamed African girl lost at sea, not yet become an African-American. (The book's memorial dedication reads simply "Sixty Million and more.") However, neither Sethe nor the others can perceive that the ghost that is haunting them is haunted herself. This would be impossible—too much—within the complicated mode of production Morrison elaborates for envisioning history or a totality and its articulations and disarticulations, in time and across time. Indeed, one major theme of the novel is this question: What is too much? What is too much self (pride) when you were not supposed to have one? What is too much to remember when there is yet more? What is too much violence (infanticide) when you are already living with too much violence (slavery)? What is too much to tell, to pass on, when "remembering seem[s] unwise" (B 274), but necessary? The double voice of the ghost will do its work, but it passes itself on as our haunting burden. *were we to look about us and discover a form, beloved, but gone hence, now sitting quietly in a streak of this magic moonshine.*

In the latter part of January 1856, Margaret Garner, the slave mother, killed her child rather than see her taken back to slavery. *Beloved, she my daughter. She mine. See. She come back to me of her own free will and I don't have to explain a thing. I didn't have time to explain before because it had to be done quick. Quick. She had to be safe and I put her where she would be* (B 200). Two moments of traumatic violence and injury are evoked in this statement: a slave mother's killing of her child and slavery. "Rather than" suggests a causal explanatory relation between these two moments, <u>one seemingly individual and private—a mother kills her child—and the other systemic and public—Slavery.</u> *I won't never let her go. I'll explain to her, even though I don't have to. Why I did it. How if I hadn't killed her she would have died and that is something I could not bear to happen to her. When I explain it she'll understand, because she understands everything already* (B 200). The elaboration of the explanation that bridges these two moments of violence, like Sethe's own language, is struggling to articulate a story that exceeds such a rationalistic and objective explanation. *I don't have to explain a thing* and yet all those things of which Sethe speaks in a rush of words that claim her relation to the child she murdered and the place she knows she cannot return herself or her children to <u>represent the failure of explanation</u>. *it had to be done quick. . . . She had to be safe. . . . Milk that belonged to my baby. . . . I was the one she didn't throw away. . . . Before I could check for the sign. . . . I looked everywhere for that hat. Stuttered. . . . After the shed, I stopped. . . . I don't believe she wanted to get to red. . . . Matter of fact, that and her pinkish headstone was the last color I recall. Now I'll be on the lookout. . . . Funny how you lose sight of some things and memory others. . . . Called me 'Jenny' when she was babbling. . . . Somebody had to know it. Hear it. Somebody. . . . Schoolteacher wouldn't treat her the way he*

*treated me. . . . I stood by her bed waiting for her to finish with the slop
jar. . . . Good God, I'm going to eat myself up. . . . She hates anything
about Sweet Home except how she was born. . . . The grape arbor. . . .
Otherwise I would have seen my fingernail prints right there . . . the
earrings. . . . Too thick, he said . . . like a daughter which is what I
wanted to be. . . . I never saw her own smile. . . . Running, you
think?. . . . When I came out of jail I saw them plain. . . . I got close. I
got close. . . . I couldn't lay down with you then. . . . Now I can. I can
sleep like the drowned. . . . She is mine* (B 200–204).

The failure of the explanation, the cultivated yet vulnerable interval
between "Slavery with a capital S" and the story of a slave mother
who killed her child, is the enabling moment of the analysis: "The
book was not about the institution—Slavery with a capital S. It was
about these anonymous people called slaves. . . . When I say *Beloved* is
not about slavery, I mean that the *story* is not slavery. The story is
these people—these people who don't know they're in an era of historical interest. They just know they have to get through the day" (Morrison in Angelo 1989: 120; Morrison 1987b: 75). The story is not Slavery with a capital S. The story is about haunting and about the crucial
way in which it mediates between institution and person, creating the
possibility of making a life, of becoming something else, in the present
and for the future. The work and the power of the story devolve from
beginning with this asymmetry, beginning with a relationship whose
evocation requires precisely refusing to reduce these two moments to
cause and effect, as if this story or history could be told simply as a
"sequence of events like the beads of a rosary" (Benjamin 1969: 263).
The work and the power of the story lie in giving all the reasons why
the reasons are never quite enough, why they cannot close the breach
between two interrelated but distinct affairs, why haunting rather than
"history" (or historicism) best captures the constellation of connections that charges any "time of the now" (ibid.) with the debts of the
past and the expense of the present, why one woman killed her child
and another was haunted by the event. "I started out wanting to write
a story about . . . the clipping about Margaret Garner stuck in my
head. I had to deal with this nurturing instinct that expressed itself
in murder" (Morrison in Clemons 1987: 75). *The clipping about Margaret Garner stuck in my head. with an aspect that would make us
doubt whether it had returned from afar, or had never once stirred
from our fireside.*

The Palimpsest

> Invisible bodies, no doubt by definition, can be done away
> with much more easily than visible ones. Since . . . ghosts . . .
> and the like take up no physical space in our empirical world,
> the liquidation of them involves no bloodletting, leaves no
> corpses and calls for no official inquiry.
>
> WILLIAM LaFLEUR, "Hungry Ghosts and Hungry Minds"[5]

"They 'forgot' many things" (Morrison in Clemons 1987: 74). The
slave narratives, that is. The slave narrative was the principal form by
which the experience of slavery was conveyed to the nineteenth-century
primarily white and female reading public. The slave narrative was an
authenticated testimony, written by slaves or former slaves in an autobiographical address, that sought to reverse for the author and for the
society the conditions of bondage it described. The slave narrative was
thus an autobiography and a sociology of slavery and freedom.[6] Like
much sociology, it combined the autobiographical (it contained the
traces of the one who scripted it), the ethnographic (it spoke in the third
person for/of someone else), the historical (its present tense was never
on its own), the literary (it was created within an available grammatology of voice and convention), and the political (it produced interested
accounts of power). The slave writers' purpose, as an instance of the sociological imagination, was to describe the "intricate connection between the patterns of their own lives and the course of world history . . .
[and] what this connection means for the kinds of men [and women]
they are becoming and for the kinds of history-making in which they
might take part" (Mills 1959: 4). In its most general outlines, the slave
narrative tried to connect its audience to the foundationally divisive social relations that underwrote the slave experience, an experience most
of its readers were able to keep at a distance from themselves. It tried to
make the agony and moral illegitimacy of slavery palpably present and
to create a relationship between reader and slave so that, in the best of
narratives (e.g., Jacobs [1861] 1987), the nexus of force, desire, belief,
and practice that made slavery possible could be exposed and abol-
ished. It accomplished its task of laying bare Slavery by producing a
morality of verisimilitude, by forging a congruence between realism
and sympathy. It told the bare, real truth of slavery, from the point of
view of the one who was or had been in it, so that the reader would be
moved to comprehend, empathize, and seek salvation for the slave and
the nation.

the appearance of being true

But the slave narrative was also produced, distributed, received, "conscripted," in John Sekora's words, into the "loose but elaborate network of abolitionist clergymen, politicians, merchants, writers, editors, printers, and advocates . . . transatlantic in scope and resources" (1988: 106, 108). Well above and beyond the usual "vagaries of American printing and bookselling" (ibid.: 106), the slave narrative, whatever else it attempted to and did accomplish, was greatly constrained by the demands placed on it by the abolition movement, its primary sponsor and its largest consumer. Sekora asks:

> Does it matter who controls the shape of the story—author or sponsor? Does it matter that the facticity demanded by sponsors may preclude individual personality? . . . Does it matter that a slave's story is sandwiched between white abolitionist documents, suggesting that the slave has precious little control over his or her life—even to its writing? Does it matter that several people . . . alleged that most black agents—including the great Douglass—had no stories until abolitionists gave them one? Does it matter that the very sponsors of slave narratives attempt to muffle the slave voice? (ibid.: 109)

And, we might add, does it matter that Margaret Garner never even wrote her own biography, which was written for her first by the newspapers and then by the prominent Cincinnati abolitionist Levi Coffin, being passed on thus at an even greater remove? The answers to these questions is undoubtedly yes.

For the majority of lay abolitionist readers, the slave narrative was popular sociology. It possessed a distinctive factual value because it told you what life was really like for the slave striving to be free. And it possessed a distinctive factual-moral value because it provided the believable proof that the slave, legally property, was a potential citizen, a human being. The slave narrative was expected to bear witness to the institution and experience of Slavery simply in plain speech and thus, by implication, sincerely. It was not to display any literary self-consciousness because "nothing that might prompt the reader to suspect that he or she was reading fiction could be allowed" (Andrews 1988: 90). This was arguably a challenge for the writer, and as William Andrews notes, "in the two decades before Emancipation, black autobiography served as a kind of sociocultural crucible in which some of the era's most interesting . . . experiments were conducted in how to tell the truth about experience. . . . By the mid-nineteenth century, black autobiographers had recognized that their great challenge was much more than just telling the truth; they had to *sound* truthful doing it" to those, including a "noted leader of the American Anti-Slavery Society," who, in his own words, "'thought that the slave, as a general thing, is a liar'" (ibid.: 89–90). How could known liars sound truthful? They would have to display, with the utmost genuineness (which often meant acknowledging the reader's suspicions about veracity), just those qualities that we associate with a conventional sociological realism: a plain unembellished style of writing that conveyed only the *believable* facts, a balanced assessment with no "exaggeration" and "nothing that smacked of 'the imagination'" (ibid.: 90). (The need for understatement was no doubt tied to the desire to distance the slave narrative, a serious, genuine, political work by and for the legally and "materially" oppressed, from sentimentality and the sentimental novel, a woman's genre, with all its emotional melodrama and claim on the reader's feelings.)[7] To be sure, to produce such a realism this popular sociology required an astute calculation of the entirety of the ideological parameters of American life itself. It required apprehending just what aspects of slavery and the slave experience would, indeed, be believable, that is, consumable by an audience who may or may not have believed in slavery, but whose parameters of knowing were certainly established within the larger confines of the existence of racial slavery itself. Sounding truthful, acquiring the condition of believability, then, was as important to the slave narrative's success as a political document as any truth about slavery it would remit.

If this sociological realism was already a very complicated venture, bound heart to hand by what it could *not say* it was further elaborated by the additional burden of attesting not simply to the slave as a reliable reporter, but also to her or his basic humanity. "The slave's texts . . . could not be taken as specimens of a black 'literary culture.' Rather, these texts could only be read as testimony of defilement: the slave's *representation* of the master's attempts to transform a human being into a commodity, and the slave's simultaneous verbal witness of the possession of a 'humanity' shared in common with Europeans" (Gates 1988b: 52). The complex articulation of this double bind—I testify to my transformation into a Slave while I testify to the existence of my shared humanity with you—is what the slave narrative was asked to express. In this scheme, where the law forbade reading and writing (literacy), but the "human community" required them as tokens of membership, slaves not only had to "steal" some learning as evidence of the *still existing*

criminal system that prevented them from acquiring it rightfully, they also had to become author(ized) as evidence of an already extant humanity.[8] Literacy became, then, as Henry Louis Gates Jr. has argued, a key trope in the slave narrative itself, as the writers displayed, referred to, and commented on the possession *and* illegality of it. The resourceful and often quite ingenious play on literacy in the slave narrative does not alter the fact that the slave narrative, by the very nature of its being a believable written document, constituted proof that the slave possessed the recognizable "*visible* sign of reason" that the European American demanded (ibid.: 53).

Beloved is not a simulated slave narrative. It is avowedly fiction; it is not written in the traditional autobiographical voice; it is not sponsored by nor is its testimony vouchsafed by a white authority; and it begins in 1873, well after Emancipation. (We will return to the significance of the opening date later.) But it does retell the story of Margaret Garner, *the slave mother who killed her child rather than see it taken back to slavery,* claiming its continuous relation to the history (slavery) and form (narrative) of the origins, in the most general sense, of African-American writing in the United States. As it retells one story and in this way summons another, it remembers some of what the slave narrative forgot, creating a palimpsest, a document that has been inscribed several times, where the remnants of earlier, imperfectly erased scripting is still detectable.

A palimpsest certainly, but is *Beloved* to be read as popular sociology today? A good deal of the exceptional scholarship on the slave narrative has amply demonstrated that the slave narrative was a literature produced by writers drawing on a range of particular conventions, styles, creative designs, and tropes that place it more accurately in the history of African-American autobiography and literature.[9] There are several reasons for this interpretive application, notwithstanding the obvious desire to study a notable part of African-American culture and one only relatively recently addressed by scholars since its virtual disappearance in American culture after the Civil War. But an important motivation concerns the troubling implications of treating black literature as *unquestioned* sociology, a concern, in part, about the sanctioned use of black literature as a teaching tool of tolerance (Morrison 1989: Morrison in Angelo 1989, 121). (Indeed, *Beloved* contains a carefully considered disquisition on tolerance that, as is Morrison's special talent, captures the lived caliber of what enables someone's magnanimity)

the quality of someone's character or the level of their ability

kindness, generosity

prevents

restraint   *appearance of being true*

what precludes its forbearance, and what registers its limitations.)
The variegated history of the use and abuse of black literature is well
beyond the scope of my pursuit here. Suffice to say that part of that
variety history takes its cue from the conjunction of verisimilitude and sympathy the abolitionist movement (and later the discipline of ethnology/
anthropology) established as the valid, legitimate, and sensible condition of knowledge and consensual political persuasion (see Cruz forthcoming; Dent forthcoming). But what other kind of popular sociology
might be warranted or invented on the basis of *Beloved*'s revisions and
way of seeing? The elaboration or the evocation of this other sociology
is what I hope this chapter, by the end of it, will have announced.

   This other sociology that *Beloved* might entitle revises the slave narrative in at least two ways germane to the discussion here. First, Morrison rejects literacy as the supreme measure of humanity, but more significantly, she refuses the task of having to prove the slave's (and by
implication her descendants') humanity.[10] Second, Morrison will prof-
fer a different type of sociological realism, one that encompasses haunting and the complexity of power and personhood that inheres in its
work. *present*
According to Davis and Gates:

> Almost all of the [slave] narratives refer to literacy in three ways: they
> recount vividly scenes of instruction in which the narrator learned to read
> and then to write; they underscore polemical admonishments against
> statutes forbidding literacy training among black slaves; and they are
> prefaced by [an] ironic apologia . . . which . . . transforms the convention
> of the author's confession of the faults of his tale . . . [into a] denunciation
> of that system that limited the development of his capacities. (1985: xxviii)

In *Beloved*, these features take an interesting turn.

   The political message of the scene of instruction was, in Ishmael
Reed's terms, to show that "the slave who was the first to read and . . .
write was the first . . . to run" (Gates 1987: 108).[11] In *Beloved*, however, the decision to run is made collectively when schoolteacher, a professional reader and writer who "was teaching us things we couldn't
learn" (B 191), becomes intolerable. Although the threshold of tolerance for schoolteacher is broken down in its own way for each person
at Sweet Home, Sethe's reason for running is most apt here. Sethe runs
not when she learns to read and write, but when she learns how she will
be read and written, when she learns how she will be represented in a

book, literacy's most prized artifact. When she hears schoolteacher's directions to his pupil that he should put her animal characteristics on the right and her human characteristics on the left, she does not know what the word *characteristics* means and has to ask, but she nonetheless understands the conjuncture of power and epistemology that is the very stakes of her representability. Sethe may not be "literate," but she can read the situation perfectly well (perhaps too well), and her reading and writing skills are explicitly located in relation to her refusal to be any part of schoolteacher's book or part of the larger economy in which this particular literate learning has value. Here, all too audaciously, literacy literally measures humanity, savagely, as only a culture schooled in racial science could dream up.

Just as *Beloved*'s scene of instruction points to the contradictory valence of the slave narrative's maxim "In literacy was power" (Gates 1987: 108), so too do the "polemical admonishments against statutes forbidding literacy training among slaves" find another connotation. For the most part, in *Beloved* the exhortations are quietly reinscribed, set not in the context of polemic but in the context of everyday talk and activity. Sethe is taught "the alphabet" by members of the black community during her "twenty-eight days . . . of healing, ease and real-talk" (B 95). Baby Suggs "always wished she could read the Bible like real preachers" (B 208). Denver discusses her father's philosophy of reading and writing—"But my daddy said, If you can't count they can cheat you. If you can't read they can beat you"—and decides that "it was good for me to learn how, and I did until it got quiet and all I could hear was my own breathing and one other who knocked over the milk jug while it was sitting on the table" (B 208).

But loudly resounding off the page is the painful irony of Sethe's making ink:

> "He [schoolteacher] liked the ink I made. It was her [Mrs. Garner's] recipe, but he preferred how I mixed it and it was important to him because at night he sat down to write in his book. It was a book about us but we didn't know that right away. We just thought it was his manner to ask us questions. He commenced to carry round a notebook and write down what we said. I still think it was them questions that tore Sixo up. Tore him up for all time." She stopped. (B 37)

When she begins again, she halts, still deciding whether or not she has the energy to beat back her tiredness. *I made the ink, Paul D. He couldn't have done it if I hadn't made the ink* (B 271). Within the violence of an

otherness

economy in which Sethe made the ink used to write her into a book that
would literally measure her alterity, the equation literacy equals power
unmasks its sinister shadow. A terrifying recognition, from inside its
embrace, of the mode of production that underwrote the laws against
slave literacy and a harbinger of a continuing problem.

Beloved begins "124 was spiteful" and ends with the refrain "This is
not a story to pass on." There are no apologies for the spite, although
some are asked for, and there are no apologies for passing on a story
that was not to be passed on. And yet, through an elaborate tapestry
of oral-become-written storytelling, stitching the movements between
past and present, between victimhood and agency, between limits and
possibilities, a system is denounced, with perhaps less irony than
the older narratives and with a great deal of studied passion. A system
is denounced, but gently so too is the need to keep refuting, in the
late twentieth century, that "*Blacks became slaves,* finally" (Robinson
1983: 176); that slavery created so total a condition of subjection that
all trace of humanity vanished; that slavery became these African-
Americans as the totality of their ontology. As Cedric Robinson and
Morrison both suggest, it is indisputable that "slavery altered the conditions of their being" but also indisputable that slavery "could not
negate their being" (ibid.: 177). Robinson's remarks about certifying or
sanctifying this point over and over again are significant and worth
quoting at length:

> The American revisionists . . . have transformed this African people into
> *human beings,* capable of judgment, injury, accommodation and heroism.
> In short, a people possessing, as Blassingame put it, 'the same range. . . .'
> To this point, their project has been successfully executed. . . . Still this
> 'political' triumph is but a partial one, for the defence of the slaves ad-
> dresses its antagonists in their terms. Expectedly, in a post-slave society
> where the historical victory of the enslaved stratum was incomplete, the
> question of the humanity of the enslaved people would linger. It would . . .
> have to be spoken to. We now 'know' what the master class certainly
> knew but for so long publicly denied only to be confronted with the truth
> in its nightmares, its sexual fantasies and rotting social consciousness: the
> enslaved were human beings. But the more authentic question was not
> whether the slaves (and the ex-slaves and their descendants) were human.
> It was, rather, just what *sort* of people they were . . . and could be. (ibid.:
> 176–77)

And thus all the liberal abolitionist pressure to get the slave writer to
display his or her humanity, hoping against hope to convince them-

selves of what was always a fragile truth, or in any event a limited one entirely compatible with a belief in the basic inequality of men, is left waiting in the wings as Morrison goes to the heart of Robinson's "more authentic question." What sort of people were the slaves and the former slaves and their descendants? What sort of people could they be? To be sure, these questions still participate in a "collective and individual reinvention of the discourse of 'slavery,'" but the perhaps unavoidable effort "attempt[s] to restore to a spatio-temporal object its eminent historicity, to evoke *person/persona* in the place of a 'shady' ideal" (Spillers 1989: 29).

verify

If the slave narrative was expected to speak for those who had no audible public voice and who had no legal access to writing or to personhood, then *Beloved* will not only retell the story of Margaret Garner, but will also imagine the life world of those with no names we remember, with no "visible reason" for being in the archive. Morrison does not speak for them. She imagines them speaking their complex personhood as it negotiates the always coercive and subtle complexities of the hands of power. The slave narrative was supposed to corroborate the vitality of American ideologies of individualism. It said, "I have transcended absolutely impossible circumstances in order for this story to reach you." But it also had to disclaim its exceptionality in order to legitimately represent those who had no publicly sanctioned right to write, but were in the same circumstances. If the slave narrative had to struggle to manage such a crisis of representation, *Beloved,* by contrast, gives individual voices and faces to those who lacked public ones, but does so within a decentered structure of storytelling that deploys the sounds and rhythms of call and response.

But *Beloved* also problematizes the retrieval of lost or missing subjects by transforming those who do not speak into what is unspeakable, so that in that marvelous power of negative dialectics it can be conjured, imagined, worked out. What gestures the unspeakable? In this other sociology, which is willy-nilly another politics, the ghost gesticulates, signals, and sometimes mimics the unspeakable as it shines for both the remembered and the forgotten. This other sociology stretches at the limit of our imagination and at the limit of what is representable in the time of the now, to us, as the social world we inhabit. Stretching to bend, the close of *Beloved* summons the challenge:

"Everybody knew what she was called, but nobody anywhere knew her name. Disremembered and unaccounted for, she cannot be lost because no one is looking for her, and even if they were, how can they call her if they don't know her name? Although she has claim, she is not claimed" (B 274).

Finally, then, if the slave narrative could not display a literary consciousness, because nothing that might prompt readers to suspect that they were reading fiction was permissible, in *Beloved* we are forced to contend with what might be the exemplar of "fictional pretenders to the real thing" (Andrews 1988: 91), that is, ghosts. Whatever can be said definitively about the long and varied traditions of African-American thought, writing, and radicalism, the social reality of haunting and the presence of ghosts are prominent features. The capacity not only to live with specters, in order to determine what sort of people they were and could be, but also to engage the ghost, heterogenously but cooperatively, as metaphor, as weapon, as salve, as a fundamental epistemology for living in the vortex of North America. The significance of ghosts and particularly spirit work in African-American culture and letters no doubt owes some of its origin to their respected place in African life and thought, "a consciousness implicated," as Robinson puts it, "in what Amos Tutuola so many generations later would name the 'bush of the ghosts'" (1983: 245; see also Christian 1993). But above and beyond the African inheritance, it is not so difficult to see that any people who are not graciously permitted to amend the past, or control the often barely visible structuring forces of everyday life, or who do not even secure the moderate gains from the routine amnesia, that state of temporary memory loss that feels permanent and that we all need in order to get through the days, is bound to develop a sophisticated consciousness of ghostly haunts and is bound to call for an "official inquiry" into them.

The Story of a Hat

> Perhaps no case that came under my notice, while engaged
> in aiding fugitive slaves, attracted more attention and aroused
> deeper interest and sympathy than the case of Margaret
> Garner, the slave mother, who killed her child rather than
> see it taken back to slavery. This happened in the latter part
> of January, 1856. The Ohio River was frozen over at the
> time . . .   *The Reminiscences of Levi Coffin*[12]

Fugitive Slaves on the Underground Railroad; or, The Underground Railroad: Levi Coffin Receiving a Company of Fugitives in the Outskirts of Cincinnati, Ohio (Charles T. Webber, 1893, exhibited at the Columbian World's Fair in Chicago in 1893; courtesy of the Cincinnati Art Museum)

"[Events] *do* occur, to be sure, but in part according to the conventions dictating how we receive, imagine, and pass them on" (Conley 1988: xvi). *It was not a story to pass on* (B 274). An event becomes the possibility of writing a story, a history; an event is passed on. *It was not a story to pass on.* The authoritative account of Margaret Garner's actions and trial has been passed on to us by the famous Ohio abolitionist Levi Coffin. Passed on between two imposing faces, staring unsmiling from the page, and The Story of a Hat.

In 1876 the Western Tract Society in Cincinnati published the REMINISCENCES OF LEVI COFFIN, *The Reputed President of the Underground Railroad; BEING A BRIEF HISTORY OF THE LABORS OF A LIFETIME IN BEHALF OF THE SLAVE, WITH THE STORIES OF NUMEROUS FUGITIVES, WHO GAINED THEIR FREEDOM THROUGH HIS INSTRUMENTALITY, AND MANY OTHER INCIDENTS.* His reputation as a Christian, exaggerated by his unsmiling face and that of his wife, Catherine, forewords his preface: "I had no desire to appear before the public as an author, having no claim to literary merit. What I had done I believed was simply a Christian duty and not for the purpose of being seen of men, or for notoriety, which I have never sought" (C i). In his own "plain, simple style," like the seeming simplicity of the portrait printed "not for the purpose of being seen of men," he "tells the stories without any exaggeration," even if they are "interesting" and "thrilling" (C i-ii).

Although Coffin has no desire to appear before the public as an over-stating author, he authorizes his story with a reputation and a geneal-ogy: the history of his patronymic and his family beginning in 1066. "In . . . 1066 Sir Richard Coffin, knight, accompanied William the Con-queror from Normandy to England, and the manor of Alwington, in the county of Devonshire, was assigned to him" (C 3). Margaret Gar-ner's story is prefaced by his reputation (*in behalf, through his instru-mentality*), an unsmiling image, the history of his father's name, and an acknowledgment of an inheritance—his antislavery principles: "Both my parents and grandparents were opposed to slavery, and none of ei-ther of the families ever owned slaves; and all were friends of the op-pressed, so I claim that I inherited my anti-slavery principles" (C 11). A valuable bequest, this patrimony. Yet Coffin does not notice that it is precisely his genealogy, a lineage of conquest and property ownership, that gifts him the possibility of a reputation—to act *in behalf* of the ones whose lives need rectification and who seemingly cannot act on their own.

"Perhaps no case that came under my notice, while engaged in aid-ing fugitive slaves, attracted more attention and aroused deeper inter-est and sympathy than the case of Margaret Garner, the slave mother, who killed her child rather than see it taken back to slavery." The event is passed on. *Through his instrumentality, in behalf. he came to my store . . . to ask counsel. . . . I told him. . . . I directed him. . . . I would make arrangements.* The event is passed on. Unexceptionably for a story of a slave woman, even if "Margaret seemed to have a dif-ferent nature" (C 564).

At the time it occurred, Margaret Garner's story was a minor news sensation. It was reported daily in the Cincinnati papers and the *New York Daily Times* and was covered nationally and in England. It was picked up as a celebrated cause by the abolitionist movement, which found in it indisputable evidence of the pathology of slavery. It was also taken up by feminist abolitionists, who highlighted the specifically gen-dered degradations of slavery: abolitionist and feminist Lucy Stone Blackwell attended the trial and black abolitionist Sarah Parker Red-mond gave a lengthy lecture on the Garner case three years later in Eng-

land.[13] The case was debated as a major precedent for the constitutionality of the 1850 Fugitive Slave Act, and it generated intense
political maneuvering between Kentucky and Ohio over the principle of
states' rights. The reports are fraught with conflicting details, although
every account repeats the structuring frame: Margaret Garner, the slave
mother who killed her child rather than see it taken back to slavery.[14]

The first report appeared in the Cincinnati papers on January 29,
1856. "The city was thrown into much excitement yesterday morning
by the information that a party of slaves . . . had made a stampede from
Kentucky to this side of the river. Other circumstances, however, which
afterward transpired, have imparted a degree of horrible interest to the
affair different to that which usually attends a stampede of negroes"
(*Cincinnati Enquirer*, January 29, 1856).[15] On a horse-drawn sleigh,
late in the night on Sunday, January 27, 1856, Margaret Garner, a
twenty-two- or twenty-three-year-old "mulatta"[16] about five feet tall
with a high forehead, finely arched eyebrows, and bright and intelligent
eyes, left Boone County, Kentucky, and headed for Cincinnati, Ohio.
Margaret Garner was pregnant at the time and fled with her husband,
Simon Garner Jr. (sometimes known as Simeon or Robert), her two boys,
Samuel and Thomas, ages four and six (or according to the *Cincinnati
Enquirer*, two and five), her less-than-one-year-old infant named Scilla
or Priscilla, and the three-year-old girl who would be killed. Accompanying the Garners were Simon Jr.'s parents, Simon and Mary Garner,
and nine friends, also slaves. Margaret Garner and her four children
were owned by Archibald K. Gaines of Boone County, Kentucky.
Margaret Garner had previously been owned by John P. Gaines, who
later became governor of Oregon Territory (Y 58). Simon Garner Sr.,
Mary Garner, and Simon Garner Jr. were owned by James Marshall of
Richwood Station, Boone County, Kentucky. After traveling about sixteen miles, they arrived at the frozen Ohio River and crossed over. The
Garners had been to Cincinnati, so the road was familiar to them, and
the frozen Ohio River was a popular crossing spot for slaves going
northward.[17]

Upon reaching Cincinnati, the eight Garners split off from the group
and after asking several people for directions made their way to the
home of their kinsman Elijah Kite, whose father, Joe Kite, had purchased Elijah's freedom. Immediately (or after breakfast, according
to Coffin), Kite set off for Sixth and Elm Streets, to the shop of Levi
Coffin, "president" of the Underground Railroad, to "ask counsel"

(C 559). Knowing the danger of the party's conspicuousness, Coffin directed Kite to take them directly to a black settlement on the western outskirts of town where fugitives were often harbored, promising to make arrangements "to forward them northward, that night, on the Underground Railroad" (C 559). Kite returned to his home but minutes afterward an arresting party surrounded his house and demanded the surrender of the fugitives. Yanuck and Coffin speculate that the Garners' whereabouts were betrayed by "someone of whom the Garners asked directions" (Y 51; C 558–59). Gaines and the son of James Marshall, Simon Garner Sr.'s owner, had arrived in Cincinnati at seven in the morning, obtained a warrant for the arrest of the slaves pursuant to the Fugitive Slave Act, and appeared at the home of Elijah Kite along with some friends and a force of deputy United States marshals. "The other nine fugitives . . . made their way up town and found friends who conducted them to safe hiding-places, where they remained until night. They were then put on the Underground Railroad, and went safely through to Canada" (C 558).

What happened next is not exactly clear. The Garners barricaded themselves inside the house and Simon Garner Jr. fired two rounds from a revolver. A deputy marshal forced a window and jumped into the cabin, losing two of his fingers and several teeth in a struggle with Simon Garner Jr. The rest of the party battered down the front door. "Margaret Garner fought wildly, but was at last overpowered" (Y 52). The arresting party found two profusely bleeding children, a badly bruised infant, and the almost lifeless girl who passed on minutes later. Sometime during the assault on the house, Margaret Garner tried to kill her children. Yanuck and the Cincinnati papers report that Margaret seized the knife *before* they entered, during the struggle outside the house:

> Suddenly, Margaret Garner seized a butcher knife and turned upon her three-year-old daughter. With swift and terrible force she hacked at the child's throat . . . until the little girl was almost decapitated. The two Garner men began to scream . . . [and run] wildly about the cabin. Now Margaret Garner turned toward one of her little boys who pleaded piteously with his mother not to kill him. She called to . . . Mary Garner, "Mother, help me to kill the children." The old woman began to wail and wring her hands. Her eyes could not endure the murder of her grandchildren and she ran for refuge under a bed. Finally, Elijah Kite's wife managed to disarm Margaret Garner who all the while sobbed that she would rather kill every one of her children than have them taken back across the river. (Y 52)[18]

Coffin, however, is adamant that Margaret seized the knife *after* the posse had entered the house and dragged her husband from it: "At this moment, Margaret Garner, seeing that their hopes of freedom were vain, seized a butcher knife that lay on the table, and with one stroke cut the throat of her little daughter, whom she probably loved the best. She then attempted to take the life of the other children and to kill herself, but she was overpowered and hampered before she could complete her desperate work" (C 559–60).

The whole party was arrested and the Garners were taken to the federal courthouse in Cincinnati where Gaines made application to John L. Pendery, a U.S. commissioner for the Southern District of Ohio, for a certificate to transport his slaves back to Kentucky. Because James Marshall's son had not brought a power of attorney, the hearings were postponed and the Garners were forced to stay in Ohio and then to walk to the Hammond Street police station house. Gaines entered the police station carrying the dead child, whom he intended to take back with him to Kentucky, prompting the *Cincinnati Gazette* to comment, "He was taking it to Covington for interment that it might rest in ground consecrated to slavery" (January 29, 1856; see Y 53 n. 28). "Margaret Garner sat as though stupefied, but she roused herself when a compliment was paid her on her fine looking little boy. She replied sadly, 'You should have seen my little girl that—that—(she did not like to say was killed) that died, that was the bird.' She had a scar on the left side of her forehead running down to her cheekbone.[19] When she was asked how she had come by this mark, she replied only, 'White man struck me'" (Y 53; *Cincinnati Gazette*, February 11, 1856).

After a considerable contest between state agents and local marshals, the hearings began on January 30. The trial lasted two weeks. John Jolliffe, a prominent antislavery attorney in Cincinnati, was the chief counsel for the Garner family, while the slave claimants were represented by Colonel Francis T. Chambers of Cincinnati and by two lawyers from Covington, Kentucky. Margaret Garner was eventually indicted for murder and the Garner men as accessories to murder. But none of them were tried for murder. The trial (actually a series of hearings) that transpired sought to determine whether they were fugitive slaves and therefore to be remanded to their owners. The defense attempted to have Margaret Garner tried for murder (and her family members for complicity) in order to challenge the constitutionality of the 1850 Fugitive Slave Act, which effectively prevented nonslave states like Ohio from harboring fugitives. Jolliffe hoped to show what "hellish" effects the Fugitive Slave Act had, in this case having "driven a frantic mother to murder her own child rather than see it carried back to the seething hell of American slavery" (C 561). In the meantime, the trial principally concerned whether the Garners were free or slaves. Gaines and Marshall's lawyers argued that they were slaves, while Jolliffe claimed that the Garners (and their children) had been made free by their previous visits to Cincinnati (in a free state) and hence were free at the time of their departure from Kentucky. Margaret Garner was even, despite the prohibition on slave testimony in court, allowed to testify on behalf of her claimed free status. Eventually, the commissioner decided that a "voluntary return to slavery, after a visit to a free State, re-attached the conditions of slavery, and that the fugitives were legally slaves at the time of their escape" (C 560).

There was a great deal of activity surrounding the trial. There was considerable protest by the black residents of Cincinnati, who were of course excluded from attending the trial unless they were called as witnesses, a prerogative it took Jolliffe some time to establish. Several newspapers reported not only efforts to rent a public hall for organized meetings,[20] but also the daily presence of protesting black women (variously described as "well-dressed Negro women," or "mulatto women," or "colored women," or "a plentiful sprinkling of sable and yellow hues," or "dark-hued damsels," or "saddle colored ladies dressed in the extreme of fashion") who gathered in the streets yelling epithets at the police and marshals and encouragement to Margaret Garner.[21] Some of these women might have been arrested. In any event, they kept daily vigil at the police station for Margaret Garner, attempting to bring her food and waving to her from the outside.

The protesters were not permitted to visit the Garners in jail, but the family had two noteworthy visitors, in addition to Coffin and the lawyers. The Reverend P. C. Bassett published his conversation with Margaret Garner in the *American Baptist:* "'I inquired' says Mr. Bassett, 'if she were not excited almost to madness when she committed the act!' 'No,' she replied, 'I was as cool as I now am; and would much rather kill them at once, and thus end their sufferings, than have them taken back to slavery and be murdered by piecemeal'" (May [1856] 1861: 43). (Coffin, on the other hand, found an "expression of settled despair" on her face, a "sorrow . . . beyond the reach of any words of encouragement and consolation" [C 564]). Another prominent visitor was Lucy Stone

Blackwell. Stone had been attending the hearings and was rumored to have asked for permission to pass a knife to Garner (or to have actually passed the knife), with which she could kill herself if the commissioner sent her back to Kentucky. The rumor was mentioned in court by the slave owner's lawyer, and Stone responded there to the accusations:

> "When I saw that poor fugitive, took her toil-hardened hand in mine, and read in her face deep suffering and an ardent longing for freedom, I could not help bid her be of good cheer. I told her that a thousand hearts were aching for her, and that they were glad one child of hers was safe with the angels. Her only reply was a look of deep despair, of anguish such as no words can speak. . . . The faded faces of the negro children tell too plainly to what degradation female slaves must submit.[22] Rather than give her little daughter to that life, she killed it. . . . With my own teeth I would tear open my veins and let the earth drink my blood, rather than wear the chains of slavery. How then could I blame her for wishing her child to find freedom with God and the angels, where no chains are?" (C 564–65)

The commissioner responded that it was not a matter of sympathy, but of property. Since the slaves had "voluntarily" returned to slavery in Kentucky after being free in Ohio, they were rightfully subject to the Fugitive Slave law.

The Garners were ordered back across the Ohio River on February 26, this time on the ferry. They stayed in the Covington jail for a few days. Ohio's governor, Salmon P. Chase, made a requisition to Governor Charles S. Morehead of Kentucky for the return of the Garners, but Gaines had already sent Margaret Garner down the river, farther south, some said to be sold in Arkansas (see May [1856] 1861: 43). On the way, the ship carrying the Garners was involved in an accident and Margaret Garner fell (or jumped) into the water with her child in her arms. Margaret Garner was rescued, but the child drowned. There were reports that Gaines had returned her to the Covington jail, but when Chase sent an officer with a requisition he was told by the jailer that Margaret Garner had been taken away the night before on Gaines's order. Gaines denied knowing her whereabouts but promised that he would let the Cincinnati papers know if he found out. There were also reports that Gaines simply defied the requisition and sent Margaret Garner to the New Orleans slave market (ibid.: 44). Whatever happened, Yanuck's conclusion lingers eerily: nothing was ever heard of Margaret Garner again.

Today, mostly tourists take the ferry across the river; everyone else

usually drives their cars across the bridges. Back and forth, I went be-
tween the Cincinnati Historical Society Research Library in the Cin-
cinnati Union Terminal and the Covington jail, stopping at the police
station and looking for the "black settlement" in what was the old
slaughterhouse district, now gone among the leftover waterfront ware-
houses. I went out to Boone County, where the Garners lived, trying to
imagine the long walk with children in tow. Now there are a couple of
small industrial parks where houses and farms used to be. Sometimes a
newer house sits there; sometimes an older house reminds you fleetingly
of the past. You are quickly back to the highway, however, without
local bearings. I found the markers for the Gaines family stuck incon-
spicuously in a roadside cemetery you could as easily pass by as stop at.
Nothing there registers Margaret Garner or her family's presence. No
one at the Covington jail had any recollection of her or the celebrated
case. And yet, I always had the distinct impression that I was bumping
into her.

"The Story of a Hat," which occurred "during the time of the Margaret
Garner trial," immediately follows Coffin's description of Margaret
Garner and goes on for seven pages. A trivial story, really. In response
to the demand by a Kentucky marshal to remove his hat in court, Levi
Coffin, as would be his habit as a Quaker, refused. Twice. During
Margaret Garner's trial, "the story of my adventure with the marshal,
respecting my hat, soon became extensively known. The accounts given
of it in the Cincinnati papers were copied by other papers in various
parts of the country. . . . For several days I could not walk the streets
without being accosted by some one who would assert that I had
whipped the marshal" (C 574).[23] Margaret Garner, wearing one and
maybe two scars on her face from a striking (a whipping?) had been
pursued by her owners from Kentucky, who crossed the same river she
did to claim their property in the name of the Fugitive Slave Act. She
"could not walk the streets without being accosted by some one who
would assert" that she belonged elsewhere. She was about to be sent
back to Kentucky and then sold, and Levi Coffin goes on for seven
pages, full of pride, that he refused a Kentucky marshal's order to remove his hat.

Coffin's Hat Story is a testament not only to his reputation as an
antislavery activist, but also to his power to claim his property, his
hat. *In spite of touching appeals, of eloquent pleadings, the Commis-*

sioner remanded the fugitives back to slavery. He said that it was not a question of feeling to be decided by the chance current of his sympathies; the law of Kentucky and of the United States made it a question of property (C 566). Remember that the failed strategy of Garner's lawyers was to attempt to have Margaret Garner tried for murder, with the hope of an acquittal. As a slave woman she was legally property or chattel and thus, according to the law, she could not be tried for murder because only a person could have committed such a crime. The counterintuitive nature of the defense is matched by the disqualification of the court: the law disallows her even the subjectivity of a criminal. In the eyes of the law, Margaret Garner is not a juridical subject. She is only what a property contract promises, a transaction of exchange value. *In spite of touching appeals*, in spite of the defiant claim she made to be a mother, a legal and social oxymoron in the context of slavery, Margaret Garner's predicament remains a question of property.[24] The court says she belongs to someone else.[25] *In spite of touching appeals*, Coffin's story is a question of property. He claims his hat and his reputation, now enhanced: a man whose reputation rests on *through his instrumentality, in behalf* can act on his own behalf to claim his property.

A man who inherited his antislavery principles passes down two events, as history, as story, both seemingly about reputation and property. A man denied fantasies of property ownership because he inherited antislavery principles displaces Margaret Garner's story, a "question of property," with a story of a hat as property claimed and defended. An event, Margaret Garner's suffering and trial, becomes the stage for a white man's fantasy of his right to own and dispose of his property as he sees fit. The Story of a Hat can only be read as Coffin's assertion of the right to claim one's property even against the state or the law. And yet the story intends to counter such an assertion over Margaret Garner's body and counter the legitimacy of owning people as if they were property. Coffin unwittingly imagines the fantasy and power of ownership of property and story as the hat becomes the trope that reads the failure of Margaret Garner's claim to self-possession and to her own story. An event becomes the possibility of writing a story, a history; an event is passed on. The story of Margaret Garner has been passed on to us between two imposing faces, staring unsmiling from the page, and The Story of a Hat.

Two events become one story. If an event is a "coded trope that 'read[s]' or allegorizes the past," but if the story is not Slavery with a capital S, what is the story, what is the event? Perhaps a "knot of half-signs that are grasped syntactically" (Conley 1988: xv). A Story of a Hat.

Paul D didn't *ask her outright*, but the question was there in *the clipping he showed* her. She was in the newspaper too, although people no longer stopped her on the street to talk or to congratulate her. She started circling around the answer he was requesting, but hadn't actually come right out and asked. *Sethe knew that the circle she was making around the room, him, the subject, would remain one. That she could never close in, pin it down for anybody who had to ask. If they didn't get it right off—she could never explain. Because the truth was simple, not a long drawn-out record of flowered shifts, tree cages, selfishness, ankle ropes and wells. Simple: she was squatting in the garden and when she saw them coming and recognized schoolteacher's hat, she heard wings. Little hummingbirds stuck their needle beaks right through her headcloth into her hair and beat their wings. And if she thought anything, it was No. No. Nono. Nonono. Simple. She just flew. Collected every bit of life she had made, all the parts of her that were precious and fine and beautiful, and carried, pushed, dragged them through the veil, out, away, over there where no one could hurt them. Over there. Outside this place. . . . And the hummingbird wings beat on* (B 163).

Twice she saw a hat, and twice she repeats her claim. *It is when she lowers her eyes to look again at the loving faces before her that she sees him. Guiding the mare, slowing down, his black hat wide-brimmed enough to hide his face but not his purpose. He is coming into her yard and he is coming for her best thing.* This second time, however, the hat Sethe sees belongs not to her former owner schoolteacher, but to Mr. Bodwin, a well-known abolitionist in town who has helped Baby Suggs, Sethe, and her family. Standing in the doorway, some eighteen years after she originally heard *wings. Little hummingbird wings stick needle beaks right through her headcloth into her hair and beat their wings* she recognizes again a hat and a man. Even though it is not the same man at all, even though this "good" man is just coming to pick up her daughter Denver for work and will survive the trip. *And if she thinks anything it is no. No no. Nonono. She flies. . . . And above them all, rising from his place with a whip in his hand, the man without skin, looking. He is looking at her* (B 261–62).

The mistake Sethe makes in thinking that Mr. Bodwin, who has done her no harm, is schoolteacher is a carefully cultivated one, the ground well laid. It is also an insightful mistake. As George Lipsitz nicely puts it, "People who appear to be 'mistaken' about another . . . sometimes really know things that can not be represented easily because their knowledge is illegitimate by existing standards and paradigms" (1994: 162). At this moment, almost twenty years after the Proclamation, Sethe knows through the powerful mediation of haunting that as a proclaimed fact abolition is not emancipation. She knows that the precarious difference between the kind man and the owning man is secured, always uncertainly, by the sympathetic heart of the liberal abolitionist's morality, its limitations registered by the arbitrariness, the accidental nature of its kindness. She knows that Emancipation was not about whites saving blacks and she knows that real freedom, real emancipation (that which would give the formal Proclamation a genuine meaning) cannot be warranted or secured on the undependable ground of a saving kindness.[26]

Paul D's meditation on the ability of Mr. Garner, his owner, a kind man, to "give" him his status as a man puts the issue most concisely:

> Nobody counted on Garner dying. . . . Everything rested on Garner being alive. Without his life each of theirs fell to pieces. Now ain't that slavery or what is it? . . . For years Paul D believed schoolteacher broke into children what Garner had raised into men. . . . Now, plagued by the contents of his tobacco tin, he wondered how much difference there really was between before schoolteacher and after. Garner called and announced them men—but only on Sweet Home, and by his leave. Was he naming what he saw or creating what he did not? . . . Oh, he did manly things, but was that Garner's gift or his own will? . . . In Sixo's country, or his mother's? Or, God help him, on the boat? Did a whiteman saying it make it so? Suppose Garner woke up one morning and changed his mind? Took the word away. . . . They had been isolated in a wonderful lie, dismissing Halle's and Baby Suggs' life before Sweet Home as bad luck. Ignorant of or amused by Sixo's dark stories. Protected and convinced they were special. Never suspecting the problem of Alfred, Georgia. (B 220–21)

Garner promises that as benevolent sponsor he can give Paul D what the institution of slavery itself disallows, his manhood. Garner's kindness, his "gift" of manhood, is both arbitrary and disingenuous when it offers itself as something more than individual kindness, a necessary but not a sufficient condition for sovereign agency. Here, the limits of kindness are marked by an urgent question of self-representation as self-determination—"Was he naming what he saw or creating what he did not?"—and of accidents becoming structural damage, "Halle's and Baby Suggs' life before Sweet Home . . . the problem of Alfred, Georgia." *Bad luck, dark stories,* and the *wonderful lie* of a structure of forgetting that Garner could wake up one morning and change his mind. In the waking of a morning, Paul D could be again neither Man nor man. Between sleeping and waking, between Garner and schoolteacher, is the margin of accident that is the ruse for authenticating slavery itself.

A woman recognizes a hat, a knot of half-signs, which weaves a story, binds the time of the now with a hungry past, and marks a limit. *No. No. Nono. Nonono.* No explanation, just a ritualistic recognition of the signs of violence and a refusal. There is no explanation not because she cannot provide one, but because what we could just call culture, a synthetic tradition of reading and responding to signs, is almost always the medium by which property relations meet their limits and their capacity to explain. A woman sees a hat and a man and she flies. There are things that cannot be remembered by Coffin's *Reminiscences.* There are things that cannot be remembered without admitting that a knot of half-signs weaving a story and marking a limit is the story, a story that exists in the profound Everywhere between "Slavery with a capital S" and a seemingly anonymous slave woman who killed her child.

"[Events] *do* occur, to be sure, but in part according to the conventions dictating how we receive, imagine, and pass them on." In the rewriting of this event, a different story or history is made possible, and we are offered some important lessons for how to counter "strategies of terministic violence and displacement . . . [and] the reincarnations of human violence in their intellectual and symbolic array" (Spillers 1987b: 176–77). In between an event that did occur and a transferential haunting, a clipping that "stuck in my head," Morrison retells a story, reinscribes an event that is no longer located between two unsmiling faces and The Story of a Hat. The hat now signs what before it only displaced. An event is passed on, reimagined, dictating different conventions. We have to interpret anew the signs of this event to grasp it, to understand why a clipping "stuck in my head," just as Sethe reads the dangerously mobile signs around her. Just as she hears some writing, is touched by three shadows, breaks water when a young girl arrives, recognizes a hat and hands around her throat, remembers, responding to a series of questions, lost objects, languages, and selves. All the intimations of this event are reread into an elaborate cultural braid of portentions and significations, fragments of events, memories, lives embodied and embedded within a System that never succeeded in making itself the world or in turning people into the inert property of its will, and that cannot then fully account for the lives made within its negating and treacherous bounds.

Yet an account takes place, neither simply description nor causal explanation, but something else. The something else is a ghost story, a story of enchantment, of "*knowing* the things behind things," as Morrison says (B 37). A story that is no longer located in the vice of the morality of verisimilitude, which the abolitionist, with honorable motivations, nonetheless demanded. And, indeed, much that distinguishes Morrison's story from Coffin's can be found in their respective hat stories: Coffin trying to hold on to it, obsessed with its property rather than its spirit, and Morrison conjuring up the complicated nexus that is the thing behind it, offering reconciliation and a future without property-tied domination. To get to the ghost story, it is necessary to understand how something as simple as a hat can be profoundly and profanely illuminating, if you know how to read the signs. To get to the ghost and the ghost's story, it is necessary to understand how the past, even if it is just the past that flickered by a moment before, can be seized in an instant, or how it might seize you first.

Bumping into a Rememory

> There is a secret agreement between past generations and the present one. Our coming was expected on earth. Like every generation that preceded us, we have been endowed with a *weak* Messianic power, a power to which the past has a claim. That claim cannot be settled cheaply. Historical materialists are aware of that.   WALTER BENJAMIN, *Illuminations*[27]

Or how it might seize you first.

> "I was talking about time. It's so hard for me to believe in it. Some things go. Pass on. Some things just stay. I used to think it was my rememory. You know. Some things you forget. Other things you never do. But it's not. Places, places are still there. If a house burns down, it's gone, but the place—the picture of it—stays, and not just in my rememory, but out there, in the world. What I remember is a picture floating around out

there outside my head. I mean, even if I don't think it, even if I die, the picture of what I did, or knew, or saw is still out there. Right in the place where it happened."

"Can other people see it?" asked Denver.

"Oh, yes. Oh, yes, yes, yes. Someday you be walking down the road and you hear something or see something going on. So clear. And you think it's you thinking it up. A thought picture. But no. It's when you bump into a rememory that belongs to somebody else. Where I was before I came here, that place is real. It's never going away. Even if the whole farm—every tree and grass blade of it dies. The picture is still there and what's more, if you go there—you who never was there—if you go there and stand in the place where it was, it will happen again; it will be there for you, waiting for you. So, Denver, you can't never go there. Never. Because even though it's all over—over and done with—it's going to always be there waiting for you." (B 35–36)

"Is there somewhere I should stand?" (copyright Jaimie Lyle Gordon, 1987, silver print,

What original instruction can we make out of this time of things that passes on or just stays? What can we make out of this rememory that forgets some things and never ever others, a memory already indicated as uncanny by its fundamental repetitiousness and by its gesture to the haunted house? We could make out of this deeply social memory the kind of historical materialism an awareness of haunting would produce. For Morrison's social memory is not just history, but haunting; not just context, but animated worldliness; not just the hard ground of

social memory = haunting

infrastructural matters, but the shadowy grip of ghostly matters. It is *not just in my rememory, but out there, in the world, right in the place where it happened.* The picture of the place is not personal memory as we conventionally understand it, private, interior, mine to hoard or share, remember or forget. The picture of the place *is* its very sociality, all the doings, happenings, and knowing that make the social world alive in and around us as we make it ours. It *is still out there* because social relations as such are not ours for the owning. They are prepared in advance and they linger well beyond our individual time, creating that shadowy basis for the production of material life. The possibility of a collectively animated worldly memory is articulated here in that extraordinary moment in which you—*who never was there* in that real place—can *bump into a rememory that belongs to somebody else.* You are walking down the road or into the building and you hear or see something so clearly, something that isn't necessarily visible to anyone else. You think, "I must be *thinking it up,* making it up." Yet in this moment of enchantment when you are remembering something in the world, or something in the world is remembering you, you are not alone or hallucinating or making something out of nothing but your own unconscious thoughts. You have bumped into somebody else's memory; you have encountered haunting and the picture of it the ghost imprints. Not only because this memory that is sociality is out there in the world, playing havoc with the normal security historical context provides, but because *it will happen again; it will be there for you.* It is *waiting for you.* We were *expected.* And therein lies the frightening aspect of haunting: you can be grasped and hurtled into the maelstrom of the powerful and material forces that lay claim to you whether you claim them as yours or not.

Denver may not care about Sweet Home: "'How come everybody run off from Sweet Home can't stop talking about it? Look like if it was so sweet you would have stayed'" (B 13). But she is concerned that "the thing that happened that made it all right for my mother to kill my sister could happen again" to her. Denver doesn't know "what it is" or "who it is," but she knows that it "comes from outside this house, outside the yard, and it can come right on in the yard if it wants to" (B 205). So, *Denver, you can never go there. Never. Because even though it's all over—over and done with—it's going to always be there waiting for you.* What does Sethe think is waiting for Denver? The what and the who Denver doesn't know and sometimes doesn't care about: Sweet

Home. Sweet Home, the name a cruel caricature, captures well "the paradigm of conflated motives" that is "antebellum slavery in the United States" (Spillers 1989: 25). Sweet Home is slavery at home, certainly capitalized, but embedded within an economy of homework and the aberrant domesticity the slave household upheld:

> Deeply embedded, then, in the heart of American social arrangements, the "peculiar institution" elaborated "home" and "marketplace" as a useless distinction, since, at any given moment, and certainly by 1850—the year of the Fugitive—the slave was as much the "property" of the collusive state as . . . she was the personal property of the slaveholder. We could say that slavery was, at once, the most public institution *and* the ground of the institution's most terrifying intimacies. (ibid.: 28)

The terrifying intimacies of Sweet Home, slavery at home: the ink, the stolen milk,[28] the hat. It is *not just in my rememory, but out there, in the world.* Public and private, home and market, the sweet home of slavery still haunts the fugitive who made the run across the river. It is *waiting for you.* ~ *Sweet home as haunting*

Beloved's appearance, the breathing presence of this beautiful ghost whose sparse talk is like a series of picture books, bears out this theory of memory as haunting. *Where I was before I came here . . . it's never going away.* And it can return, expectantly and incarnate, to settle claims that cannot be adjudicated easily or cheaply, to settle claims that are clamoring, haunting the house. Sethe is thinking Sweet Home and she will try to make amends, taking advantage of Beloved's return, creating a cocoon of protectiveness around the ghost she is sure is her dead baby. Denver thinks it is the baby too and in sisterly fashion decides that "maybe it's still in her the thing that makes it all right to kill her children. I have to tell [Beloved]. I have to protect her" (B 206). But you can bump into somebody else's memory and *not even know it.* This too happens because Beloved always shines twice; she means more than what they hear. That more is the very condition of possibility for Sweet Home: the impersonal and seemingly abstract system of the exchange of captured bodies as mercantile and later propertied capital. This slavery is never at home. It travels internationally (it is what Weber called wandering trade), becoming that second nature of a society that "assures us that human beings make a mess of it when they try to control their destinies . . . and that we are fortunate in possessing an interpersonal mechanism—the market—which can substitute for human hubris and planning and replace human decisions altogether" (Jameson 1991:

Shines twice as possibility

273). The replacement of situated human decision making about the production and reproduction of social life (with all the messiness any self-government entails) with an impersonal, unquestionable, uncontrollable thing called the market is modern enslavement in the general sense. The genealogy of the conceptual abstraction and its fortunes traces it back to the concrete form in which it arrived here in the United States, the passage of captive Africans to America. Morrison's gentleness and ruthlessness, her sadness and anger, as she figures this passage across what Paul Gilroy (1993) has called the Black Atlantic, is beautifully moving as it makes concrete the abstract: A woman walked out of the water breathing hard, speaking to herself of "circle[s] around . . . neck[s]," "small rats," "hill[s] of dead people" and "they never knew where or why she crouched, or whose was the underwater face she needed like that. Where the memory of the smile under her chin might have been and was not, a latch latched and lichen attached its apple-green bloom to the metal. What made her think her fingernails could open locks the rain rained on?" (B 210–12, 274–75).   *Proximity*

Spectrality is . . . what makes the present waver (Jameson 1995: 85). The emphasis on the wavering present, on the propinquity of hard-to-touch, hard-to-see abstractions powerfully crisscrossing our concrete quotidian lives is key. The presence of the ghost informs us that the over and done with "extremity" of a domestic and international slavery has not entirely gone away, even if it seems to have passed into the register of history and symbol. Haunting the post–Civil War and by allegorical reference the post–civil rights era, the presence of a ghost who is herself haunted tells us that although we may not be able to grasp all of what the ghost is trying to communicate to us, "taking the dead or the past back to a symbolic place is connected to the labor aimed at creating in the present a place (past or future) . . . 'a something that must be done'" (de Certeau 1988: 101). What is to be done? First the ghost that haunts 124 Bluestone Road in 1873 will have to be evicted so that home can be moved finally from Sweet Home to 124. The ghost is not living in the spirit world. It is living, and not too graciously at that, in the real world of day jobs, burnt toast, sibling rivalry, sought-after love and companionship, adjudging neighbors, and something will have to be done about that. *What made her think her fingernails could open locks the rain rained on?* The second task involves confronting the trauma of the Middle Passage, confronting what reaches down deep beneath the waters or beneath the symbolics of emancipation, free labor,

free citizen. This trauma links the origin of Slavery with a capital S to
the origin of modern American freedom, to the paradigmatic and value-
laden operations of the capitalist market.[29] This is a market whose
exchange relations continue to transform the living into the dead, a system of social relations that fundamentally objectifies and dominates in
a putatively free society. The Middle Passage is the decisive episode
that establishes the amnesiac conditions of American freedom: emancipation as enslavement. In order to manage this "remembering which
seems unwise," it will be necessary to broach carefully and cautiously
the desires of the ghost itself. The ghost's desires? Yes, because the
ghost is not just the return of the past or the dead. The ghostly matter is
that always "waiting for you," and its motivations, desires, and inter-
ventions are remarkable only for being current.

A Long Way

> Denver looked at her shoes. "At times. At times I think she
> was—more."   TONI MORRISON, *Beloved*[30]

Slave Ship (Slavers Throwing Overboard the Dead and Dying, Typhoon Coming On)
(Joseph Mallord William Turner, 1840, oil on canvas, 90.8 × 122.6 cm, courtesy Museum
of Fine Arts, Boston, Henry Lillie Pierce Fund)

A woman walked out of the water thirsty and breathing hard having traveled a long distance looking for a face. Nobody counted on her walking out of the water. Especially the ones who counted.[31] The others were more generous and took her for one of their own, even though she had not made the first passage, but arrived late, speaking in a language they recognized, but had needed to forget. They made her language their own and fell in love with her, but she was thirsty and breathing hard having traveled a long distance looking for a face. She remembered a ship men without skin iron waters angry limbs protruding wild sea beasts and the smell and look of the color red. They all had reasons to avoid remembering red and they all had reasons they never spoke to avoid remembering why the woman arrived late. *How bad is the scar?*[32] But the woman saw a face in the waters she was desperate to find and so she walked out of the water thirsty and breathing hard having traveled a long distance looking for that face. She found one but it was not the one she saw in the waters, even though the face she found was also looking for a face she had lost. The woman drank the stories belonging to the face she found, trying to satisfy a hunger the other only fed. She was bound to be unforgiving. After all, she'd traveled a long distance, holding a memory the waters did not drown. *How bad is the scar?* But she was also bound to be forgotten again because her hunger was insatiable and the living could not afford to feed her. A woman walked out of the water thirsty and breathing hard having traveled a long distance looking for a face. Nobody counted on her walking out of the water, but when she did, she reminded them of things they had forgotten or hadn't even got around to remembering yet. *How bad is the scar?* A woman walked out of the water thirsty and breathing hard having traveled a long distance looking for a face. Nobody counted on her walking out of the water. Nobody counted her until she forced an accounting. But even then, she had come too far and they had their own memories that were looking for a story. *How bad is the scar?*

The ghost's desires? It is already a lot to deal with what keeps jarring and jamming the reconstructive efforts demanded by 1873, a bad and depressing year all around.

> She shook her head from side to side, resigned to her rebellious brain. Why was there nothing it refused? No misery, no regret, no hateful picture too rotten to accept? Like a greedy child it snatched up everything. Just once, could it say, No thank you? I just ate and can't hold another

bite? . . . No thank you. I don't want to know or have to remember that. I have other things to do. (B 70)

The other things Sethe has to do involve refashioning her life and becoming a different somebody than she was before, hardly minor tasks; the whole project exacerbated by, if not doubly motivated by, the ghost in the haunted house. In this very personal process of reconstruction, which is intimately linked to the Reconstruction the date 1873 signs yet at a certain daily remove from it, the pressing problem of the present is the disjunction between a historical rupture (Emancipation) and the remaking of subjects. In a context in which History is said to be in the making all the exhilarating and troubling "choices and passions" that define an individual's life world—the things I have to do—converge on just that point where "determinism" or a collective logic of history spirals around them (Jameson 1991: 328). The relationship between subjection and subjectivity is an old problem, but not any less prevalent for being so persistent.

The year 1873 forms a crossroads in post–Civil War history. In the summer, the War Department and the Department of the Interior sponsored "competitive surveying expeditions" in South Dakota's Black Hills (Slotkin 1985: 329). These expeditions marked a turning point in the ongoing continuation of the Civil War as a Western war on Indian tribes. They consolidated the military's control of Indian policy and initiated extermination raids against the Sioux. The government surveys were the first step in opening Sioux lands to economic development, and 1873 advanced the alliance of white supremacism, industrial expansion, and permanent war. The year also brought industrial expansion to a halt in a collapse so protracted and severe that it was known until the 1930s as the Great Depression. Recent advances in wages and working conditions were swept away by an increasingly Darwinian business environment that starved or crushed tens of thousands of small businesses and accelerated the concentration of ownership and economic control (Foner 1988: 513). Finally, the opposition to these fusions of racism, poverty, coercion, and violence known as Radical Reconstruction had entirely exhausted itself. Racial violence had pushed the Republican Congress to pass the rather strong Enforcement Acts and Ku Klux Klan Act in 1870 and 1871, but the rise of the Liberal Republicans prior to the election of 1872 had further weakened Republican support of Reconstruction. When the voice of reform itself spoke to the former slaves, as embodied in Liberal presidential candidate Horace Greeley, it said, "Root, Hog, or Die!" Radical Reconstruction had tried to combine the formal, legal freedom of Emancipation with the political self-rule and social resources that would make freedom secure and powerful. By 1873, these efforts were dead.

Morrison's oblique focus on the period in American history we call Reconstruction is instructive here. While only the crudest of structuralists (or the laziest of ideologues) reads a pronouncement as experiential reality, for many it has not been as obvious as it may seem that freedom is not secured when the state proclaims it thus. The pronouncement only inaugurates the lengthy walk into the discriminating contradictions of the newly heralded modernity. And indeed, no one in the novel (or, we can surely say, in real life) gained freedom from the pure fact of the Emancipation Proclamation. They either ran, were bought out of slavery by a relative, or were freeborn and actively assisted fugitives as they dealt with the Northern version of free racism in the post-Emancipation United States. Twenty years after the Emancipation Proclamation, the characters in *Beloved* are struggling with the knowledge that "freeing yourself was one thing; claiming ownership of that freed self was another" (B 95).

The novel takes on this crucial task of shifting the historical and analytic burden away from the Civil War and the Emancipation Proclamation as the decisive moment when America solved the problem, eliminated enslaving conditions, affirmed a new morality of the state, and made everyone free to Reconstruction. The "twenty awful years" (Du Bois [1935] 1992) from 1854 to 1877 enfold Morrison's story, a story about ordinary black people, now free and living in Ohio, trying to remake their lives in the shadow of a Reconstruction that turned out to be expansionist, militaristic, and subjugating. In this regard, the presence of Sixo, an Indian and slave at Sweet Home who "stopped speaking English because there was no future in it" (B 25), and the sick and dying fugitive Cherokee Paul D meets escaping from prison in Alfred, Georgia, who refused to walk to Oklahoma on the "trail of tears" when the discovery of gold in the Appalachians forced their removal in 1838, links east and west in the story of the regenerative violence (Slotkin 1973) that founds the United States in the crucible of the Civil War and the Emancipation Proclamation. Between 1860 and 1890, the West was finally "won" from the remaining free tribes in a series of wars that were absolutely essential to yet remain ideologically unassimilable to the Civil War, which constructed a nation freed from the tyranny and political-economic limitations of a slave economy. The Civil War and the appropriation of Indian Territory—a liminal category in which *Indian* is the foreign possessive name for a category, territory, which is the white man's future: a state to be—were the joint imperatives of a manifest destiny that enabled the official Reconstruction of the United States as a modern racial capitalist enterprise. This manifest destiny was already prophesied, and even the Sioux's Ghost Dance in 1890, a ceremonial hope for a "new land" where only Indians and the ghosts of their ancestors would live among "sweet grass," "running water and trees," and "great herds of buffalo and wild horses," could not prevent it (see D. Brown 1970: 389–412).

Reconstruction ratified a prevailing but limited notion of freedom as the freedom to own property, to sell one's labor, and to not be owned as property. From slave labor to wage labor, what kind of freedom did capitalist freedom produce? Although Baby Suggs is surprised and excited by the prospect of money—"Money? Money? They would pay her every single day? Money?" (B 144)—by the time Stamp Paid is tired enough to understand why, when they came into her yard, Baby Suggs got weary and just had to go to bed, he is already smelling "skin, skin and hot blood" (B 180). Smelling the lynchings and the long march of those now possessing "free" status into the twentieth century. Reconstruction was a failure politically, socially, and economically, and we still live today with the consequences of the great divide between legal right and substantive freedom.

Reconstruction is American History, but it also must perforce be fashioned by people who unavoidably make their long or short way—who remember and forget—in the vortex of those spiraling determinations. The inevitable but intrusive presence of spiraling determinations creates the haunting effect but also sets limits on what can be remembered and what needs to be reckoned with now in the very charged present. At the start of the novel, some seventeen years after she has murdered her baby, Sethe is immobilized. She cannot move forward and she is holding fast to her steely determination to keep the past at bay, hoping against hope that repressing it will bring the peaceful comfort she longs for. But Paul D lovingly touches (enlivens) the tree of scars on her back, which Sethe knows is there but cannot see or feel; Beloved arrives, the fleshy talking return of the repressed; and despite the fact that Paul D has run the specters out of the house, it is haunted again. In

1873 what haunts revolves around what can be remembered right then and there in Sethe's contemporaneity as she negotiates the complex and dangerous transferential relations that Beloved's arrival has generated. What can be remembered in 1873 is broadly contained in the statement passed down to us, *Margaret Garner, the slave mother . . . killed her child rather than seeing it taken back to slavery.* Yet we know there is more. Sethe cannot remember the more of Beloved's story, even though she believes that remembering and telling her own will explain Beloved's and reconcile the damage. There is a limit, the nature of which is lived history, to what Sethe and the community can remember or confront. *No thank you. I just ate and can't hold another bite.* This limit restricts our ability to rest secure in history as determinate context. (Indeed, it sets us the challenge of always taking the so-called answer, the determinate context, as the contentious soliciting question.) But such a limit also harbors the ineluctable promise of making contact with the ghostly haunt. *For taking the dead or the past back to a symbolic place is connected to the labor aimed at creating in the present a place (a past or future), a something that must be done.* Almost at the end of the Reconstruction that will be a failure, excited about new prospects but also tired, the memories and nightmares of Sweet Home all too vivid, the baby ghost living in the house, what could Sethe and Paul D and the rest possibly remember if not that which would create a hospitality for the present?

Yet we know there is more. We know that it is Beloved's *how can I say things that are pictures* (B 210) that marks the other side of the limit of what Sethe's rebellious brain refuses to accept. And we also know that a conflict is readied between Sethe and Beloved because despite the seeming saturation of having remembered it all—of thinking that everything repressed has returned made patently clear to Sethe by the ghost's very live manifestation—there is more. Unfortunately (for it would be simpler), it is not a question of assuming that if Sethe could only remember the more of Beloved's story she would have the whole story. The whole story is always a working fiction that satisfies the need to deliver what cannot possibly be available. You might recall that Beloved had two dreams, *exploding and being swallowed,* and these are monitory premonitions for us all. Morrison makes us aware here of the problem of exploding or being swallowed as she operationalizes her haunting theory of rememory. As we approach Beloved from Sethe's point of view, we can see how she acts as a screen for the memory of

Sethe's dead child (Freud 1899). As Sethe grapples with the memory of the child and why she killed her, Beloved as ghost is a haunting reminder of what Sethe and not Beloved must contend with. And in a sense she couldn't be otherwise because Beloved's return and the repetition and displacement of memory the whole text stages must remain partial to the living, to 1873. *When the living take the dead or the past back to a symbolic place, it is connected to the labor aimed at creating in the present a something that must be done.* But we also approach Beloved now in the late twentieth century under different conditions, and when we do we are reminded of what Morrison's characters cannot remember or digest in 1873: the more of Beloved's story as a slave-to-be who never arrived, a history of barely legible traces imagined or conjured up out of Documents Illustrative of the Slave Trade. *They never knew where or why she crouched* or quite understood that the ghost haunting them could be haunted too. We can admit the haunted ghost into evidence and she gives notice, paradoxically, to the unspeakability of her story and to her yearnings:

> "Ain't you got no brothers or sisters?"
> . . . "I don't have nobody."
> "What was you looking for when you came here?"
> . . . "This place. I was looking for this place I could be in."
> "Somebody tell you about this house?"
> "She told me. When I was at the bridge, she told me."
> . . . "How'd you come? Who brought you?". . . "I asked you who brought you here?"
> "I walked here. . . . A long, long, long, long way. Nobody bring me. Nobody help me." (B 65)

And if we shift perspective, begin to approach the ghost's desires, what will we find?

An Engraving

> The clearest memory she had, the one she repeated, was the bridge—standing on the bridge looking down.
> TONI MORRISON, *Beloved* [33]

how can I say things that are pictures. Beloved is trying desperately to remind them, to tell them something about a passage they have mostly forgotten, but "the repressed is not easily discerned; its language is a

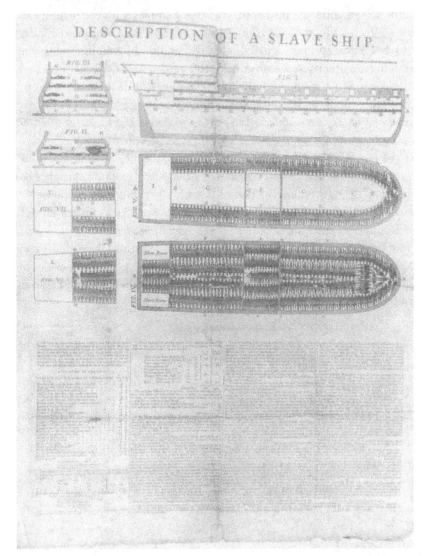

Plan and cross section of a slaver, the *Brookes* of Liverpool (1789, copper engraving, 604 × 504 mm, by permission of Wilberforce House, Hull City Museums, Art Galleries and Archives, U.K.)

graphic presence of bodies conjured up from visions or memories of other worlds" (Conley 1988: xix). She has pictures of another world she is trying to conjure up for them so that she may find calmer waters. *the man on my face the men without skin small rats crouching stand-*

ing the little hill of dead people the circle around her neck the bridge flowers a face song is gone (B 210–13). A ghostly presence, she has come a long way alone to haunt their present, to quench her thirst, to listen to their stories, to ask them questions, to find the face she lost. She is looking for them. She is looking for a place to be in. Somebody told her to look there. *The clearest memory she had . . . was the bridge—standing on the bridge looking down.*

I look for her in the archive, and among the charters, ship logs, and cash receipts I find an engraving. The engraving of the plan and cross section of the slaver *Brookes*, "officially sponsored by the Abolitionist Society," was "sent 'to the Members of both Houses of Parliament & to such other persons as may be thought expedient by the Committee of Distribution'" on the occasion of "William Wilberforce's speech in the House of Commons on 12 May [1789] proposing a resolution for the abolition of the slave trade" (Honour 1989: 64–65). The purpose of the engraving is to create an impression of the violence of the slave trade so that we—who were not on the ship—can apprehend its essence. The engraving does create an impression of the dehumanization of the slave trade, but it does so unwittingly, by being able to represent only the plan of the ship and the space for its cargo. The invisibility and the insignificance of the men, women, and children who inhabited the *6 feet by 1 foot 4 inches* (men), *5 feet 10 in. by 1 foot 4 in.* (women), *5 feet by 1 foot* (boys), and *4 feet 6 in. by 1 foot* (girls) allotted them is an offense that cannot be avowed in the representation itself. Were it to be allowed, the "historical and social consciousness of these Africans," what *they* carried in their nakedness on the ship with them, the ship that supposedly carried only cargo and not culture, would have to be present in some form.

> These cargoes . . . did not consist of intellectual isolates or deculturated blanks—men, women and children separated from their previous universe. African labour brought the past with it, a past which had produced it and settled on it the first elements of consciousness and comprehension. . . . It would be through the historical and social consciousness of these Africans that the trade in slaves and the system of slave labour was infected with its contradiction. (Robinson 1983: 173; emphasis in the original)

And so the signs of this consciousness, the cultural "seeds" of contradiction and "opposition" (Cabral in Robinson 1983: 174), were removed from the Description, an example if there ever was one of that civilizing document that is at the same time a document of barbarism.

Our ghost—and she is our ghost because we do see her *how can I say things that are pictures* there where these things have been removed—is buried alive in this scriptural tomb of a Description although her "absence [is] so stressed, so ornate, so planned [it] call[s] attention to [itself]" (Morrison 1989: 11). The call to attention is our inheritance of the history of an exchange of people whose official history leaves only the Description of a Slave Ship, a description that forces us to imagine what it only gestures toward; that forces us to call again for an "official inquiry," this time into the condition of the haunting remainder of the ship, its ghosts.

To perſons unacquainted with the mode of carrying on this ſyſtem of trading in human fleſh, theſe Plans and Sections will appear rather a fiction, than a real repreſentation of a ſlave-ſhip.[34] A recognition that real representations are fictions too enables us to find the "imaginary zone . . . every culture has . . . for what it excludes," for what is personally, historically, and sociologically unspeakable (Cixous and Clément 1986: 6). A recognition that real representations are fictive too disrupts the illusion that we could find the real woman precisely where she will not be, in the "Description" that is the real representation. Lost on the way from there—Africa—to here—America—Beloved is a sign without a referent for those to whom her return is addressed. *Everybody knew what she was called, but nobody anywhere knew her name. Disremembered and unaccounted for, she cannot be lost because no one is looking for her, and even if they were, how can they call her if they don't know her name? Although she has claim, she is not claimed* (B 274). Claimed or not, "somewhere every culture has an imaginary zone for what it excludes and it is that zone we must try to remember today." We must try to remember today if for no other reason than that a ghost is haunting the living, forcing us in that uncanny way hauntings have to "track the image" or the apparition "back to a *point of density*"—the engraving—and toward a "*potentiality* induced from a *dispersion* of gestures" (Spillers 1989: 51). And in this sense, haunting is essential to this laborious work. After all, we need to know that something is missing in order to even begin to look for it or its dispersion of gestures anywhere, in the archive or in the imaginary zone. The ghostly haunt gives precisely this notification. *The clearest memory she had . . . was the bridge—standing on the bridge looking down.* The ghostly haunt says, Something is happening you hadn't expected. It says, Something is making an appearance to you that had been kept from view. It says, Do something about the wavering present the haunting is creating.

If we make a leap I realize is not easy and try to grasp the ghost's standpoint, its voice only ever fragmentary fantastic pictures, we are led to conclude that the ghost is a living force. It may reside elsewhere in an otherworldly domain but it is never intrinsically Other. It has a life world, in the strongest sense of the term, of its own. And it carries this life world with all its sweet things, its nastiness, and its yearnings into ours as it makes its haunting entry, making itself a phenomenological reality. There is no question that when a ghost haunts, that haunting is real. The ghost has an agency on the people it is haunting and we can call that agency desire, motivation, or standpoint. And so its desires must be broached and we have to talk to it. *The ghost's desire,* even if it is nothing more than a potent and conjectural fiction, must be recognized (and we may be able to do no more than simply feel its haunting impact) if we are to admit that the ghost, particularly as it functions as a figure for that which is invisible but not necessarily not there, is capable "of strategy towards us" (Spivak 1989b: 273). *Sethe's is the face that left me . . . her smiling face is the place for me* (B 213).

[margin handwritten note: haunting as desire ↓ recognition]

But the modus operandi of a ghost is haunting, and haunting makes its only social meaning in contact with the living's time of the now. As Barbara Christian (1993) suggests, the need of the dead to be remembered and accommodated, and these are two of Beloved's cravings, is inseparable from the needs of the living. In other words, the ghost is nothing without you. In this sense, the ghost figures what systematically continues to work on the here and now. When a ship, a bridge, a face, an inert object, an ordinary building, a familiar workplace, a patch of grass, a photograph, a house becomes animated, becomes haunted, it is the complexities of its social relations that the ghostly figures. This sociality, the wavering present, forces a something that must be done that structures the domain of the present and the prerogatives of the future.

The Living

Most understandings of ghosts and phantoms, including Sethe and Denver's deep belief in the identity of Beloved, conceive the ghost as the return of a lost loved one, what Freud called the familiar stranger. A familiar stranger is a vivid characterization of the commanding meeting

"Fighting the Horizon" (copyright Jaimie Lyle Gordon, 1990, silver print, 16 × 20 inches)

haunting:
familiar
&
also
strange

of familiarity and strangeness that defines haunting. But the ghost is not just the lost loved one. Indeed, if haunting was only ever about our own lost loved ones, the return of the ghost to the living would be the end—albeit a dramatic one—of the story. This is the crucial point, as we saw in chapter 3, on which the Mothers of the Plaza de Mayo insisted. Sethe and Denver lost their daughter/sister Beloved. Beloved comes back. She is not a bag of bones but a living, breathing entity. They feed her, make amends, and restore the family. What more could there be? This is not the end of the story because when the ghost's information, so to speak, is relayed back only to the familial and the familiar, it leads to the "displaced acceptance of the phantom as part of . . . life which . . . in turn leads to bizarre and even delirious acts" (Abraham [1975] 1988: 80).

Bizarre and even delirious acts? A readied conflict. The house has gone quiet not only because the ghost has come out of the shadows, but also because the women have closed themselves up inside it. At first, it was all so many games and the pleasure of the sweets and the days taken off from work. But then Sethe loses her job, the arguments begin, and Beloved gets more and more demanding, bossing Sethe around and taking "the best of everything—first" (B 241), until she's taken over. Taking and taking and then accusing, *how could she have left her?* (B 241), making Sethe cry and offering no forgiveness for *the milk* and the headstone and Sethe's mournful suffering described over and over again. A fundamental misunderstanding, tearing them apart, binding them to each other, that won't budge: *That before leaving Sweet Home Beloved slept every night on her chest or curled on her back? Beloved denied it. Sethe never came to her, never said a word to her, never smiled and worst of all never waved goodbye or even looked her way before running away from her* (B 242). Round and round they go in this ghost dance, *beribboned, decked-out, limp and starving but locked in a love that wore everybody out*, oblivious to Denver, oblivious to the empty larder, oblivious to what has become the incommensurability of their hauntings, a mortal conflict.

The ghost is hungry and selfish (understandably greedy is how Denver at an earlier moment describes it) and lost and bearing all the weight of the world it carries. *And no one understands.* Denver is the first to see the tip of Beloved's scar and she is the first to see the aberrant mourning:

> Beloved sat around, ate, went from bed to bed. Sometimes she screamed, "Rain! Rain!" and clawed her throat until rubies of blood opened there. . . . Then Sethe shouted, "No!" and knocked over chairs to get to her and wipe the jewels away. Other times Beloved curled up on the floor, her wrists between her knees, and stayed there for hours. . . . Then it seemed to Denver the thing was done: Beloved bending over Sethe looked the mother, Sethe the teething child, for other than those times when Beloved needed her, Sethe confined herself to a corner chair. (B 250)

Denver is also the first to see the mortal conflict with the living that will never end if something isn't done: "Sethe was trying to make up for the handsaw; Beloved was making her pay for it. But there would never be an end to that" (B 251). The ghost will have to be dispatched. As Denver learns this crucial lesson about haunting, she, the one who wouldn't leave the yard, becomes the intrepid angel of history, head looking forward, forward, forward. Denver will stop protecting Beloved from *the thing that happened that made it all right for my mother to kill my sister* and begin to protect her mother from Beloved's thing, even though she is still not sure what or who that is either.

The expulsion of Beloved begins when Denver leaves the yard, "inaugurate[s] her life in the world as a woman" (B 248), and slowly becomes a member of the community again. Some gifts of food, a few thank-yous, a warm smile, shared better memories of 124 lead up to the visit with Janey Wagon about getting a job. Janey makes Denver explain the trouble, and it is a very short gossipy distance from Janey to everybody else and finally to Ella, who "thought it through" (B 255). And Ella decided that although she "didn't mind a little communication between the two worlds," "the idea of past errors taking possession of the present" was simply not acceptable when "everyday was a test and trial" (B 257, 256). And so thirty women abandoned the judgment against Sethe's "misdirected prideful rage" they had held onto for seventeen years and "walked slowly, slowly toward 124." The women see Sethe and the ghost that "had taken on the shape of a pregnant woman." Sethe sees them and also Mr. Bodwin on his way to collect Denver for work and *It is when she lowers her eyes to look again at the loving faces before her that she sees him. Guiding the mare, slowing down, his black hat wide-brimmed enough to hide his face but not his purpose. He is coming into her yard and he is coming for her best thing. She hears wings. . . . And if she thinks anything, it is no. No no. Nonono. She flies* (B 261–62).

And what of Beloved? *Beloved is smiling. But now her hand is empty. Sethe is running away from her . . . and she feels the emptiness in the hand Sethe has been holding. Now she is running into the faces of the people out there, joining them and leaving Beloved behind. Alone. Again. . . . And above them all, rising from his place with a whip in his hand, the man without skin, looking. He is looking at her* (B 262). Backward and forward, time is scrambling, things are repeating as the haunting scenes finally merge, the women's voices a chorus of convergences they will never inhabit together. Sethe runs again. Beloved disappears.

Morrison's resolution of the struggle between Sethe and Beloved helps us to see that haunting as a way of life, or as method of analysis, or as a type of political consciousness, must be passed on or through. (This lesson can be aptly applied to other contemporary versions of endless mourning, such as left pessimism or cynicism, political paralysis, or DeLillo's telecommunicative indifference.) To remain haunted is to remain partial to the dead or the deadly and not to the living. Morrison provides a stunning example of how to hospitably and delicately talk to ghosts and through hauntings, which we must do. Because when ghosts appear to you, the dead or the disappeared or the lost or the invisible are demanding their due. They are, for better or worse, very much alive and present. But Morrison also tells us that the ghost must be collectively exorcised so that, to reverse de Certeau, if the *dead* start to take the *living* back to the past, *it is connected to the labor aimed at*

*creating in the present a place (a past or future), a something that must
be done.*

The collective exorcism of Beloved is crucial to establishing that
"what haunts are . . . the gaps left within us by the secrets of others"
(Abraham [1975] 1988: 75) or the articulated and often disarticulated
traces of that abstraction we call a social relationship of power. The
significance of Morrison's double-voiced ghost rests on the extent to
which it cannot be reduced simply to an individual's memorable biography, but rather signals, however obliquely, the very conditions that
make that biography historically possible and imaginable. These conditions, however, become "'phantom effect[s]' . . . [that] fade during . . .
transmission from one generation to the next and that, finally . . . disappear" (ibid.: 80). *They forgot her like a bad dream. . . . Like an unpleasant dream during a troubling sleep. . . . By and by all trace is gone.*
They didn't have any choice but to forget her because *remembering . . .
the breath of the disremembered and unaccounted for . . . seemed unwise.* But the last word remains, Beloved. And we are thus left with the
lesson that "shared . . . phantoms find a way to be established as social
practices along the lines of *staged words*" (ibid.). To stage a shared
word like *Beloved* is not only to reckon with the ghost by placing its
"effects . . . in the social realm" (ibid.). To stage the final word as
Beloved also notifies us that even after the "fixing ceremony" (Christian
1993), haunting remains. We are still left to wrestle with what they
have forgotten: "not only the footprints but the water too and what . . .
is down there" (B 275).

We are asked, then, to consider two counterintuitive features of
haunting. The first is that the ghost cannot be simply tracked back to an
individual loss or trauma. The ghost has its own desires, so to speak,
which figure the whole complicated sociality of a determining formation that seems inoperative (like slavery) or invisible (like racially gendered capitalism) but that is nonetheless alive and enforced. But the
force of the ghost's desire is not just negative, not just the haunting and
staged words, marks, or gestures of domination and injury. The ghost is
not other or alterity as such, ever. It is (like Beloved) pregnant with unfulfilled possibility, with the something to be done that the wavering
present is demanding. This something to be done is not a return to the
past but a reckoning with its repression in the present, a reckoning with
that which we have lost, but never had. The ghost always also figures
this utopian dimension of haunting, encapsulated in the very first lines

of Jacques Derrida's book on specters: "Someone, you or me, comes forward and says: *I would like to learn to live finally*" (1994: xvii).

The second feature of haunting we are asked to consider involves this wavering yet determinate social structure, or what we could call history. History, Morrison suggests, is that ghostly (abstract in the Marxist sense) totality that articulates and disarticulates itself and the subjects who inhabit it. It is, in contrast to sociology and other modern retrieval enterprises, never available as a final solution for the difficulties haunting creates for the living. It is always a site of struggle and contradiction between the living and the ghostly, a struggle whose resolution has to remain partial to the living, even when the living can only partially grasp the source of the ghost's power. What is not so counterintuitive is Morrison's broadest claim that we should beware forgetting the enslavement or domination that persists and that often masquerades as emancipation or freedom.

A woman walked out of the water breathing hard, and we are reminded that when ghosts haunt, that haunting is material. A woman walked out of the water breathing hard having traveled a long distance looking for a face, and we are reminded that her desires will make all the difference to those she meets. A woman walked out of the water thirsty and breathing hard having traveled a long distance looking for a face, and we are reminded that she returned to a place and a time she never was. A place and a time where her arrival could only be understood within the memoryscape her haunting both produced and interrupted. A woman walked out of the water thirsty and breathing hard and within the gap between more memories than seem tolerable and there being still more, we are reminded of haunting's affliction and its yearning for a something that must be done.

If You Were Me and I Were You

> The American dream is innocence and clean slates and the future.
> TONI MORRISON, "A Conversation with Miriam Horn"

He was writing in a book about them, with the ink she made. Asking them questions, observing their behavior, measuring their attributes, calculating their worth, establishing their race for science. He was in a scene of research, ethnographic research, creating a story, producing a record,

"If you were me, and I were you" (copyright Jaimie Lyle Gordon, 1988, silver print, 30 × 40 inches)

with the ink she made. He wanted to get it all down, a complete record, a book with all the facts, with the ink she made. *I didn't care nothing about the measuring string. We all laughed about that—except Sixo.... Schoolteacher'd wrap that string all over my head, 'cross my nose, around my behind. Number my teeth.* When she heard his questions she ran, but his book remains. Like "Delia, a slave belonging to B. F. Taylor, [who] was ordered to pose in the nude for the benefit of Louis Agassiz's scientific studies" (Sterling 1984: 18–19), she was just a piece of data waiting for his words to write her up, to pass her down to us as social science. (Louis Agassiz arrived from Switzerland in the United States in 1846. Influenced by the anatomist Dr. Samuel Morton, author of two books on the science of racial separation, Agassiz went to Columbia, South Carolina, in 1850 to study the racial characteristics of African-born slaves. At the request of Dr. Robert W. Gibbes, who hosted Agassiz and accompanied him on his trip, J. T. Zealy photographed the slaves Agassiz examined. The fifteen photographs of unclothed slave women and men that remain are collected at Harvard University's Peabody Museum of Archaeology and Ethnology. They were found in the museum's attic in 1976. Each photograph lists a first name and place of residence [plantation], and in three cases the tribe or region of origin.)

Of course, he missed everything. Everything that might have made him notice that she was alive and would stop making the ink and run away, even kill her children, probably kill him too. Even with his professional method (1. Defining what counts as evidence. 2. Collecting evidence. 3. Generalizing from specifics. 4. Drawing conclusions.), even with all his documentation and will to find the errors, even with Agassiz's fifteen photographs, he misread all the signs and could only count as evidence what occurred within his very limited field of vision. *Number my teeth. I thought he was a fool. And the questions he asked was the biggest foolishness of all.* A problem of perspective, he thought, and so he returned to claim his data, his story, his property. But it was too late, she ran out of his book (and his clutches) and landed in a different one—more caring, more careful, more able to understand that it was inevitable that she would stop making the ink and run away, even kill her children, probably kill him too.

He was writing in his book about them, with the ink she made. She would never speak for him, a deliberate refusal to satisfy his desire to complete his book. All his book will ever teach us is how, caught within his limited field of vision, he misread all the signs and produced a story in which her refusal to speak is its noisiest silence. *I commenced to walk backward, didn't even look behind me to find out where I was headed. I just kept lifting my feet and pushing back. . . . Like somebody was sticking fine needles in my scalp.* Yet she seems to have spoken to the woman writer who, with her ear to her ghostly presence, put her into a book where the ink spills words that haunt us with a story forgotten and now remembered. A story not at all like the dream of social science. *And the questions he asked was the biggest foolishness of all.*

He was writing in a book about them, with the ink she made. I am also writing in a book about her, a book that investigates the shadows from which our texts often flee. Few teachers, especially sociology teachers, reading *Beloved* today would identify with schoolteacher, the educated master. Like Levi Coffin over one hundred years ago, most would repudiate schoolteacher and announce themselves, as he did, "friends of the oppressed." They might even claim to have inherited such principles from the oppressed themselves. However, the repudiation of schoolteacher and the sympathetic identification with the slaves and their descendants assert an interest that is double-edged. *"'This is your ma'am. This,' and she pointed. 'I am the only one got this mark now.'"* The repudiation of schoolteacher registers a desire to be included in one of the very crucial political questions *Beloved* poses: How can we be accountable to people who seemingly have not counted in the historical and public record? " '*But how will you know me? How will you know me?*'" After all, the question—how can we be accountable to people who have seemingly not counted?—has been a major impetus for a range of collectively organized efforts in critical scholarship. The rejection of the master and the concomitant identification with the slaves and their descendants produce a sense of inclusivity that such a question invites. " '*Mark me, too,*' I said. '*Mark the mark on me too.*'" But this desire for inclusion, which is the essential quality of sympathetic identification, is a treacherous mistake. " '*Did she?*'" asked Denver. " '*She slapped my face.*'"

It is a treacherous mistake for two reasons. The first is that it displays a basic misunderstanding of (and in this a fundamental disrespect for) the unequivocal need, however it is expressed and whether or not you approve of the expressions, that people who are subjugated or exploited or relentlessly taxed have to be *done with all that.* Holding them to their identity as marked (or wanting to join them) is not only to hold them back from moving on, it also locks the repudiation in place, solid and secure that I am not that other Schoolteacher. The second reason this kind of identification is mistaken is that haunting always gets the better of this "psychologizing social glue," whose logic is the American dream of innocence and clean slates and the future: If you were me and I were you.[35]

The call for accountability that Morrison raises in *Beloved* is set against slavery's accounting of the person as property belonging to another:

> Shackled, walking through the perfumed things honeybees love, Paul D hears the men talking and for the first time learns his worth. He had always known, or believed he did, his value—as a hand, a laborer who could make profit on a farm—but now he discovers his worth, which is to say he learns his price. . . . Remembering his own price, down to the cent, that schoolteacher was able to get for him, he wondered what Sethe's would have been. . . . When he thought about it now, her price was greater than his; property that reproduced itself without cost. . . . What had Baby Suggs' been? How much did Halle owe? . . . What did Mrs. Garner get for Paul F.? More than nine hundred dollars? How much more? Ten dollars? Twenty? Schoolteacher would know. He knew the worth of everything. It accounted for the real sorrow in his voice when he pronounced Sixo unsuitable. (B 226, 228)

The relationship between accountability and accounting that slavery establishes means that those who do not count are those whose worth is literally measured by their price. Who can answer Paul D's questions? *Schoolteacher would know. He knew the worth of everything.* It is not insignificant that schoolteacher both knows "the worth of everything" and counts, measures, and analyzes Sethe's characteristics in the name of a masterful science that seems all too frequently surprised by the political and economic investments that others notice quite readily. It is also significant that Sethe's mother slaps her when she asks her mother, in the brief moment of a longing encounter, to "mark me too." And in the significance of what schoolteacher and Sethe's mother know, we had better shift the question. How are we accountable for the people who do the counting?

In a text as evocative and successful in creating a sociological and mythical reality as *Beloved,* it is perhaps too easy to distance ourselves from the ones who count, to disclaim this onerous inheritance by sympathetically identifying with the others or by denying any identification whatsoever. (This book is not about me.) Yet Morrison's call for accountability suggests that it is our responsibility to recognize just where we are in this story, even if we do not want to be there. She also suggests that we cannot decline to identify as if such an (albeit worthy) act can erase or transcend the sedimented power relations in which we lived then and live now. Thus, we will have to contend not only with those who do not count but are counted; we will also have to contend with those who have the right to count and account for things. In order to continue to displace claims made *in behalf for a reputation,* in order to grapple with the shadows from which our texts have fled, some of us will have to contend with the ghosts of schoolteacher, Mr. and Mrs. Garner, Mr. Bodwin, and all the rest whose names we do not know, and contend with the *real sorrow* in their pronouncements.

Morrison names and remembers the anonymous slave and in doing so she also inscribes within each unique individual name a genealogy of the anonymous. Denver is named after the white girl who helped deliver her; Sethe is named after the only man her mother "put her arms around"; Baby Suggs names herself after her husband; Stamp Paid signs himself all accounts paid. When we read these names, their anonymity is disclosed as a historical construction, making the name sign a life, a set of memories, a history. Yet each name also offers a story of why the people who hold these names are anonymous, why they have not counted, even if they have against all odds counted for themselves.[36] For white readers in particular, such a genealogical project is only the start of a related but different one: the project that delves into why the white name seems to announce itself as if it did not harbor precisely this same history. *The American dream is all innocence and clean slates and the future.* Despite the best intentions and political hopes, to repudiate the genealogy that traces the white name to its seemingly unspeakable origins is to continue to forget that white people are in the story too. This is without doubt a way of counting, but it is mostly our own shadows that such an accounting eclipses. How are we accountable for those who do the counting?

Nobody saw them falling. But fall they did, a woman and a double-voiced ghost who kept forcing the woman to "[pick] meaning out of a code she no longer understood" (B 62). The voices of these women could be heard emanating from the spiteful, then loud, now quiet house. These voices spoke volumes—of passages made and not made, of markings visible and invisible, of memories remembered and forgotten, of limits and possibilities, of burdens and responsibilities. But in these voices a secret, "recognizable but indecipherable," could sometimes be heard:

> Whitepeople believed that whatever the manners, under every dark skin was a jungle. Swift unnavigable waters, swinging screaming baboons, sleeping snakes, red gums ready for their sweet white blood. In a way, he thought, they were right. The more coloredpeople spent their strength trying to convince them how gentle they were, how clever and loving, how human, the more they used themselves up to persuade whites of something Negroes believed could not be questioned, the deeper and more tangled the jungle grew inside. But it wasn't the jungle blacks brought with them to this place from the other (livable) place. It was the jungle whitefolks planted in them. And it grew. It spread. In, through and after life, it spread, until it invaded the whites who had made it. Touched them every one. Changed and altered them. Made them bloody, silly, worse than even they wanted to be, so scared were they of the jungle they had made. The screaming baboon lived under their own white skin; the red gums were their own. Meanwhile, the secret spread of this new kind of whitefolks' jungle was hidden, silent, except once in a while when you could hear its mumbling in places like 124. (B 198–99)

The secret spread of this new kind of whitefolks' jungle was hidden, silent, except once in a while when you could hear its mumbling in places like 124. Perhaps white readers would be wise to read *Beloved* as a ghost story of this unspeakable moment in the narrative of the history and inheritance of slavery. To speak of this secret, that whites have already been touched and invaded as if from the outside by a world of their own making, is one crucial testimony the slave narrative could not utter but Morrison does. What Morrison is saying in this spectacular passage is that if we listen carefully to the voices of 124, we will hear not only "their" story, the old story of the past, but how we are in this story, even now, even if we do not want to be. To be in the seemingly old story now scared and not wishing to be there but not having anywhere else you can go that feels like a place you can belong is to be haunted. And haunting is exactly what causes declarative repudiations and voluntaristic identifications eventually to fail, although it must be said that they can be sustained for quite some time. Reckoning with ghosts is not like deciding to read a book: you cannot simply choose the ghosts with which you are willing to engage. To be haunted is to make choices within those spiraling determinations that make the present waver. To be haunted is to be tied to historical and social effects. To be haunted is to experience the glue of the "If you were me and I were you" logic come undone. Though you can repeat over and over again, as if the incantation were a magic that really worked, I am not Schoolteacher / He is not me, the ghostly matter will not go away. It is waiting for you and it will shadow you and it will outwit all your smart moves as that jungle grows thicker and deeper. Until you too stage a shared word, a something to be done in time and for another worlding.

The last word. Beloved. Who is the beloved?

having
no
place
to belong: haunted

There are crossroads where ghostly signals flash from the traffic ("Migrant Mother," copyright Jaimie Lyle Gordon, Continuous Series 1986–92, silver print 30 x 40 inches)

5

there are crossroads

We began with the analytic importance of life's complications, with the complexities of power and personhood, with the meddlesome fictive, with the impositions of the barely visible, and with our own affective involvement in these matters and in the knowledge we create about them. We end with haunting in our contemporary world, which is also where we began, and about which I will have a few final words to offer. These are the bookends because when I started writing this book I knew without question, a sign of an important advance in scholarly knowledge, that domination and resistance are basic and intertwined facts of modernity. I had been well schooled in this point by sociology, by a number of radical traditions of thought and action, and by my own experiences. But I had also become increasingly troubled by the taken-for-grantedness of this fact, the way it is more often an answer than a question, and I felt that our predominant modes of expressing and communicating the enormity and the intricacies of this fact are wanting.

Book after book, conference after conference, interaction after interaction, I was more and more convinced, to use Cedric Robinson's eloquent words, that "something more than objective material forces were responsible for 'the nastiness' . . . that something of a more profound nature than the obsession with property was askew in a civilization which could organize and celebrate—on a scale beyond previous human experience—the brutal degradations of life and the most acute violations of human destiny" (1983: 442). Robinson is discussing the motivation for the black radical tradition whose genealogy and historical origins he has been tracing, its active rejection of the "systematic privations" of racial capitalism (and in an expanded version its rejection of the privations of a racially gendered capitalism) and also its critique of the inadequacies of Marxism. He says, "It seemed a certainty that the system of capitalism was part of it, but as well symptomatic of it. . . . It was not simply a question of outrage or concern for Black survival. It was a matter of comprehension" (ibid.). Yes, something more hinged on the question of comprehension, hinged absolutely on understanding, in a manner most scholars have not quite effectuated, that the very tangled way people sense, intuit, and experience the complexities of modern power and personhood has everything to do with the character of power itself and with what is needed to eradicate the injurious and dehumanizing conditions of modern life. Ghostly matters are part of the "something more" because haunting is one of the most important places where meaning—comprehension—and force intersect.

At the heart of *Ghostly Matter*'s meditation on haunting is an engagement with novels by Luisa Valenzuela and Toni Morrison. I have learned a great deal from what these women say and how they say it. They changed my way of thinking and they have helped me to better articulate what were initially stammering and inchoate suspicions and disappointments. The completion of this project confirms my belief that Valenzuela and Morrison's way of seeing—their way of negotiating the always unsettled relationship between what we see and what we know—has tremendous significance for social analysis and for those who write with critical intentions and, at least in part, to effect social and political change. I have hoped that by sharing the lessons I learned, which coalesce around haunting, sociologists and other social analysts might be more willing to rise to their challenges. These challenges are all too often like the rising of "renegade ghosts" (T. Davis 1978: 43). Perhaps by now, you will at least be willing to entertain the idea that when ghosts arise, it is not necessary to flee from "the craft of their ways / or the gentleness that drove them / before invisible steeds took them" (ibid.). It might even be worthwhile to talk to them . . . for a little while at least, until the something to be done their arrival announces takes its course.

By way of a necessarily incomplete summary, let me try to review what we learn when we look at the world through Valenzuela's and Morrison's eyes. The most obviously striking feature of their way of seeing is that Luisa Valenzuela, Toni Morrison, and Sabina Spielrein too, can see what is usually invisible or neglected or thought by most to be dead and gone. They recover "the evidence of things not seen," that paradoxical archive of stammering memory and witnessing lost souls (Baldwin 1985: xiii). They recover the evidence of things not seen and they show that ordinary people ascertain these evidentiary things not also, but more often than professional seers. These women possess a vision that can not only regard the seemingly not there, but can also see that the not there is a seething presence. Seething, it makes a striking impression; seething, it makes everything we do see just as it is, charged with the occluded and forgotten past. These women comprehend the living effects, seething and lingering, of what seems over and done with, the endings that are not over.

Perceiving the lost subjects of history—the missing and lost ones and the blind fields they inhabit—makes all the difference to any project trying to find the address of the present. And it is the writing of the history of the present that is, I think, the sociologist's special province. The history of the present, which "would play the role of a kind of 'internal ethnology of our culture and our rationality,'" is always a project for those looking toward the future (Sheridan 1980: 205). To write a history of the present requires stretching toward the horizon of what cannot be seen with ordinary clarity yet. And to stretch toward and beyond a horizon requires a particular kind of perception where the transparent and the shadowy confront each other. As an ethnographic project, to write the history of the present requires grappling with the form ideological interpellation takes—"we have *already* understood"—and with the difficulty of imagining beyond the limits of what is already *understandable*. To imagine beyond the limits of what is already understandable is our best hope for retaining what ideology critique traditionally offers while transforming its limitations into what, in an older Marxist language, was called utopian possibility.

Such a double take establishes the importance of thinking in terms of shadows and acts, to paraphrase Ralph Ellison. Only such a context, which is our history of the present project, that third-class travel between the synchronic—the sociological—and the diachronic—the historical—can broach the effectivity of marginality and invisibility, its pall and its spell. Only such a context can call into question the demand for the "unequivocal accusation of the real" without turning into decontextualized relativism or a free-market pluralism. Only such a context can approach the intermingling of fact, fiction, and desire as it shapes us and the public knowledge we create.

Sabina Spielrein grasped something crucial, in part what was grabbing her, about the unseen transfer of force and sentiment between analyst and patient. Luisa Valenzuela saw, without any hindsight whatsoever, writing as she was in the midst of it all, the terrifying and conjuring power of the state to which most in her class were blind. She shows us how the repression AZ, the professional analyst, could not or would not see was enveloping him, drawing him to it as he was looking elsewhere. Toni Morrison saw slavery living in the aftermath of its abolition. She saw the anonymous, the phantom subjects of history, and imagined their talk, feelings, and habits, in all their concreteness and contradictions. Morrison saw how grappling with a real ghost who is herself haunted is a crucial and necessary part of the American history we call Reconstruction.

It would be wrong to suggest that we possess no paradigms for seeing the unseen or for uncovering the work of unseen forces. Psychoanalysis, for example, does attempt to provide a scientific approach to the unconscious and to those symptomatic effects whose origins lie elsewhere, repressed, out of our conscious grasp. It has much to say about the processes, such as displacement, projection, denial, rationalization, and wishing, by which things appear and recede. Marxism too provides a paradigm for understanding the impact of unseen forces. Marxism calls the ensemble of these unseen forces a mode of production, which never can be located as such, but that produces real, often quite phantasmatic, effects: objects that come alive only when you can't see the labor that made them; markets that are ruled by invisible hands; value that is a surplus of what has been appropriated from you; groups of people, classes, that are bound to each other in a wrenching division. Both Marxism and psychoanalysis provide important directions for analyzing unseen forces, their harm, and the constricting parameters within which they force us to live.

But Valenzuela and Morrison comprehend something more and qualitatively different than these paradigms do, and this comprehension makes their contributions both special and essential. It is essential to see the things and the people who are primarily unseen and banished to the periphery of our social graciousness. At a minimum it is essential because they see you and address you. They have, as Gayatri Spivak remarked, a strategy toward you. Absent, neglected, ghostly: it is essential to imagine their life worlds because you have no other choice but to make things up in the interstices of the factual and the fabulous, the place where the shadow and the act converge. It is essential to write about societies and people enthralled by magic, enchanted, possessed and entranced, disappeared, and haunted because, well, it is more common than you might have considered. Valenzuela and Morrison are willing to go through *the other door* with its *flood of tears and consolation enclosed* or to collect *the footprints* and dive for *the water too and what is down there,* and thus they see that all these ghostly aspects of social life are not aberrations, but are central to modernity itself.

While Valenzuela and Morrison could not possibly speak to all the different facets of the profound and elemental deprivations of modernity they address—slavery and racism, state authoritarianism, Enlightenment science, gendered repression—they capture a crucial element that many have missed and that most social science rejects as extraneous or irrelevant. Valenzuela and Morrison see with a remarkable clarity and with an extraordinary generosity of apprehension the haunting way systematic compulsions work on and through people in everyday life. They see into the abstractions: they comprehend the elusive concreteness of ghostly matter. They capture those singular and yet repetitive instances when home becomes unfamiliar, when your bearings on the world lose direction, when things are animated, when the over and done with comes alive, when the blind field comes into view, when your own or another's shadow shines brightly.

And in this, Valenzuela and Morrison understand the fundamental sociality of haunting, that we are haunted by worldly contacts. Luisa Valenzuela tells a story of, among other things, the disastrous blindness of a psychoanalytic science of human contact. A science that cultivates and values transference but treats animism—the belief in and experience of the incitements of the things of the world—as childish primitive superstition; a science of human contact without a social unconscious. Valenzuela shows us a psychoanalyst desperately seeking the essence of the feminine who cannot see the most obvious fact about the woman with whom he is involved. She warns us that one of the more psychoanalytically sophisticated middle classes in the world turned a blind eye to the massive terror, "the nervous system," exhausting and repressing the society at large. By contrast, Morrison's Sethe sees the tactile materiality of social relations, especially their dangers, "out there" in those rememories that you can bump into, even if they did not happen to you personally, that are waiting for you, even if you think they are finished and gone. Since for Morrison individual memory is congealed social memory (the way the commodity is congealed labor for Marx), she offers us a conception of a collectively animated worldly memory that is our shared sociality, our loving and deadly contacts.

This collectively animated worldliness is crucial because the ghostly matter does not just appear and recede as a supplemental effect of real "objective material conditions." The ghostly matter is itself a historical materialism with its own particular mode of causality that does not usually look very much like context, influence, reflection. It looks like a structure of feeling.

Structure of feeling is a concept Raymond Williams invented to capture "actively lived and felt" meaningful social experience as it intricately interacts with and defies our conceptions of formal, official, and fixed social forms. A structure of feeling is a way of designating "those elusive, impalpable forms of social consciousness which are at once as evanescent as 'feelings' suggests, but nevertheless display a significant configuration captured in the term 'structure'" (Eagleton 1991: 48). Williams says, "We are talking about characteristic elements of impulse, restraint, and tone; specifically affective elements of consciousness and relationships: not feeling against thought, but thought as felt and feeling as thought: practical consciousness of a present kind, in a living and interrelating continuity. We are then defining these elements as a 'structure': as a set, with specific internal relations, at once interlocking and in tension" (1977: 132).

Three problems with our most common modes of social and cultural analysis led Williams to develop his idea of a structure of feeling. These are problems to which we have already given some attention. The first problem is the reduction of the "specifically and definitively" lived experience of the social to fixed forms, the treatment of a vibrant pulsating living present as an inert past tense. When we "convert" "relationships, institutions and formations in which we are still actively involved . . . into formed wholes rather than forming and formative processes . . . only the fixed explicit forms exist, and living presence is always . . . receding" (128). By contrast, a structure of feeling gives notice not, for example, to the cold influence of a given and discernible ideology or class structure upon individual thinking, but rather to the proceeding looming present. *We are talking about . . . affective elements of consciousness and relationships: not feeling against thought, but thought as felt and feeling as thought: practical consciousness of a present kind, in a living and interrelating continuity* (132).

The second problem involves a related tendency to define the social as the known, and then, in compensation for the evacuations thus rendered, to define the personal or the subjective as the moving present: "If the social is always past in the sense that it is always formed [the known relationships, institutions, formations, positions], we indeed have to find other terms for the undeniable experience of the present: not only the . . . realization of this and this instant, but the specificity of present being . . . within which we may indeed discern and acknowledge institutions, formations, positions, but not always as fixed . . . [and] defining products" (128). What do we call the undeniable experience of the present that gets lost when we treat the social as if it were a hard-edged immobile past? "All that escapes [us] . . . is grasped . . . as the personal: this, here, now, alive, active, 'subjective'" (128). A structure of feeling defines not only, then, "a social experience that is still in *process*," but also social experiences that are often not "recognized as social but taken to be private, idiosyncratic, and even isolating" (132). A structure of feeling gives notice to the necessarily social nature of what we call the subjective; it gives notice to the texture and skin of the *this, here, now, alive, active* contemporaneity of our lives.

The third problem occurs as a result of the first two. When we reduce the social to fixed past-tense forms and when we then segregate the subjective and what Williams calls the "explicit," we end up with highly reified asocial abstractions that fail to capture just the conflagration of "social" and "personal" that is the living present. When the "complexities, the experienced tensions, shifts, and uncertainties, the intricate forms of unevenness and confusion" (129) are set against the reductions as their aberrant supplements, then, says Williams, they disappear from social analysis altogether: "Social forms are then often admitted for generalities but debarred, contemptuously, from any possible relevance to this immediate and actual significance of being" (130). Where do these complexities and tensions and confusions go? As social analysis flees from recognizing their very sociality, these complexities and tensions do not just disappear or become silent or become settled into an asocial unconscious. "The actual alternative to the received and produced fixed forms is not silence: not the absence, the unconscious, which bourgeois culture has mythicized. It is a kind of feeling and thinking which is indeed social and material" (131). This feeling, structured and effervescent, is social and material, and it is also "embryonic," by which Williams means that it is not "fully articulate" or yet part of a "defined exchange." *Its relations with the already articulate and defined are then exceptionally complex* (131).

And thus we come to the core of the conceptual comprehension that is not only the structure of an affective social experience and consciousness, but also the spellbinding material relations of exchange between the defined and the inarticulate, the seen and the invisible, the known and the unknown. A structure of feeling is not the subjective or the personal as we have conventionally understood them as the self-contained other of the sociological object. A structure of feeling is precisely that conception, or sensuous knowledge, of a historical materialism characterized constitutively by the tangle of the subjective and the objective, experience and belief, feeling and thought, the immediate and the general, the personal and the social (129). A structure of feeling "articulates *presence*" (135) as the tangled exchange of noisy silences and seething absences. Such a tangle—as object and experience—is haunting. And haunting describes a practical consciousness that "is always more than a handling of fixed forms and units." Haunting describes just those "experiences to which the fixed forms do not speak at all, which . . . they do not recognize" (130).

The historical materiality of the tangle is what our cases have highlighted. The example of Spielrein shows not only that psychoanalysis loses the woman it claims to have analytically grasped, but also that the easy invisibility of the gendered object of professional desire, the disposability of the loved one, plagues Freud and returns to haunt psychoanalysis and its history. Luisa Valenzuela shows us not only that a Latin American authoritarian state violated the human rights of its people to secure a capitalist, Christian, and patriarchal order, but also that its primary modus operandi, disappearance, worked by haunting and by creating a haunted society in which the disappeared still wander, leaving almost everything of this modernization project unresolved. Toni Morrison shows us not only that Slavery was violent and exploitative, a System, but also that even when it was supposed to be over, it could return to haunt the living, forcing them to coexist with ghosts in a very real material way by eating, sleeping, dressing, playing, and talking with them, making Reconstruction and the "freedoms" it passes on to us today our haunting inheritance.

A structure of feeling "methodologically . . . is a cultural hypothesis, actually derived from attempts to understand . . . specific feelings, specific rhythms . . . and yet to find ways of recognizing their specific kinds of sociality, thus preventing that extraction from social experience which is conceivable only when social experience itself has been categorically (and at root historically) reduced" (Williams 1977: 132–33). I have offered a cultural hypothesis: haunting is a shared structure of feeling, a shared possession, a specific type of sociality. I might even suggest that haunting is the most general instance of the clamoring return of the reduced to a delicate social experience struggling, even unaware, with its shadowy but exigent presence. Haunting is the sociality of living with ghosts, a sociality both tangible and tactile as well as ephemeral and imaginary.

Such a cultural hypothesis eludes "analysis couched only in terms of the well-scored categories of material life, social organization, and the dominant ideas of an epoch" (Taussig 1987: 288). Thus, we must find a way to express the structure of feeling that is haunting "where the true social content is . . . of this present and affective kind, which cannot without loss be reduced to belief-systems, institutions, or explicit general relationships, though it may include all of these as lived and experienced, with or without tension, as it also evidently includes elements of social and material . . . experience which may lie beyond, or be uncovered or imperfectly covered by, the elsewhere recognizable systematic elements" (Williams 1977: 133). These are vague but well-intentioned caveats about presuming too much about haunting and the ghost. But the basic point remains that a knowledge of the materialism that is this affective exchange of haunting requires engagement with its very features, requires grappling with Valenzuela and Morrison's crucial insight: the ghostly phantom objects and subjects of modernity have a determining agency on the ones they are haunting, which is everyone, making our lives just what they are at any given moment—a tangle of structured feelings and palpable structures.

Raymond Williams goes one crucial step further. A structure of feeling, a haunting in particular, is a social experience "*in solution,* as distinct from other semantic formations which have been *precipitated* and are more evidently and more immediately available" (ibid. 133–34). There is something unique about haunting as a structure of feeling. It is "emergent." That is to say, it does not "have to await definition, classification, or rationalization before [it] exert[s] palpable pressures and set[s] effective limits on experience and on action" (132). The emergent quality of a haunting does not, as we have seen, just set limits; it simultaneously relates to a solution (134). Williams's language here provides a precision we need. He does not describe dissolution, such as melancholia, for example, but an emergent solution. He says, "Yet this specific solution is never mere flux. It is a structured formation," or, in our words, a something to be done, which is at the "very edge of semantic availability" (134). The "new articulations," the somethings to be done, are always discovered in material practices, although "often, as it happens, in relatively isolated ways, which are only later seen to compose a significant generation" (134). Fading footprints, fading photographs. It is thus that Valenzuela and Morrison insist not only on the unavoidability of dealing with State Power or Slavery or Racism or Capitalism or Science or Patriarchy, with their capital letters, but also on the unavoidability of reckoning with the structure of feeling of a haunting, of reckoning with the fundamentally animistic mode by which worldly power is making itself felt in our lives, even if that feeling is vague, even if we feel nothing.

Reckoning is about knowing what kind of effort is required to change ourselves and the conditions that make us who we are, that set limits on what is acceptable and unacceptable, on what is possible and impossible. Both Valenzuela and Morrison are concerned with change and transformation. Transformation means something distinct from resistance, rapidly becoming an all-purpose word encompassing everything from the ordinary capacity of people to make meaning out of things they use or enjoy but did not make to organized social movements to large-scale revolutions. Distinctions of scale and scope are helpful for knowing whether you are identifying a basic electrified current of social life—meaning—or whether you are analyzing the reconfiguration of social institutions or the shifting of underground historic fault lines. It must be said, it is true, that often time and perspective play havoc with our ability to know which of these things are happening at a given moment. Valenzuela and Morrison focus on the way a solution, a something to be done, emerges from haunting and the *very edge of semantic availability* to manifest its inexorability for us. It is the precarious but motivated transition from being troubled, often inexplicably or by repetitively stuck explanations, to doing something else that they chart with exquisite fidelity. It is the necessarily experiential and embodied quality of the transformation upon which they insist. In both the stories they tell, change begins slowly with individuals who are unsettled and haunted by forces that are much greater than themselves and barely visible. AZ and Sethe, in particular, are altered and are transported beyond their individual troubles and their circumscribed worlds. But this change is not intellectual; it is extremely difficult and must become incarnate. The kind of transformation evoked and called for by Valenzuela and Morrison is about going beyond what you already know just so. It involves being taken beyond a dull curiosity or a detached know-it-all criticism into the passion of what is at stake. It is not individualistic, but it does acknowledge, indeed it demands, that change cannot occur without the encounter, without the *something you have to try for yourself*. There are no guaranteed outcomes for an encounter; much is uncertain and the results may be very limited. But if you think you can fight and eliminate the systems' complicated "nastiness" without it, you will not get very far because it will return to haunt you.

AZ is taken on a long journey; he makes contact with a ghostly woman, tries to talk to her, and really does learn something after all. When The Discovery begins, AZ is already dead, not because the army has killed him on Page zero, but because he is living in a stupor of denial and fear and the only life he has is a romantic obsession with the other woman. You think he is going to be blown up at the end, but he comes alive only then and there because he has lost himself and the exotic psychoanalyzed other woman, reckoned with what he had been missing before, and become someone else. Sethe sees a hat and has to kill her child. She is also numb and stuck between past and present when her story begins. It is the presence of the beloved ghost and the reckoning with her, the living and loving and dispatching her, accomplished only with the assistance of the community, that moves Sethe to the something that must be done, her reconstructed future.

Valenzuela and Morrison apprehend the magic of social reality and they offer a way of seeing for a world where "social relations are stripped of an aura everywhere reinstated by the [ghosts] they generate" (Eagleton 1981: 27). This way of seeing is a transformative, perhaps even revolutionary, knowledge. Why? Because their way of seeing does not just disclose the evidence of things not seen, neglected and banished: it illuminates profanely. I hope it is clear by now that I take their way of seeing to be a sociological imagination and not a strictly literary or aesthetic one, as if these could be disaggregated so easily. The sociological imagination demonstrated here does not just declare the basic social link between the biographical and the historical. It does not just demonstrate the influence of operationally controlled social structures. It does not just collect the conscious thoughts and bounded practices of ordinary people. It does not just assert the importance of the subjective. This socio-logical imagination does not just give us the halfway house of known and confessed transferential investments and interests. This sociological imagination does not just describe or rationally explain or tell us what to do. It also does not treat social construction—the making and making up of the social world and of us—as a professional curiosity or as the al-ready available final answer to our most pressing questions. This other sociological imagination conjures, with all the affective command the word conveys, and it does so because it has a greatly expanded impres-sion of the empirical that includes haunted people and houses and soci-eties and their worldly and sometimes otherworldly contacts.

Profane illumination is a concept that Walter Benjamin used to de-scribe the "materialist, anthropological inspiration" (1978: 179) of the surrealists' experience of Parisian urban everyday life and its new, out-moded, and sometimes forlorn object world. In their efforts to "win the energies of intoxication for the revolution" (ibid.: 189), the surrealists hoped to "bring . . . to the point of explosion . . . the immense forces of 'atmosphere' concealed in" everyday things (ibid.: 182). It was the em-phasis on phenomenal forms, our habitual relation to them, and their capacity, upon a certain kind of contact, to shatter habit—"because only at the depth of habit is radical change effected, where unconscious strata of culture are built into social routines as bodily disposition" (Taussig 1993a: 25)—that motivated Benjamin to become himself a most astute theoretician and unusual ethnographer of the profane illu-mination, to make out of it a whole dialectics of seeing replete with an optical unconscious (see Buck-Morss 1977, 1989; Taussig 1993a).

"There . . . are crossroads where ghostly signals flash from the traffic, and inconceivable analogies and connections between events are the order of the day" (Benjamin 1978: 183). What are these ghostly sig-nals? We have encountered quite a few of them: a sunken couch, a hand, a photograph, a wolf, an open door, a hat. These are the flashing half-signs ordinarily overlooked until that one day when they become animated by the *immense forces of atmosphere concealed in them*. These illuminations can be frightening and threatening; they are pro-fane but nonetheless charged with the spirit that made them. Sometimes you feel they are grabbing you by the throat, sometimes you feel they are making you disappear, sometimes you are willing to talk to them, as Sabina Spielrein did with the wolf. Whether it appears unexpectedly or whether you cultivate and invite its arrival, the profane illumination is a discerning moment. It describes a mode of apprehension distinct from critique or commentary. The profane illumination describes when "thought presses close to its object, as if through touching, smelling, tasting, it wanted to transform itself" (Adorno in Taussig 1992: 145). The profane illumination captures the medium by which we have a different kind of access to the "density of experience" (Adorno 1981: 240). Proximate and vibrant, the profane illumination captures just that experience of the ghostly matter. Profane illumination is a kind of conjuring that "initiates" (Benjamin 1978: 192) because it is telling us something important we had not known; because it is leading us somewhere, or elsewhere.

This mode of apprehension that notices and comprehends the ghostly matter of the sunken couch, the hat, the photograph, the reflection in the mirror, the open door is a sensuous knowledge. Sensuous knowledge is a different kind of materialism, neither idealistic nor alienated, but an active practice or passion for the lived reality of ghostly magical invented matters. Sensuous knowledge is receptive, close, perceptual, embodied, incarnate (see Marx [1888] 1970: 121, [1844] 1975: 389–90). It tells and it transports at the same time. Sensuous knowledge is commanding: it can spiral you out of your bounds, it can hollow out, with an x-ray vision, the seemingly innocuous artifacts of the master. To experience a profane illumination is to experience the sensate quality of a knowledge meaningfully affecting you. To experience a profane illumination is to experience a something to be done: talking to a wolf; replacing your fearful self and the invisible fathers; protecting your child from what is waiting for her; living with, loving, and dispatching a ghost. Sensuous knowledge always involves knowing and doing. Everything is in the experience with sensuous knowledge. Everything rests on not being afraid of what is happening to you.

For profane illumination is a way of encountering the ghostly presence, the lingering past, the luminous presence of the seemingly invisible. When you see, in a photograph or in a hat or in a footprint, the hand of the state, the other door, the water and what is down there, you have seen the ghostly matter: the lost beloveds and the force that made them disposable. When you have a profane illumination of these matters, when you know in a way you did not know before, then you have been notified of your involvement. You are *already* involved, implicated, in one way or another, and this is why, if you don't banish it, or kill it, or reduce it to something you can already manage, when it appears to you, the ghost will inaugurate the necessity of doing something about it.

There is more to social life than haunting. It would be foolhardy and self-serving to suggest that haunting is the only measure of the world. Similarly, all knowledge does not strive and should not be expected to illuminate profanely, or intoxicate, or win energies for a revolution. And even on its own terms, we have seen that profane illumination can take different forms: it can be quiet and understated or deafening and dramatic. But I hope I have conveyed that haunting, with its characteristic spellbinding experience of the animated effectivity of the blind field, is a constituent feature of contemporary modern life. I hope I have also conveyed that much is at stake in our recognition of and engagement with ghostly matters, in our ability to stop fleeing from the recognition of the something more.

Today scholars know more than they ever have about the subtleties of domination, about the intersections of the modern systems that organize the production, reproduction, and distribution of social life, about the edifice of constructions upon which culture sings and weeps, about the memories and the overflowing accounts of the disremembered and the unaccounted for. Yet our country's major institutions—the corporation, the law, the state, the media, the public—recognize narrower and narrower evidence for the harms and indignities that citizens and residents experience. The most obvious violations—the poverty, the gaping inequalities of resources, the brutality of the police, the corruption of democratic politics, the hunger and homelessness, the hateful beatings and batterings—are everywhere to be seen only in the disappearing hypervisibility of their fascinating anomalousness. The more subtle violations are unseen and denied with a sanction only their perverted and inverted returns evidence adequately: the sublimating insecurities and the exorbitant taxes for our unquestioned behavior; the wear and tear of long years of struggling to survive; the exhausting anger and shame at patiently and repetitively explaining or irritably shouting about what can certainly be known but is treated as an unfathomable mystery; the deep pain of always having to compete in a contest you did not have any part in designing for what most matters and merits; the sinking demoralization and forlorn craziness of exchanging everything with the invisible hands of a voracious market; the quiet stranglehold of a full-time alertness to benevolent rule; and the virtually unspeakable loss of control, the abnegation, over what is possible.

Today, the nation closes its eyes neither innocently nor without warning. It has renewed a commitment to blindness: to be blind to the words *race, class,* and *gender* and all the worldliness these words carry in their wakes; to be blind to only the most shrunken, formal, and value-laden official empirical actualities. This is a commitment struck, as has historically been the case, when fear of loss gets the better of what could be gained. What does it mean for a country to choose blindness as its national pledge of allegiance? Choosing blindness has serious consequences for all of us because race, class, and gender, already reifications of force and meaning, can be turned into what Patricia Williams calls "phantom words." But as phantoms, they return to haunt. They create a confined but powerful room in which to live:

> The power of that room . . . is deep, angry, eradicated from view, but strong enough to make everyone who enters the room walk around the bed that isn't there, avoiding the phantom as they did the substance, for fear of bodily harm. They do not even know they are avoiding; they defer to the unseen shapes of things with subtle responsiveness, guided by an impulsive awareness of nothingness, and the deep knowledge and denial of witchcraft at work. . . . Blindly formalized constructions . . . are the creation of a space that is filled in by a meandering stream of unguided hopes, dreams, fantasies, fears, recollections. They are the presence of the past in imaginary, imagistic form—the phantom-roomed exile of our longing. (P. Williams 1991: 49)

And thus we return to end with that paradoxical feature of haunting. Haunting always harbors the violence, the *witchcraft* and *denial* that made it, and the *exile of our longing,* the utopian. When I am a spooky phantom you want to avoid, when there is nothing but the shadow of a public civic life, when bedrooms and boardrooms are clamorous ghost chambers, deep "wounds in civilization" are in haunting evidence. But it is also the case that some part of me in abeyance of the injury and some part of the missing better life and its potentialities are in haunting evidence too. The ghost always registers the actual "degraded present" (Eagleton 1991: 131) in which we are inextricably and historically entangled *and* the longing for the arrival of a future, entangled certainly, but ripe in the plenitude of nonsacrificial freedoms and exuberant unforeseen pleasures. The ghost registers *and* it incites, and that is why we have to talk to it graciously, why we have to learn how it speaks, why we have to grasp the fullness of its life world, its desires and its standpoint. When a ghost appears, it is making contact with you; all its forceful if perplexing enunciations are for you. Offer it a hospitable reception we must, but the victorious reckoning with the ghost always requires a partiality to the living. Because ultimately haunting is about how to transform a shadow of a life into an undiminished life whose shadows touch softly in the spirit of a peaceful reconciliation. In this necessarily collective undertaking, the end, which is not an ending at all, belongs to everyone.

Notes

1. her shape and his hand

1. This list is not complete. Others who could be added include Felman and Laub (1992), Haraway (1989), Minh-ha (1989, 1991), and M. B. Pratt (1984). If we were to include Silko (1977, 1991) or Wideman's recent work (1994) or Baldwin (1985) or Du Bois ([1940] 1984, [1903] 1989) or Ellison ([1952] 1981, 1964) or . . . well, then, a whole field begins to emerge whose broad expanse is cause for a serious analytic pause.

2. See Charles Lemert's recent book *Sociology after the Crisis* (1995), especially chapters 5 and 8, for a wonderfully thoughtful discussion of taking the measure of the social world.

3. My focus on social practices is written in the spirit of a crucially important point Harvey Molotch makes in his excellent article on the state of sociology, "Going Out" (1994: 222, 224): "One of the things wrong with sociology, in our country, is that we need a better country. . . . We really have to change America to change us."

4. There is a certain degree of repetition to this sentiment, even if one takes a fairly short historical perspective. Here is C. Wright Mills, in 1959: "We are at the ending of what is called The Modern Age . . . so now The Modern Age is being succeeded by a post-modern period. Perhaps we may call it: The Fourth Epoch.

"The ending of one epoch and the beginning of another is, to be sure, a matter of definition. But definitions, like everything social, are historically specific. And now our basic definitions of society and of self are being overtaken by new realities. I do not mean merely that we *feel* we are in an epochal kind of transition. I mean that too many of our explanations are derived from the great historical transition from the Medieval to the Modern Age; and that when they are generalized for use today, they become unwieldy, irrelevant, not convincing" (236).

That Mills's statement was written at the height of the New American Century is not without a certain significance since one persuasive periodization of postmodernity links it to the end of the century, most usually indicated by the OPEC oil crisis of 1973. Mills's statement should be read in the context of then current debates on postindustrialism, to which he contributed significantly with his seminal work on class, *White Collar* (1951), and that bear a striking resemblance to current attempts to define the contours of a late capitalism. It should also be read in the context of the 1950s version of the politically motivated claim, most prominently made by Daniel Bell in *The End of Ideology* (1960) and repeated in the 1990s by Francis Fukuyama (1992), that history had ended and ideology become bankrupt, the proof being the preeminence of worldwide U.S. hegemony. Mills's most direct and pointedly acerbic response to Daniel Bell was "The New Left" (1960 [1963]).

5. Taussig (1993a: 98–99) and Pietz (1993: 141–43) offer intriguing speculations on "communist fetishism" and postcapitalist animism that have potentially interesting implications for haunting's future. To quote Taussig, "*Post-capitalist animism* means that although the socioeconomic exploitative function of fetishism . . . will supposedly disappear with the overcoming of capitalism, fetishism as an active social force inherent in objects will remain. Indeed, it must not disappear, for it is the animate quality of things in post-capitalist society without the 'banking' mode of perception that ensures what the young Marx envisaged as the humanization of the world" (1993a: 99). See also T. Keenan (1993) on commodity fetishism and ghosts.

6. In this respect, *Ghostly Matters* differs from the important work by James C. Scott (1990) on domination and resistance. But his very potent notion of the "hidden transcript" that "helps us understand those rare moments of political electricity when, often for the first time in memory, the hidden transcript is spoken directly and publicly in the teeth of power" (xiii) is clearly necessary to understand haunting. Indeed, one could argue that the ghost mediates between the public and hidden transcripts, producing a particular kind of valence to the operation of and "study of power that uncovers contradictions, tensions, and immanent possibilities" (xii).

7. Jacques Derrida has now written a theory of the specter in direct engagement with Marx's texts in a moving and beautiful book about Marx's ambivalent yet obsessive relationship to ghosts. *Specters of Marx* (1994) is a very significant book of philosophy and a crucial political intervention by perhaps the most influential European philosopher living today. But it is not, I think, despite its similarly motivated distress at the claim of history's end, quite the theory of ghosts Horkheimer and Adorno would have written. See Jameson's (1995) generous and learned review essay of Derrida's book.

8. The history of the origins of American sociology (see Ross 1991; M. Smith 1994) could be reconceived such that what I am here calling the fictive would be more central to our historic mission. Acknowledging and incorporating the foundational role of W. E. B. Du Bois would be a first step (see the virtually unparalleled efforts of Lemert 1993, 1994, and 1995, especially chapters 6 and 8). Although this is not the place for an extended review of Du Bois, which in any event would have to account for the developments and refinements in his thought subsequent to his early and heavily emphasized work, *The Souls of*

Black Folk, suffice it to say that the profession might have developed otherwise had Du Bois's notion of double consciousness become sociology's common sense, rather than its suppressed history. Double consciousness is a sociological imagination, in the most profound sense in which Mills deployed the term. It is an imagination bound to a dialectics of shadows and acts, approaching our gravest social problems from the "second sight" of "being" the problem itself and thereby confounding, in that very moment, the boundary between subject and object (see the especially astute conclusion to chapter 5, "The Concept of Race," in *Dusk of Dawn* [1940] 1984). Double consciousness is a sociological imagination that fixes its sight on that very remainder of the tangible or the factual that haunting signifies and that an attention to its sign-work captures: "But after all that has been said on these more tangible matters of human contact, there still remains a part essential to a proper description of the South which it is difficult to describe or fix in terms easily understood by strangers. It is, in fine, the atmosphere of the land, the thought and feeling, the thousand and one little actions which go to make up life. In any community or nation it is these little things which are most elusive to the grasp and yet most essential to any clear conception of the group life taken as a whole. What is thus true of all communities is peculiarly true of the South, where, outside of written history and outside of printed law, there has been going on for a generation as deep a storm and stress of human souls, as intense a ferment of feeling, as intricate a writhing of spirit, as ever a people experienced. Within and without the sombre veil of color vast social forces have been at work,—efforts for human betterment, movements toward disintegration and despair, tragedies and comedies in social and economic life, and a swaying and lifting and sinking of human hearts which have made this land a land of mingled sorrow and joy, of change and excitement and unrest. . . . But if he lingers long enough there comes the awakening: perhaps in a sudden whirl of passion which leaves him gasping at its bitter intensity; more likely in a gradually dawning sense of things he had not at first noticed. Slowly but surely his eyes begin to catch the shadows of the color line" ([1903] 1989: 127–28).

2. distractions

1. Freud 1919: 242–43. All further references to Freud's essay "The Uncanny," trans. James Strachey, in *The Standard Edition of the Complete Psychological Works of Sigmund Freud*, vol. 17, London: Hogarth Press, 1919, will be given in parentheses as U.

2. See Freud's extended discussion (U 220–26) of the meaning of the word *heimlich,* homely, "a place free from ghostly influences" (225) and how its "meaning . . . develops in the direction of ambivalence, until it finally coincides with its opposite, *unheimlich*" (226), " 'seeming quite . . . ghostly to him' " (224).

3. On "phantom objectivity," see Georg Lukács (1971: 83, 100) and Karl Marx (1976: 128).

4. U 250.

5. *A Secret Symmetry: Sabina Spielrein between Jung and Freud* contains Spielrein's diary from the years 1909 to 1912, her letters to Jung written between 1911 and 1918, her letters to Freud, and his to her. Almost all of this material is fragmentary. Although Carotenuto makes reference in his extended analysis of these documents to Jung's letters to Spielrein, permission to publish them was not granted. See also Kerr (1993) for an analysis of Spielrein's relationship to Jung, Freud, and the "unconscious" of psychoanalysis. All further references to Carotenuto, *A Secret Symmetry: Sabina Spielrein between Jung and Freud,* will be given in parentheses as S.

6. U 236–37.

7. *This Sex,* 125.

8. As is probably evident by now, my evocation and use of psychoanalysis is somewhat idiosyncratic and to the side of an enormously diverse tradition of theory and clinical practice, which now includes a rather large body of feminist psychoanalytic work. In general, I try to move within and between some of what I take to be the important insights of psychoanalysis, especially its critique of empiricism and its emphasis on haunting, transference, and memory. With respect to feminist psychoanalysis, despite its range, most of it has concentrated on the narratives of normal sexual identity formation among white middle-class women that Freud invented and various others, including Jacques Lacan, have embellished and revised. My concern has not been with the developmental narratives of psychoanalysis, but rather with psychoanalysis as a model of analysis more generally. I recognize the limits of my approach, but I also hope that these very same limits free us up to develop enhanced social-psychoanalytic faculties.

9. S 85.

10. *Order of Things,* 374.

11. All further references to "The Unconscious," trans. James Strachey, in *The Standard Edition of the Complete Psychological Works of Sigmund Freud,* will be given in parenthesis as Ucs.

12. See Erich Fromm's classic essay "The Social Unconscious" in *Beyond the Chains of Illusion* (1962). Using Marx, Fromm goes well beyond Freud's notion of the unconscious to define it as "the whole man—minus that part of him which corresponds to his society" (139). See chapter 3 for a discussion of Marxism and psychoanalysis and chapter 4 for a discussion of Toni Morrison's theory of rememory, which is, in its own way, a social unconscious.

13. See William Pietz's (1993) discussion of animism and aesthetic judgment in Kant for clarification of Freud's reference, especially 137–40.

14. These include the distinction between "the uncanny we actually experience and the uncanny that we merely picture or read about" (U 247). This distinction is partially a holdover from Freud's initial presumption that uncanny experiences are qualities of feeling, aesthetic experiences, which he modestly claims a lack of qualification to investigate. This distinction is partially due to Freud's belief that "fiction presents more opportunities for creating uncanny feelings than are possible in real life" (U 251). In the end, this distinction does

not hold up too well, not only because in real life we are always reading and picturing experiences, but also because Freud's whole analysis rests on what we feel when the "world of common reality" is confronted with the presence of something that is not supposed to be there, that is not "factual."

15. See also Claude Lévi-Strauss, "The Science of the Concrete," in *The Savage Mind* (1966), especially 10–11, for an interesting discussion of magic's nonscientific understanding of causality.

16. *Specters*, 175.

3. the other door, it's floods of tears with consolation enclosed

1. The title of this chapter is from Luisa Valenzuela's *He Who Searches (Como en la Guerra)*, 30. All further references to *He Who Searches* will be given in parentheses as V.

This chapter is dedicated to Luisa Valenzuela in appreciation of her gifts and her enormous generosity to me.

2. Born in Buenos Aires in 1938, Luisa Valenzuela is reportedly the most translated contemporary Latin American woman author (Garfield 1988: 281). Work translated into English includes the novels *He Who Searches* (1979a); *Black Novel (with Argentines)* (1992), an exploration of the relationship between sadomasochism as sexual pleasure and sadomasochism as political terror set in New York City; and *The Lizard's Tail* (1983). *The Lizard's Tale* is a wild fiction about José López Rega, Juan Perón's public welfare minister. In 1956, Perón, in exile, met his third wife, Isabel (María Estela Martínez), in a Panama City nightclub, the Happy Land Bar. She was a dancer in the floor show there. The manager of the bar, Raúl Lastiri, would become one of the most important members of the returning government, as would Lastiri's father-in-law, José López Rega, a witch doctor and "obscure ex-corporal in the Argentine police" known for his writings on the love charms of Venus and Saturn. López Rega learned his magic in Brazil from the practitioners of the macumba. López Rega was perhaps the most powerful man in Argentina. In the many photographs of him he is always a shadowy presence, behind or to the side of Juan and Isabel Perón. His post as minister of social welfare gave him access to a large budget and a nationwide network of officials. It was at the ministry that he put together a powerful death squad called the Triple A (Alianza Anti-Comunista Argentina, the Argentine Anti-Communist Alliance). Its first operation was at Ezeiza Airport on the day of Perón's return from exile in 1973 (Simpson and Bennett 1985: 62–63). See "The Encounter" in chapter 3.

Several collections of Valenzuela's short stories have also been published in English: *Clara: Thirteen Short Stories and a Novel* (1976), *Strange Things Happen Here* (1979b), *Other Weapons* (1985), and *Open Door* (1988a). Valenzuela has published many short stories in English-speaking periodicals, including the stunning "Symmetries" (1988b). A special issue about her writing was published in 1986 by the *Review of Contemporary Fiction*. Work remaining untranslated includes *Los Heréticos* (1967), *El Gato Eficaz* (1972), *Libro Que No Muerde* (1980), and *Donde Viven Las Aguilas* (1983).

For literary criticism on *He Who Searches,* which tends to be heavily psychoanalytic, see Glantz (1986), Hicks (1991), Hoeppner (1992), Maci (1986), and Magnarelli (1988). For literary criticism on Valenzuela's other works, see Addis (1989), Craig (1991), Garcia-Moreno (1991), Hart (1993), Magnarelli (1988), Martinez (1986), and Rubio (1989).

One might almost describe a genre of nonnaturalist fiction by Southern Cone women writers that asks us to contemplate how and why we tolerate the most abominable violence. See Orphée (1985), Peri Rossi (1989), and Ortiz (1986–87). On Gambaro, see Garfield (1988) and D. Taylor (1990). Two recent books add to our knowledge of Latin American women writers: García Pinto (1991) consists of interviews and analysis; Castro-Klaren, Molloy, and Sarlo (1991) is an anthology.

3. See Beverley (1993: 69–99), Beverley and Zimmerman (1990), Harlow (1987), Jara and Vidal (1986), and Yúdice (1991) on the *testimonio.* We will see in chapter 4 that a good deal of contemporary literary scholarship on the slave narrative, itself a type of testimony, places it in the history of African-American literature, while pioneering scholars of the *testimonio,* such as John Beverley, make a case for the reverse: "I want to argue that testimonio involves a break or split with the novel and fictionality as such. . . . *Testimonio is not a form of the novel*" (1993: 154).

4. As Guillermo Maci (1986) notes, this character is "almost without a name. He has a frame for a name: AZ. A chain of signifiers. . . . Perhaps AZ is the ironic sign of the possession of absolute knowledge. . . . The inquisitorial traits assumed by AZ in the effort to sound out the other, to dominate the other, sanction with the irony of the letter (AZ) the infatuation of a knowledge which becomes lost on that same road which it seeks to conquer" (67–68).

5. Alfredo Navoni is a recurring character in Valenzuela's writing. He appears in the stories collected in *Other Weapons* (1985) and in *The Lizard's Tale* (1983).

6. Luisa Valenzuela was in self-imposed exile during most of Argentina's military rule. See her interview in Katz (1983: 60–70). In addition to public and private book seizures and burnings, the military government passed censorship decrees. The first, communiqué No. 19, issued by the junta on March 24, 1976, made "anyone who by any means emits, spreads, or propagates news, communiqués or images with a view to upsetting, prejudicing or demeaning the activity of the Armed, Security, or Police Forces . . . liable to a punishment of up to ten years in prison" (Argentine National Commission on the Disappeared 1986: 363). Later, in 1977, the Argentine Penal Code was revised to include rules so sweeping "it [was] no longer necessary to ban any book by decree. The new Penal Code penalize[d] . . . the printer (so that no one [would] dare to print a text that [was] merely doubtful) and the distributor and the bookstore (so that no one [would] dare sell it); and as if this weren't enough, it also penalize[d] the reader, so that no one [would] dare read it, much less keep it. Thus the consumer of a book [got] the same treatment the law applie[d] to consumers of

drugs" (Galeano 1978: 306–7). Journalists, in particular, were the object of special scrutiny by the military government. Many were imprisoned and disappeared; foreign journalists were expelled. Shortly after the coup, the military seized and took over the journalists' union, the Argentine Journalists' Federation (Argentine National Commission on the Disappeared 1986: 362–68). See also Andersen (1993: 194–204) on the total war to "conquer minds," as General Vilas put it, and its educational and cultural front.

7. *The Disappeared*, 401. Simpson and Bennett cite this case from a condensed summary the Argentine National Commission on the Disappeared issued at the time they were writing their book. AZ is a pseudonym for Dr. Teresita Hazurun. A slightly longer version of her ordeal can be found in Argentine National Commission on the Disappeared (1986: 28–29).

8. Major works in English documenting the system of disappearance and its historical precedents include Amnesty International (1980, 1981, 1994), Argentine National Commission on the Disappeared (1986), and Berman and Clark (1983). Additional studies include Andersen (1993), Hodges (1991), and Simpson and Bennett (1985). Weschler (1990) provides a comparative (Uruguay) journalistic account, Guest (1990) emphasizes the role of the United Nations, and Pion-Berlin (1989) investigates the relationship between economic doctrine and the ideology of state terror in Argentina and Peru. Partnoy (1986) and Timerman (1981) are the two most widely known English-language testimonies of the experience of being disappeared. The Chilean poet and writer Marjorie Agosin has written extensively on disappearance in Argentina and elsewhere in Latin America, combining poetry and prose (1988, 1989, 1990).

9. There is some disagreement over the actual numbers of people disappeared and the methods for calculating the figures. The Argentine National Commission on the Disappeared appointed by Raúl Alfonsín in 1983 stated that nine thousand had disappeared. Colonel Ramón Camps, police chief for the province of Buenos Aires, claimed more than forty-five thousand disappeared. The Mothers of the Plaza de Mayo estimated at least thirty thousand. See Bouvard (1994: 31–32).

10. As part of the military government's cultural war to reorganize and control university and secondary education, the junta banned all student activity and targeted students, including high school students, for disappearance. Although many students were tortured and killed, perhaps the best-known incident of student repression was the *La Noche de Los Lápices* (Night of the Pencils), named after the Third Reich's Night of the Long Knives and after the 1966 raid on the Argentine universities known as the Night of the Long Sticks. Shortly after the coup, students in Buenos Aires province organized protests against the elimination of the half-rate bus fare they had won in a campaign the year before. "On September 16, 1976, in the Buenos Aires provincial capital of La Plata, police chief Col. Ramón Camps—a man the Alfonsín government later charged was responsible for the 'direct participation in the deaths of thousands of people'—ordered the deaths of those who participated in the protest. Throughout the province more than twenty adolescents were kidnapped"

(Andersen 1993: 201). Only three of the students, one of whom was only fourteen years old, survived.

All further references to Argentine National Commission on the Disappeared, *Nunca Más. The Report of the Argentine National Commission on the Disappeared* will be given as CONADEP.

11. See Fisher (1989) and Bouvard (1994) on the Mothers of the Plaza de Mayo's criticism and rejection of the CONADEP report. The commission did not have the authority to subpoena military personnel; their effective immunity (especially from being named) led the Mothers to conclude not only that the report was inadequate, but also that "'the book was paralysing because they describe all this horror and they don't give a way out'" (Graciela de Jeger in Fisher 1989: 131).

12. In her analysis of how, in the 1960s and 1970s, the Southern Cone authoritarian regimes both continued long-standing forms of repression and invented new ones, Jean Franco identifies four aspects of the "new terror." It "1) was more systematic and anonymous in nature, characterized by a certain 'regularity' in the proceedings; . . . 2) involved the use of disappearance as a novel method of social control and in contrary fashion, the random appearance of dead bodies was meant to act as a warning to the general population; 3) involved the mutilation, burning or drowning of bodies in order to prevent identification, and thus the elimination of identity and also the impossibility of martyrdom (contrast this, for example with the funerals in South Africa); 4) involved the staging of events in order to produce calculated effects on the general population" (Franco 1986: 9). I treat these four characteristics as part of the general system of disappearance.

13. The Transfer was the name given not to release or to being moved to another site, but to mass assassination, usually involving the dumping of persons who were drugged and unconscious, but alive, into the sea. Detainees were aware of the signs indicating that a transfer was imminent and aware that transfer meant death. See Amnesty International (1980: 22–28) and Andersen (1993: 206).

14. Neither is it adequately framed as the aberrant suspension of law, as Julie Taylor (1994) has shown.

15. Why has literature played such an important role? "Because it was blocked from making contributions to the development of scientific thought [and because of the political suppression of social scientists], the intelligentsia was forced into the one area that did not require professional training and the institutionalization of knowledge—that is, into literature. It is here, therefore, that the confrontation between metropolitan discourse and the utopian project of an autonomous society takes place" (Franco 1988: 504). The complex nature of this confrontation is beyond the scope of my considerations, but it is brilliantly explored by Jean Franco (1986, 1988, 1989). See also Beverley and Oviedo (1993), Galeano (1978, 1985, 1987, 1988), Schwarz (1992), Shumway (1991), Sommer (1991), and Weiss (1991). It is interesting to note that while seminal scholarship has been produced on the crucial role literature and the literary intelligentsia have played in debates on nationalism and modernization,

virtually no work exists in English on the similar role played by psychoanalysts in Argentina. See my discussion, "Psychoanalytic Implications," in chapter 3 and Hollander's (1990) unique contribution.

16. See Hollander (1990) for a brief and Rock (1985) for an extensive history of the role of European immigration and its demise in the late 1930s in creating the explosive mix of class, race, and state politics that has long characterized Argentine culture.

17. Angel Garma, born in Spain and a friend of Salvador Dalí and Federico García Lorca, had trained at the Berlin Psychoanalytic Institute with Theodor Reik, Otto Fenichel, and Wilhelm Reich. Ernesto Carcamo, an Argentine doctor, studied psychoanalysis in France. Arnaldo Rascovsky, born in Argentina into a left-liberal Jewish family, was initially schooled in the classics and Russian literature. Enrique Pichon Riviere, a French-born Argentine, was involved as a student in support work for the Spanish Republic and worked with writers and artists to found the Goya Socialist Party (Hollander 1990: 891–93). Marie Langer, who played a crucial role in later developments, was from an assimilated liberal bourgeois Jewish family in Vienna; her "education . . . included attendance at the famous Schwerzwald School, where she had become versed in Marxism and feminism. After finishing medical school, she spent several years at the Vienna Psychoanalytic Institute, where she completed a training analysis with Richard Sterba and attended classes taught by Helene Deutsch and Jeanne Lampl de Groot. With the rise of Austro-fascism, Langer's antifascist political activism led her to . . . Spain, where she participated in an international medical brigade. . . . Forced ultimately to flee Europe, she spent five difficult years in Uruguay before coming to Buenos Aires, where she once again took up her professional commitment to psychoanalysis" (Hollander 1990: 893–94).

18. The thorough and revisionist history Hollander has fashioned from interviews and various documents is all the more important since "the interpretation of the break offered in the official history of APA, published eleven years later by those who remained, depicted the activists as individuals who had fallen into confusion by considering political and ideological questions to be central to psychoanalytic theory and practice" (Hollander 1990: 905).

19. Treating the psychological effects of torture and disappearance continues to this day in Argentina. This effort is led by Dr. Diana Kordon, Dr. Lucila Edelman, and their colleagues in the Psychological Assistance to Mothers of Plaza de Mayo Group (see Kordon et al. 1988). For comparative cases, see Felman and Laub (1992) on their work with Holocaust survivors and Fanon (1967: 249–310) on the "mental disorders" resulting from the colonial war in Algeria. Fanon's work is particularly interesting because, unlike the Argentines, he treated victims and perpetrators.

20. For an interesting study on the detail and its gendered connotations, see Schor (1987).

21. Bouvard's excellent (1994) work provides the most thorough and up-to-date study of the Mothers. The sources for her original research can be found in her bibliography. Fisher's (1989) politically astute book is also based on original research and is organized around extensive interviews with the Mothers.

No other book on the Mothers offers better access to their own voices and analyses as they developed over time. Fisher provides a particularly compelling description by the Mothers themselves of how they met, wandering from prison to police station to the Ministry of the Interior, waiting and being deceived by all the authorities. See also Simpson and Bennett (1985), Agosin (1990), Franco (1986, 1988), Arditti and Lykes (1993), Chelala (1993), Carlson (1993), Elshtain (1992), and Schirmer (1988). Agosin (1993) includes general essays on women and human rights in Latin America and essays on women and state terror in Chile and El Salvador.

22. The issue of what was already known was a particularly important one for the Mothers since they had for years been an active archive. And although they appreciated that most information had been kept from the public, they did not excuse the state's indifference to their knowledge and to the information and accounting they demanded.

23. See Taylor (1994) and the response by Marcus (1994) on the trials. On the military's response to the trials, which included two uprisings, and on the *Punto final* (Full Stop) and Due Obedience laws, see Fisher (1989: 135-48).

24. See Dabat and Lorenzano (1984) for an analysis of these ongoing conditions, the democratic movement, and its prospects.

25. On psychoanalysis and shamanism, see Clément (1987) and Lévi-Strauss (1963), especially the quite amazing chapter "The Sorcerer and His Magic," which begins, by the way, with the story of a shaman who has disappeared, and the more widely cited "The Effectiveness of Symbols." Clément's lyrical analysis of what was lost to psychoanalysis, and by extension to social science in general, when science replaced the core of what Lévi-Strauss calls the shamanistic complex—the ability of the shaman to summon the group's power for abreaction—is quite breathtaking.

26. The ERP and the various armed rebel groups miscalculated the nature of the struggle, particularly with regard to their stance toward Peronism. See Andersen (1993: 127-30) for a description and analysis of the blind spots and failures of the political strategies and activities of the ERP in Tucumán, especially their unpreparedness for the forthcoming military dictatorship. See also Castañeda (1993).

27. See Michael Taussig's discussion of the fear of Indian cannibalism further north in Columbia, a fear that "fed a colonially paranoid mythology in which dismemberment, cannibalism, and the exposure of body parts and skulls grinned wickedly" (Taussig 1987: 104). Taussig superbly describes the hunger, as well as the boundaries, of a world being grotesquely redrawn for a second time, fed by the ritualistic quality of the inverted mirror of cannibalism, colonialism itself. For a different angle, see Sigmund Freud's (1913) story of the founding of culture, *Totem and Taboo,* which also involves eating and brothers. Emily Hicks (1991: 73) analyzes "The long night of the thespians" as a parody of the totemic meal described by Freud.

28. Many of the armed revolutionary groups were composed of students, former students, and the children of the middle class.

29. Despite Jimmy Carter's election as president and his administration's

commitment to human rights, General Videla's dictatorship received $500 million from private U.S. banks and $415 million from the World Bank and the Bank of International Development in 1977. Argentina's rights for International Monetary Fund loans increased from $64 million in 1975 to $700 million in 1977 (Galeano 1978: 295). On the issue of lending and foreign debt, see Payer (1974, 1982).

Henry Kissinger took the opportunity of his five-day trip to Buenos Aires in 1978 to assure General Videla not only that he approved of disappearing people (provided it was efficient), but also that President Carter's human rights policies were the foolish sentiments of a one-term president. See Agosin (1990: 38, 40) and Simpson and Bennett (1985: 273). For David Rockefeller's congratulatory letter to Videla, see Galeano (1988: 246). On human rights and Washington's role in supporting authoritarian regimes, see Chomsky and Herman (1979).

30. On the fear of falling, see Ehrenreich (1989), and on loving authority see Newfield (1996).

4. not only the footprints but the water too and what is down there

1. The title of this chapter is from Toni Morrison's *Beloved*, 275. All further references will be given in parentheses as B. The epigraph is from Morrison's "Unspeakable Things Unspoken," 12.

2. *Scarlet Letter*, 31.

3. Toni Morrison is the author of six novels, *The Bluest Eye* (1970), *Sula* (1973), *Song of Solomon* (1977), *Tar Baby* (1981), *Beloved* (1987a), and *Jazz* (1992a), which was inspired by a James Van Der Zee photograph. (Of Van Der Zee's photographs of the dead, Morrison has written, "One can only say, 'How living are his portraits of the dead'" [Morrison in Van Der Zee, Dodson, and Billops 1978].) She has also published a collection of critical essays, *Playing in the Dark: Whiteness and the Literary Imagination* (1992b), and edited a book of essays on Anita Hill and Clarence Thomas (1992c). Morrison has received worldwide popular and critical acclaim. *Song of Solomon* won the National Book Critics Circle Award in 1978, *Beloved* won the Pulitzer Prize in 1988, and Toni Morrison was awarded the Nobel Prize in Literature in 1993. *Beloved* was widely discussed and reviewed in the press; I refer to several substantial interviews with Morrison throughout the chapter. There is a very large body of literary criticism on *Beloved*. In addition to the special issue of *Modern Fiction Studies* 39:3-4 (Fall–Winter) 1994 and the special section of *Cultural Critique* 24 (Spring) 1993, which includes Christian (1993), Moglen (1993), and Mohanty (1993), see the following for a representative sample: Bhabha (1992), Broad (1994), Fields (1989), Gates and Appiah (1993), Harris (1991, 1993), Henderson (1991), Hirsch (1994), Holloway (1990), Horvitz (1989), House (1990), S. Keenan (1993), Krumholz (1992), Lawrence (1991), Mobley (1993), Mullen (1992), Rhodes (1990), Rigney (1991), Smith (1993), Travis (1992).

4. All further references to Levi Coffin's *Reminiscences of Levi Coffin: The Reputed President of the Underground Railroad* will be given in parentheses as C.

5. "Hungry Ghosts," 271.

6. Gina Dent pointed out to me that Mary Louise Pratt calls the slave narrative "autoethnography" in her study of travel writing and transculturation. Pratt uses the term to refer to "instances in which colonized subjects undertake to represent themselves in ways that *engage with* the colonizer's own terms" (1992: 7).

7. Contemporary writers repeat the critique of sentimentality; a pointed example is Stanley Crouch's (1987) review of *Beloved,* itself arguably hysterical. In this review, which begins with a sneering commentary on the elevation of suffering and martyrdom that James Baldwin is held responsible for inaugurating and black women writers for perpetuating opportunistically, Crouch summarizes *Beloved* as if it were a television miniseries, including visual analogs: "Meet Sethe, an ex-slave woman who harbors a deep and terrible secret that has brought terror into her home. [Adolescent sons are shown fleeing]" (41). This description is prefaced by what he must take to be the clinching evidence of *Beloved*'s mawkishness and political vacuity: "It is designed to placate sentimental feminist ideology, and to make sure that the vision of black woman as the most scorned and rebuked of the victims doesn't weaken" (40). Crouch would do well to read Wahneema Lubiano's excellent essay on Alice Walker's *The Color Purple,* in which she analyzes the politics of affect and sentimentality: "It seems to me that it is useful to consider engagement in the sentimental as the excessive, the surplus corrective, to an imposed stoicism on Afro-Americans. . . . Given the dearth of attention . . . to the emotional well-being of marginalized others, such whole-hearted engagement with emotion is a way of asserting a previously denied right to feel. . . . Emotional disenfranchisement has been part, an overlooked part, of the total costs borne by objects of marginalization" (1989: 7, 8–9).

Crouch's obsession with white women notwithstanding, the need for "affective reenfranchisement" that Lubiano describes finds a similar political articulation in *Beloved:* "I am going to move us from a consideration of sentimentality and bourgeois white women to those who are perceived as crudely 'materially' oppressed in order to examine the too neatly and simply separated areas of the material and the non-material, the economic and the non-economic in regard to sentimentality" (ibid.: 1).

It is worth noting that the title of Crouch's essay, "Aunt Medea," harks back to the first use of that reference in relation to the story *Beloved* tells. In 1867 Thomas Satterwhite Noble, "the son of a wealthy hemp plantation owner and rope manufacturer in Lexington," exhibited his painting titled *Margaret Garner* at the National Academy of Design (McElroy 1990: 67). On May 18, 1867, *Harper's Weekly* ran a brief column on the exhibition and published an engraved version of the painting with the caption "The Modern Medea—The Story of Margaret Garner." The *Harper's* engraving is reproduced in this chapter.

8. The slave is not gendered in Gates's account, and I leave it at that for the

moment. That the female slave had to contend with another ideology of person-hood, the cult of true womanhood, is the premise of the work of A. Davis (1983), Carby (1987), Spillers (1987a), and Sánchez-Eppler (1993), among others.

9. There is a vast literature on the slave narrative as genre and about vari-ous slave narratives, including a substantial body of revisionist and original in-terpretive work by black women literary critics. See, for example, Andrews (1986, 1989, 1993), Baker (1984, 1991), Blassingame and Henderson (1984), Braxton (1989), Carby (1987), Davis and Gates (1985), Foster (1994), Gates (1987, 1988a), McDowell and Rampersad (1989), Mullen (1992), Sekora and Turner (1982), V. Smith (1987, 1990), Spillers (1987b, 1989), Starling (1988), Stuckey (1987).

10. Harryette Mullen's thoughtful essay on "resistant orality" makes some similar points, albeit in a different context. Mullen's essay provides a sustained comparative discussion of *Beloved*'s "critique of literacy as an instrumentality of white male domination" and its "alternative to the binary opposition of predatory literacy and institutionalized illiteracy" (1992: 258). See also Mobley (1993).

11. The passage from Ishmael Reed's *Flight to Canada* reads as follows: "Raven was the first one of Swille's slaves to read, the first to write and the first to run away. Master Hugh, the bane of Frederick Douglass, said, 'If you give a nigger an inch, he'll take an ell. If you teach him how to read, he'll want to know how to write. And this accomplished, he'll be running away with him-self'" (1976: 14).

12. *Reminiscences,* 557.

13. See Gilroy (1993: 66–68) for a discussion of Redmond's lecture and "the power of this narrative in the development of a distinctly feminine abolitionist discourse" (67). See also Sánchez-Eppler (1993) for a sustained critical analysis of feminist-abolitionism. On Lucy Stone Blackwell, see Blackwell (1930). On Sarah Parker Redmond, see Gilroy (1993: 234 nn. 79, 80, 81).

14. In addition to the sources listed in the following note, see Campbell (1970), Coleman (1940), Dabney ([1926] 1970), Knepper (1989), and Wilson (1879).

15. My account of the Garner case is based on the following sources: May ([1856] 1861), Coffin ([1876] 1968), Yanuck (1953), and my reading of the daily coverage of the events in the *Cincinnati Enquirer,* the *Cincinnati Daily Times,* the *Cincinnati Commercial,* the *Liberty Hall and Cincinnati Gazette,* and the *New York Daily Times.* Yanuck offers the most thorough account, drawing together Coffin, the local newspapers, and other versions and reports from such sources as the Boston *Liberator.* All further references to Yanuck will be given in parentheses as Y.

16. Margaret Garner is also described as a "dark Mulatto" (*Cincinnati Com-mercial,* January 29, 1856). Coffin and the various newspapers describe her as showing "one fourth or one third white blood." Hortense Spillers's comments are apt here: "The mulatto/a embodied an alibi, an excuse for 'other/otherness' that the dominant culture could not (cannot now either) appropriate or wish

away. An accretion of signs that embody the 'unspeakable,' of the Everything that the dominant culture would forget, the mulatto/a as term designates a disguise; covers up, in the century of Emancipation and beyond, the social and political reality of the dreaded African presence. Behind the African-become-American stands the shadow, the insubstantial 'double' that the culture dreamed *in the place of* that humanity transformed into its profoundest challenge and by the impositions of policy, its deepest 'un-American' activity.

"To understand . . . the American invention of the mulatto . . . is to understand more completely . . . the false opposition of cultural traits that converge on the binary distribution of 'black' and 'white'" (1987b: 176–77).

17. Coleman relays the following from Wilbur H. Siebert's spring 1893 interview with former President Rutherford B. Hayes, who was a practicing lawyer in Cincinnati at the time of the trial. According to Hayes: "When the Ohio River was frozen over there was terror among the slaveholders of Kentucky. During the winters of 1850–51, 1852–53, and 1855–56, the river was frozen over and numerous crossings were made, especially at Ripley, Ohio and at Cincinnati" (1940: 208, n. 31). The regularity with which slaves were trying to leave Kentucky, whose northern border bounded on several free states, and the well-known route of the frozen Ohio River makes one pause at the suggestion, made by Yanuck on the basis of a *New York Daily Times* story, that two Englishwomen who were visiting guests at the Gaines residence encouraged ("their determination to escape was strengthened") the slaves to run (Y 50 n. 18). The suggestion that the Garners and their friends needed the encouragement of two English "ladies" or other white intermediaries—rather than simply some practical assistance or political mobilization—in order to run away has a long history, its most general drift not confined to the more blatant self-serving benevolence of nineteenth-century white abolitionists. Gara (1967) provides an unembellished but effective exposé of the stereotypes of black passivity and white agency that surround our popular conceptions of fugitive slaves and of the Underground Railroad in particular. On the general topic of the ubiquity of slave resistance and revolt, see Aptheker (1943), Berlin (1974), Blassingame (1972), A. Davis (1983), Fredrickson ([1971] 1987, 1988), Genovese (1976) and his bibliographic essay in (1979), Gutman (1976), Levine (1977), Litwack (1979), Owens (1976), and Rawick (1972).

18. According to the *Cincinnati Enquirer,* Mary Garner said that Mary Kite did not take the knife away (January 30, 1856).

19. Or two scars, some said (Dabney [1926] 1970: 65; *Cincinnati Gazette,* February 14, 1856).

20. Yanuck (56) and the *Cincinnati Gazette* (February 1, 1856) reported that not a single room or hall would be rented for a public meeting, which was to include entertainment by a singing group, the Hutchinson Family, who had an abolitionist repertory. Coffin, by contrast, says not only that the antislavery singers performed several concerts, but also that "Smith and Nixon's hall, on Fourth Street, the best public hall in the city at that time, was kindly offered by the proprietors for the occasion. A part of the committee met next morning" (C 568).

21. As would be expected, there are wild and wildly varying accounts of the women protesters. See Y 56; *New York Daily Times*, February 4, 1856; *Cincinnati Commercial*, January 30, 1856; *Cincinnati Gazette*, January 30 and February 13, 1856; and, for the lengthiest description, the *Cincinnati Enquirer*, January 31, 1856.

22. The coroner's report on the death of Margaret Garner's daughter stated that "the murdered child was almost white" (Y 56). Coffin described the surviving infant as "much lighter in color than [Margaret Garner], light enough to show a red tinge in its cheeks" (C 563). Any mention of Margaret Garner, her daughters, or the black women of Cincinnati is elaborately color-coded, sometimes for lurid descriptive effect, sometimes to highlight Stone's accusation of "degradation," by which she means to refer to the rape of slave women by their owners and other white men.

23. Having read all of the coverage of the case in all the Cincinnati papers and in the *New York Daily Times*, I could find no reference to the hat incident anywhere.

24. On slavery and motherhood, see A. Davis (1983), Spillers (1987a), and Carby (1987).

25. "'A slave is one who is in the power of a master *to whom he belongs*. The master may *sell him, dispose of his person*, his industry and his labor. He can do nothing, *possess nothing, nor acquire* any thing, but what must belong to his master.' (Louisiana Civil Code, Art. 35)" (Goodell [1853] 1968: 23; emphasis in the original). And thus the law declares as an article of civil society what it can never deliver: the total ownership of another.

26. Even Amy, the young "raggediest-looking" white girl who helps Sethe deliver Denver as she is trying to get across the river, her feet so swollen she cannot walk, is met up with accidentally, under the brush, as it were.

27. "Theses on the Philosophy of History," 254.

28. Paul D, learning what he did not know, asks Sethe, "'They used cowhide on you?'" She replies, "'And they took my milk.'" He asks again, focusing on what is familiar to him, the beating, "'They beat you and you was pregnant?'" Her exclamation tries to get Paul D to comprehend an important difference between them that matters a great deal for what Sweet Home meant to each: "'And they took my milk!'" (B 17).

29. See Robinson (1983: 145–72) for a thorough analysis of the constitutive role African slavery played in the development of modern racial capitalism.

30. *Beloved*, 266.

31. "'You haven't asked about the 60 million,' says Toni Morrison. . . . She explains that the figure is the best educated guess at the number of black Africans who never even made it into slavery—those who died either as captives in Africa or on slave ships" (Clemons 1987: 75). But only certain deaths counted. Since the insurance only paid those who owned a right to claim and only for those lost at sea, anyone who disappeared because of "natural death," disease, starvation, murder, homesickness, or the privation of language or culture did not count (see Donnan [1931] 1965 vol. 2: 555–57; volumes 2 and 3 contain considerable data, including logs and accounts of slavers' insurance

records). The practice of throwing slaves overboard to "throw the loss upon the insurers" (ibid.: 555), which may have inspired the Turner painting, was not an uncommon practice. See Honour (1989: 162) on the Turner painting; see Donnan ([1931] 1965 vol. 2: 460) for one example of slaves throwing themselves overboard.

32. "They are then marked; this is done with a hot pipe sufficiently heated to blister the skin. . . . The object of this disagreeable operation is done only when several persons ship slaves in one vessel. . . . This disgusting duty is one of those forcible cruelties which cannot be avoided. When several proprietors ship in one vessel it is indispensable to mark them, in order that on the arrival the consignees may know them. Also, when death takes place in the passage, by the mark it is ascertained whose loss it is, as every Negro thrown over the board during the voyage is registered in the log book" (Conneau [1853] 1976: 96). Captain Theophilus Conneau had a long career as a slave trader, all of it illegal under American and British law. In 1827 Conneau received a consignment to load the Spanish vessel *Fortuna* with "an assorted cargo of slaves, for which they had shipped 200 thousand Havana cigars and 500 ounces or doubloons in Mexican coin" (ibid.: 90). As part of his description of his responsibilities and the trip, Conneau described the marking procedures.

33. *Beloved, 119.*

34. The quotation is from the text accompanying the plan and cross section of the slaver *Brookes.*

35. The phrase "psychologizing social glue" is Christopher Newfield's.

36. I have conflated somewhat here the differences between the initial renaming of Africans when they were captured and became slaves, the names slaves called themselves, and the names given to children both during enslavement and after. Eugene Genovese (1976: 443–50) provides a fuller discussion of the range of, and reasons for, naming and self-naming practices, distinguishing between surname and first name. See also Patterson (1982: 54–58) for an analysis of the politics of resistance that name changing implied within the context of slavery.

Bibliography

Abraham, Nicolas. [1975] 1988. "Notes on the Phantom: A Complement to Freud's Metapsychology." Trans. Nicholas Rand. In *The Trial(s) of Psychoanalysis*, ed. Francoise Meltzer, 75–80. Chicago: University of Chicago Press.

Addis, Mary. 1989. "Fictions of Motherhood: Three Short Stories by Luisa Valenzuela." *Romance Languages Annual* 1:353–60.

Adorno, Theodor W. 1967. "Sociology and Psychology-I." *New Left Review* 46:67–80.

_____. 1968. "Sociology and Psychology-II." *New Left Review* 47:79–96.

_____. 1981. *Prisms*. Trans. Samuel and Shierry Weber. Cambridge, Mass.: MIT Press.

Adorno, Theodor W., Else Frenkel-Brunswik, Daniel J. Levinson, and R. Nevitt Sanford. [1950] 1969. *The Authoritarian Personality*. New York: Norton.

Agger, Ben. 1989a. *Reading Science: A Literary, Political, and Sociological Analysis*. Dix Hill, N.Y.: General Hall.

_____. 1989b. *Socio(onto)logy: A Disciplinary Reading*. Urbana: University of Illinois Press.

_____. 1990. *The Decline of Discourse: Reading, Writing, and Resistance in Postmodern Capitalism*. New York: Falmer.

_____. 1991. *A Critical Theory of Public Life: Knowledge, Discourse, and Politics in an Age of Decline*. New York: Falmer.

_____. 1992. *Cultural Studies as Critical Theory*. Washington, D.C.: Falmer.

_____. 1993. *Gender, Culture, and Power: Toward a Feminist Postmodern Critical Theory*. Westport, Conn.: Praeger.

Agosin, Marjorie. 1988. *Zones of Pain/Las Zonas Del Dolor*. Trans. Cola Franzen. Fredonia, N.Y.: White Pine.

_____. 1989. *Women of Smoke: Latin American Women in Literature & Life*. Trans. Janice Molloy. Stratford, Ontario: Williams-Wallace.

_____. 1990. *The Mothers of Plaza de Mayo (Linea Fundadora): The Story of Renée Epelbaum 1976–1985*. Trans. Janice Molloy. Trenton, N.J.: Red Sea.

225

Agosin, Marjorie, ed. 1993. *Surviving beyond Fear: Women, Children and Human Rights in Latin America*. Fredonia, N.Y.: White Pine.

Alarcón, Norma. 1990. "Chicana Feminism: In the Tracks of the Native Woman." *Cultural Studies* 4, 3:248–56.

Amnesty International. 1980. *Testimony on Secret Detention Camps in Argentina*. London: Amnesty International Publications.

_____. 1981. *"Disappearances": A Workbook*. New York: Amnesty International Publications.

_____. 1994. *Les Disparitions*. Paris: Amnesty International Publications.

Andersen, Martin Edwin. 1993. *Dossier Secreto: Argentina's* Desaparecidos *and the Myth of the "Dirty War."* Boulder, Colo.: Westview.

Andrews, William L. 1986. *To Tell a Free Story: The First Century of Afro-American Autobiography, 1760–1865*. Urbana and Chicago: University of Illinois Press.

_____. 1988. "Dialogue in Antebellum Afro-American Autobiography." In *Studies in Autobiography*, ed. James Olney, 89-98. New York: Oxford University Press.

_____. 1989. "The Representation of Slavery and the Rise of Afro-American Literary Realism, 1865–1920." In *Slavery and the Literary Imagination*, ed. Deborah E. McDowell and Arnold Rampersad, 62-80. Baltimore: Johns Hopkins University Press.

Andrews, William L., ed. 1993. *African-American Autobiography: A Collection of Critical Essays*. Englewood Cliffs, N.J.: Prentice-Hall.

Angelo, Bonnie. 1989. "'The Pain of Being Black': An Interview with Toni Morrison." *Time*, May 22, 120–22.

Aptheker, Herbert. 1943. *American Negro Slave Revolts*. New York: Columbia University Press.

Arditti, Rita, and M. Brinton Lykes. 1993. "The Disappeared Children of Argentina: The Work of the Grandmothers of Plaza de Mayo." In *Surviving beyond Fear: Women, Children and Human Rights in Latin America*, ed. Marjorie Agosin, 168–75. Fredonia, N.Y.: White Pine.

Argentine National Commission on the Disappeared. 1986. *Nunca Más: The Report of the Argentine National Commission on the Disappeared*. New York: Farrar, Straus & Giroux.

Baker, Houston A. Jr. 1984. *Blues, Ideology, and Afro-American Literature: A Vernacular Theory*. Chicago: University of Chicago Press.

_____. 1991. *Workings of the Spirit: The Poetics of Afro-American Women's Writing*. Chicago: University of Chicago Press.

Baldwin, James. 1985. *The Evidence of Things Not Seen*. New York: Holt, Rinehart & Winston.

Barnes, John. 1978. *Evita, First Lady: A Biography of Eva Perón*. New York: Grove.

Barthes, Roland. 1981. *Camera Lucida: Reflections on Photography*. Trans. Richard Howard. London: Fontana.

_____. 1986. *The Rustle of Language*. Trans. Richard Howard. New York: Hill & Wang.

Bauman, Zygmunt. [1988] 1994. "Is There a Postmodern Sociology?" In *The Postmodern Turn: New Perspectives on Social Theory*, ed. Steven Seidman, 187–204. Cambridge: Cambridge University Press.

———. 1992. *Intimations of Postmodernity*. New York: Routledge.

———. 1993. *Postmodern Ethics*. Oxford: Basil Blackwell.

Bell, Daniel. 1960. *The End of Ideology: On the Exhaustion of Political Ideas in the Fifties*. Glencoe, Ill.: Free Press.

Bell, Derrick. 1992. *Faces at the Bottom of the Well: The Permanence of Racism*. New York: Basic Books.

Benjamin, Walter. 1969. "Theses on the Philosophy of History." In Walter Benjamin, *Illuminations*. Trans. Harry Zohn, ed. Hannah Arendt, 253–64. New York: Schocken.

———. 1978. "Surrealism: The Last Snapshot of the European Intelligentsia." In Walter Benjamin, *Reflections: Essays, Aphorisms, Autobiographical Writings*. Trans. Edmund Jephcott, ed. Peter Demetz, 177–92. New York: Harcourt Brace Jovanovich.

Berger, John. 1972. *Ways of Seeing*. London: British Broadcasting Corporation and Penguin Books.

Berlin, Ira. 1974. *Slaves without Masters: The Free Negro in the Antebellum South*. New York: Pantheon.

Berman, Maureen R., and Roger S. Clark. 1983. "State Terrorism: Disappearances." *Rutgers Law Journal* 13:531–77.

Beverley, John. 1993. *Against Literature*. Minneapolis: University of Minnesota Press.

Beverley, John, and José Oviedo, eds. 1993. Special issue: "The Postmodernism Debate in Latin America." Trans. Michael Aronna. *boundary 2* 20, 3.

Beverley, John, and Marc Zimmerman. 1990. *Literature and Politics in the Central American Revolutions*. Austin: University of Texas Press.

Bhabha, Homi. 1992. "The World and the Home." *Social Text* 31/32:141–53.

Blackwell, Alice Stone. 1930. *Lucy Stone: Pioneer of Women's Rights*. Boston: Little, Brown.

Blassingame, John. 1972. *The Slave Community: Plantation Life in the Antebellum South*. New York: Oxford University Press.

Blassingame, John, and Mae G. Henderson, eds. 1984. *Antislavery Newspapers and Periodicals*. Boston: Hall.

Blockson, Charles L. 1989. *The Underground Railroad*. New York: Berkley Books.

Bouvard, Marguerite Guzman. 1994. *Revolutionizing Motherhood: The Mothers of the Plaza de Mayo*. Wilmington, Del.: Scholarly Resources.

Braxton, Joanne M. 1989. *Black Women Writing Autobiography: A Tradition within a Tradition*. Philadelphia: Temple University Press.

Brenkman, John. 1987. *Culture and Domination*. Ithaca, N.Y.: Cornell University Press.

Broad, Robert L. 1994. "Giving Blood to the Scraps: Haints, History, and Hosea in *Beloved*." *African American Review* 28, 2:189–96.

Brown, Dee. 1970. *Bury My Heart at Wounded Knee*. New York: Washington Square.

Brown, Richard Harvey. 1987. *Society as Text: Essays on Rhetoric, Reason, and Reality*. Chicago: University of Chicago Press.

_____. 1989. *Social Science as Civic Discourse: Essays on the Invention, Legitimation, and Uses of Social Theory*. Chicago: University of Chicago Press.

Buck-Morss, Susan. 1977. *The Origin of Negative Dialectics: Theodor W. Adorno, Walter Benjamin, and the Frankfurt Institute*. New York: Free Press.

_____. 1989. *The Dialectics of Seeing: Walter Benjamin and the Arcades Project*. Cambridge, Mass.: MIT Press.

Butler, Judith. 1992. "Contingent Foundations: Feminism and the Question of 'Postmodernism.'" In *Feminists Theorize the Political*, ed. Judith Butler and Joan W. Scott, 3–21. New York: Routledge.

Campbell, Stanley W. 1970. *The Slave Catchers: Enforcement of the Fugitive Slave Law, 1850–1860*. Chapel Hill: University of North Carolina Press.

Carby, Hazel. 1987. *Reconstructing Womanhood: The Emergence of the Afro-American Woman Novelist*. New York: Oxford University Press.

Carlson, Marifran. 1993. "A Tragedy and a Miracle: Leonor Alonso and the Human Cost of State Terrorism in Argentina." In *Surviving beyond Fear: Women, Children and Human Rights in Latin America*, ed. Marjorie Agosin, 71–85. Fredonia, N.Y.: White Pine.

Carotenuto, Aldo. 1984. *A Secret Symmetry: Sabina Spielrein between Jung and Freud*. Trans. Arno Pomerans, John Shepley, and Krishna Winston, commentary Bruno Bettelheim. New York: Pantheon.

Castañeda, Jorge. 1993. *Utopia Unarmed: The Latin American Left after the Cold War*. New York: Vintage.

Castro-Klaren, Sara, Sylvia Molloy, and Beatriz Sarlo, eds. 1991. *Women's Writing in Latin America: An Anthology*. Boulder, Colo.: Westview.

Charcot, M, par Bourneville, et P. Regnard. 1876–80. *Iconographie photographique de la Salpêtrière*. Paris: Aux Bureaux du Progres Medical.

Chelala, César. 1993. "Women of Valor: An Interview with the Mothers of Plaza de Mayo." In *Surviving beyond Fear: Women, Children and Human Rights in Latin America*, ed. Marjorie Agosin, 58–70. Fredonia, N.Y.: White Pine.

Chomsky, Noam, and Edward Herman. 1979. *The Washington Connection and Third World Fascism: The Political Economy of Human Rights*. Boston: South End Press.

Christian, Barbara. 1993. "Fixing Methodologies: *Beloved*." *Cultural Critique* 24 (Spring):5–15.

Cixous, Hélène, and Catherine Clément. 1986. *The Newly Born Woman*. Trans. Betsy Wing. Minneapolis: University of Minnesota Press.

Clément, Catherine. 1987. *The Weary Sons of Freud*. Trans. Nicole Ball. London: Verso.

Clemons, Walter. 1987. "A Gravestone of Memories." *Newsweek*, September 28, 74–75.

Clifford, James. 1988. *The Predicament of Culture: Twentieth-Century Ethnography, Literature, and Art.* Cambridge, Mass.: Harvard University Press.

Clifford, James, and George E. Marcus, eds. 1986. *Writing Culture: The Poetics and Politics of Ethnography.* Berkeley: University of California Press.

Clough, Patricia T. 1986. "Understanding Subjugation: The Relation of Theory and Ethnography." *Studies in Symbolic Interaction* 7A:3–11.

_____. 1992. *The End(s) of Ethnography: From Realism to Social Criticism.* Newbury Park, Calif.: Sage.

Coffin, Levi. [1876] 1968. *Reminiscences of Levi Coffin: The Reputed President of the Underground Railroad.* New York: Augustus M. Kelley.

Coleman, J. Winston Jr. 1940. *Slave Times in Kentucky.* Chapel Hill: University of North Carolina Press.

Conley, Tom. 1988. "Translator's Introduction: *For a* Literary *Historiography.*" In Michel de Certeau, *The Writing of History,* trans. Tom Conley, vii-xxviii. New York: Columbia University Press.

Conneau, Theophilus. [1853] 1976. *A Slaver's Log Book; or, 20 Years' Residence in Africa.* Introduction by Mabel M. Smythe. New York: Avon.

Craig, Linda. 1991. "Women and Language: Luisa Valenzuela's *El Gato Eficaz.*" In *Feminist Readings on Spanish and Latin American Literature,* ed. Lisa Condé and Stephen Hart, 151-60. New York: Edwin Mellen.

Crenshaw, Kimberlé. 1991. "Demarginalizing the Intersection of Race and Sex: A Black Feminist Critique of Antidiscrimination Doctrine, Feminist Theory and Antiracist Politics [1989]." In *Feminist Legal Theory: Readings in Law and Gender,* ed. Katharine Bartlett and Rosanne Kennedy, 57–80. Boulder, Colo.: Westview.

Crouch, Stanley. 1987. "Aunt Medea." *New Republic,* October 19, 38–43.

Cruz, Jon. Forthcoming. *Culture on the Margins.* Princeton, N.J.: Princeton University Press.

Dabat, Alejandro, and Luis Lorenzano. 1984. *Argentina: The Malvinas and the End of Military Rule.* Trans. Ralph Johnstone. London: Verso.

Dabney, Wendell P. [1926] 1970. *Cincinnati's Colored Citizens, Historical, Sociological and Biographical.* New York: Negro Universities Press.

Darling, Marsha Jean. 1988. "In the Realm of Responsibility: A Conversation with Toni Morrison." *Women's Review of Books* 5, 6:5–6.

Davis, Angela Y. 1983. *Women, Race & Class.* New York: Vintage.

Davis, Charles T., and Henry Louis Gates Jr., eds. 1985. *The Slave's Narrative.* New York: Oxford University Press.

Davis, Thulani. 1978. *All the Renegade Ghosts Rise.* Washington, D.C.: Anemone.

de Certeau, Michel. 1983. "History: Ethics, Science, and Fiction." In *Social Science as Moral Inquiry,* ed. Norma Haan et al., 125-52. New York: Columbia University Press.

_____. 1988. *The Writing of History.* Trans. Tom Conley. New York: Columbia University Press.

Deleuze, Gilles, and Félix Guattari. 1983. *Anti-Oedipus: Capitalism and Schizo-*

phrenia. Trans. Robert Hurley, Mark Seem, and Helen R. Lane. Minneapolis: University of Minnesota Press.

DeLillo, Don. 1985. *White Noise*. New York: Viking.

Dent, Gina. "Developing Africa into America: The Role of Anthropology in the Literary History of Blackness." Forthcoming Ph.D. dissertation, Columbia University.

Denzin, Norman. 1986. "Postmodern Social Theory." *Sociological Theory* 4 (Fall):194–204.

_____. 1991. *Images of Postmodern Society: Social Theory and Contemporary Cinema*. Newbury Park, Calif.: Sage.

Derrida, Jacques. 1991. "Geopsychoanalysis: '. . . and the rest of the world.'" *American Imago* 48, 2:199–231.

_____. 1994. *Specters of Marx: The State of the Debt, the Work of Mourning, and the New International*. Trans. Peggy Kamuf. New York: Routledge.

Donnan, Elizabeth, ed. [1931, 1932] 1965. *Documents Illustrative of the History of the Slave Trade to America*. Vols. 2 and 3. New York: Octagon.

Du Bois, W. E. B. [1903] 1989. *The Souls of Black Folk*. New York: Bantam.

_____. [1935] 1992. *Black Reconstruction in America*. New York: Atheneum.

_____. [1940] 1984. *Dusk of Dawn: An Essay toward an Autobiography of a Race Concept*. New Brunswick, N.J.: Transaction.

Eagleton, Terry. 1981. *Walter Benjamin; or, Towards a Revolutionary Criticism*. London: Verso.

_____. 1991. *Ideology: An Introduction*. New York: Verso.

Ehrenreich, Barbara. 1989. *Fear of Falling: The Inner Life of the Middle Class*. New York: HarperCollins.

Ellison, Ralph. [1952] 1981. *Invisible Man*. New York: Vintage.

_____. 1964. *Shadow and Act*. New York: Random House.

Elshtain, Jean Bethke. 1992. "The Passion of the Mothers of the Disappeared in Argentina." *New Oxford Review* 59, 1:4–10.

Fanon, Frantz. 1967. *Black Skin White Masks*. Trans. Charles Lam Markmann. New York: Grove.

_____. 1968. *The Wretched of the Earth*. Trans. Constance Farrington. New York: Grove.

Felman, Shoshana, and Dori Laub, M.D. 1992. *Testimony: Crises of Witnessing in Literature, Psychoanalysis, and History*. New York: Routledge.

Fields, Karen. 1989. "To Embrace Dead Strangers: Toni Morrison's *Beloved*." In *Mother Puzzles: Daughters and Mothers in Contemporary American Literature*, ed. Mickey Pearlman, 159–69. Westport, Conn.: Greenwood.

Fisher, Jo. 1989. *Mothers of the Disappeared*. Boston: South End Press.

Flax, Jane. 1992. "The End of Innocence." In *Feminists Theorize the Political*, ed. Judith Butler and Joan W. Scott, 445–63. New York: Routledge.

Foner, Eric. 1988. *Reconstruction: America's Unfinished Revolution 1863–1877*. New York: Harper & Row.

Foster, Frances Smith. 1994. *Witnessing Slavery: The Development of Antebellum Slave Narratives*. 2d ed. Madison: University of Wisconsin Press.

Foucault, Michel. 1973. *The Order of Things: An Archaeology of the Human Sciences.* Trans. Alan Sheridan. New York: Vintage.

Franco, Jean. 1986. "Death Camp Confessions and Resistance to Violence in Latin America." *Socialism and Democracy* 2 (Spring/Summer):5–17.

———. 1988. "Beyond Ethnocentrism: Gender, Power, and the Third-World Intelligentsia." In *Marxism and the Interpretation of Culture,* ed. Cary Nelson and Lawrence Grossberg, 503–15. Urbana: University of Illinois Press.

———. 1989. *Plotting Women: Gender and Representation in Mexico.* New York: Columbia University Press.

Frankfurt Institute for Social Research. [1956] 1973. *Aspects of Sociology.* Trans. John Viertel. Boston: Beacon.

Fredrickson, George M. [1971] 1987. *The Black Image in the White Mind: The Debate on Afro-American Character and Destiny, 1817–1914.* Middletown, Conn.: Wesleyan University Press.

———. 1988. *The Arrogance of Race: Historical Perspectives on Slavery, Racism, and Social Inequality.* Middletown, Conn.: Wesleyan University Press.

Freud, Sigmund. [1899] 1953–74. "Screen Memories." Trans. James Stratchey. *The Standard Edition of the Complete Works of Sigmund Freud (SE),* vol. 3. London: Hogarth Press and the Institute of Psycho-Analysis.

———. 1913. *Totem and Taboo.* In *SE,* vol. 13.

———. 1914. "Observations on Transference Love (Further Recommendations on the Technique of Psycho-Analysis III)." In *Papers on Technique, SE,* vol. 12.

———. 1915. "The Unconscious." In *SE,* vol. 14.

———. 1919. "The Uncanny." In *SE,* vol. 17.

———. 1920. *Beyond the Pleasure Principle.* In *SE,* vol. 18.

———. 1921. *Group Psychology and the Analysis of the Ego.* In *SE,* vol. 18.

———. 1922. "Dreams and Telepathy." In *SE,* vol. 18.

———. 1927. *The Future of an Illusion.* In *SE,* vol. 21.

———. 1930. *Civilization and Its Discontents.* In *SE,* vol. 21.

———. 1937–39. *Moses and Monotheism.* In *SE,* vol. 23.

Fromm, Erich. 1962. *Beyond the Chains of Illusion: My Encounter with Marx and Freud.* New York: Pocket Books.

Fukuyama, Francis. 1992. *The End of History and the Last Man.* New York: Free Press.

Galeano, Eduardo. 1978. *Open Veins of Latin America: Five Centuries of the Pillage of a Continent.* Trans. Cedric Belfrage. New York: Monthly Review Press.

———. 1985. *Memory of Fire: I. Genesis.* Trans. Cedric Belfrage. New York: Pantheon.

———. 1987. *Memory of Fire: II. Faces and Masks.* Trans. Cedric Belfrage. New York: Pantheon.

———. 1988. *Memory of Fire: III. Century of the Wind.* Trans. Cedric Belfrage. New York: Pantheon.

Gara, Larry. 1967. *The Liberty Line: The Legend of the Underground Rail-road*. Lexington: University of Kentucky Press.

Garcia-Moreno, Laura. 1991. "Other Weapons, Other Words: Literary and Political Reconsiderations in Luisa Valenzuela's *Other Weapons*." *Latin American Literary Review* 19, 38:7–22.

García Pinto, Magdalena. 1991. *Women Writers of Latin America: Intimate Histories*. Austin: University of Texas Press.

Garfield, Evelyn Picon, ed. 1988. *Women's Fiction from Latin America: Selections from Twelve Contemporary Authors*. Detroit: Wayne State University Press.

Gates, Henry Louis Jr. 1987. *Figures in Black: Words, Signs, and the 'Racial' Self*. New York: Oxford University Press.

_____. 1988a. *The Signifying Monkey: A Theory of Afro-American Literary Criticism*. New York: Oxford University Press.

_____. 1988b. "James Gronniosaw and the Trope of the Talking Book." In *Studies in Autobiography*, ed. James Olney, 51–72. New York: Oxford University Press.

Gates, Henry Louis Jr., and Kwame Anthony Appiah, eds. 1993. *Toni Morrison: Critical Perspectives Past and Present*. New York: Amistad.

Genovese, Eugene. 1976. *Roll, Jordan, Roll: The World the Slaves Made*. New York: Vintage.

_____. 1979. *From Rebellion to Revolution: Afro-American Slave Revolts in the Making of the Modern World*. Baton Rouge: Louisiana State University Press.

Gilroy, Paul. 1993. *The Black Atlantic: Modernity and Double Consciousness*. Cambridge, Mass.: Harvard University Press.

Glantz, Margo. 1986. "Luisa Valenzuela's *He Who Searches*." *Review of Contemporary Fiction* 6, 3:62–66.

Goodell, William. [1853] 1968. *The American Slave Code in Theory and Practice: Its Distinctive Features Shown by Its Statutes, Judicial Decisions, and Illustrative Facts*. New York: American and Foreign Anti-Slavery Society, reprinted by Johnson Reprint Corp.

Gordon, Avery. 1992. "Marketing Differences: Feminism as Cultural Capital." *Mediations* 16, 2:37–41.

_____. 1993. "Twenty-Two Theses on Social Constructionism: A Feminist Response to Ibarra and Kitsuse's 'Proposal for the Study of Social Problems.'" In *Reconsidering Social Constructionism: Debates in Social Problems Theory*, ed. James A. Holstein and Gale Miller, 301–26. New York: Aldine de Gruyter.

Guest, Iain. 1990. *Behind the Disappearances: Argentina's Dirty War against Human Rights and the United Nations*. Philadelphia: University of Pennsylvania Press.

Gutman, Herbert. 1976. *The Black Family in Slavery and Freedom, 1750–1925*. New York: Pantheon.

Haraway, Donna. 1985. "Manifesto for Cyborgs: Science, Technology, and Socialist Feminism in the 1980's." *Socialist Review* 80:65–108.

_____. 1989. *Primate Visions: Gender, Race, and Nature in the World of Modern Science.* New York: Routledge.

Harlow, Barbara. 1987. *Resistance Literature.* New York: Methuen.

Harris, Trudier. 1991. *Fiction and Folklore: The Novels of Toni Morrison.* Knoxville: University of Tennessee Press.

_____. 1993. "Escaping Slavery but Not Its Images." In *Toni Morrison: Critical Perspectives Past and Present,* ed. Henry Louis Gates Jr. and Kwame Anthony Appiah, 330–41. New York: Amistad.

Hart, Stephen. 1993. *White Ink: Essays on Twentieth Century Feminine Fiction in Spain and Latin America.* London: Tamesis.

Harvey, David. 1989. *The Condition of Postmodernity: An Enquiry into the Origins of Cultural Exchange.* New York: Blackwell.

Haug, Frigga, et al. 1987. *Female Sexualization: A Collective Work of Memory.* Trans. Erica Carter. London: Verso.

Hawthorne, Nathaniel. [1850] 1978. *The Scarlet Letter,* 2d ed. Ed. Sculley Bradley et al. New York: Norton.

Henderson, Mae. 1991. "Toni Morrison's *Beloved:* Re-Membering the Body as Historical Text." In *Comparative American Identities: Race, Sex, and Nationality in the Modern Text,* ed. Hortense J. Spillers, 62–86. New York: Routledge.

Hennessy, Rosemary. 1993. *Materialist Feminism and the Politics of Discourse.* New York: Routledge.

Hertz, Neil. 1985. *The End of the Line: Essays on Psychoanalysis and the Sublime.* New York: Columbia University Press.

Hicks, D. Emily. 1991. *Border Writing: The Multidimensional Text.* Minneapolis: University of Minnesota Press.

Hirsch, Marianne. 1994. "Maternity and Rememory: Toni Morrison's *Beloved.*" In *Representations of Motherhood,* ed. Donna Bassin, Margaret Honey, and Meryle Mahrer Kaplan, 92-110. New Haven, Conn.: Yale University Press.

Hodges, Donald C. 1991. *Argentina's "Dirty War": An Intellectual Biography.* Austin: University of Texas Press.

Hoeppner, Edward Haworth. 1992. "The Hand that Mirrors Us: Luisa Valenzuela's Re-Writing of Lacan's Theory of Identity." *Latin American Literary Review* 20, 39:9-17.

Hollander, Nancy Caro. 1990. "Buenos Aires: Latin Mecca of Psychoanalysis." *Social Research* 57, 4:889–919.

Holloway, Karla. 1990. "*Beloved:* A Spiritual." *Callaloo* 13, 3:516–25.

Honour, Hugh. 1989. *The Image of the Black in Western Art,* Vol. 4, Part 1: *Slaves and Liberators.* Cambridge, Mass.: Harvard University Press.

Horkheimer, Max, and Theodor Adorno. [1944] 1987. *Dialectic of Enlightenment.* Trans. John Cumming. New York: Continuum.

Horvitz, Deborah. 1989. "Nameless Ghosts: Possession and Dispossession in *Beloved.*" *Studies in American Fiction* 17, 2:157–67.

House, Elizabeth. 1990. "Toni Morrison's Ghost: The Beloved Who Is Not Beloved." *Studies in American Fiction* 18, 1:17-26.

Ibarra, Peter, and John Kitsuse. 1993. "Vernacular Constituents of Moral Discourse: An Interactionist Proposal for the Study of Social Problems." In *Reconsidering Social Constructionism: Debates in Social Problems Theory*, ed. James A. Holstein and Gale Miller, 25–58. New York: Aldine de Gruyter.

Irigaray, Luce. 1985. *This Sex Which Is Not One*. Trans. Catherine Porter with Carolyn Burke. Ithaca, N.Y.: Cornell University Press.

Jacobs, Harriet A. [1861] 1987. *Incidents in the Life of a Slave Girl. Written by Herself*. Ed. Jean Fagan Yellin. Cambridge, Mass.: Harvard University Press.

Jacoby, Russell. 1975. *Social Amnesia: A Critique of Conformist Psychology from Adler to Laing*. Boston: Beacon.

_____. 1983. *The Repression of Psychoanalysis: Otto Fenichel and the Political Freudians*. New York: Basic Books.

Jameson, Fredric. 1991. *Postmodernism: or, The Cultural Logic of Late Capitalism*. Durham, N.C.: Duke University Press.

_____. 1995. "Marx's Purloined Letter." *New Left Review* 209 (January/February):75–109.

Jara, René, and Hernán Vidal, eds. 1986. *Testimonio y literatura*. Minneapolis: Institute for the Study of Ideologies and Literature.

Jardine, Alice. 1985. *Gynesis: Configurations of Woman and Modernity*. Ithaca, N.Y.: Cornell University Press.

Jung, Carl. 1954. "Psychology of the Transference." Trans. R. F. C. Hull. In *The Practice of Psychotherapy: Essays on the Psychology of the Transference and Other Subjects. Collected Works*, vol. 16. New York: Pantheon.

_____. 1965. *Memories, Dreams, Reflections*. Recorded and edited by Aniela Jaffe, trans. Richard and Clara Winston. New York: Vintage.

Katz, Jane. 1983. *Artists in Exile*. New York: Stein and Day.

Keenan, Sally. 1993. "'Four Hundred Years of Silence': Myth, History, and Motherhood in Toni Morrison's *Beloved*." In *Recasting the World: Writing after Colonialism*, ed. Jonathan White, 45–81. Baltimore: Johns Hopkins University Press.

Keenan, Thomas. 1993. "The Point Is to (Ex)Change It: Reading *Capital*, Rhetorically." In *Fetishism as Cultural Discourse*, ed. Emily Apter and William Pietz, 152–85. Ithaca, N.Y.: Cornell University Press.

Kerr, John. 1993. *A Most Dangerous Method: The Story of Jung, Freud, and Sabina Spielrein*. New York: Knopf.

Kingston, Maxine Hong. 1977. *The Woman Warrior: Memoirs of a Girlhood Among Ghosts*. New York: Vintage.

Kipnis, Laura. 1988. "Feminism: The Political Conscience of Postmodernism?" In *Universal Abandon? The Politics of Postmodernism*, ed. Andrew Ross, 149–66. Minneapolis: University of Minnesota Press.

Knepper, George W. 1989. *Ohio and Its People*. Kent, Ohio: Kent State University Press.

Kordon, Diana, et al. 1988. *Psychological Effects of Political Repression*. Trans. Dominique Kliagine. Buenos Aires: Sudamericana/Planeta.

Krumholz, Linda. 1992. "The Ghosts of Slavery: Historical Recovery in Toni Morrison's *Beloved*." *African American Review* 26, 3:395–408.

Laclau, Ernesto, and Chantal Mouffe. 1985. *Hegemony and Socialist Strategy: Towards a Radical Democratic Politics.* Trans. Winston Moore and Paul Cammack. London: Verso.

LaFleur, William R. 1989. "Hungry Ghosts and Hungry People: Somaticity and Rationality in Medieval Japan." In *Fragments for a History of the Human Body, Part One,* ed. Michel Feher with Ramona Naddaff and Nadia Tazi, 270–303. New York: Urzone.

Laplanche, J., and J.-B. Pontalis. 1973. *The Language of Psycho-Analysis.* Trans. Donald Nicholson-Smith. New York: Norton.

Lash, Scott. 1990. *Sociology of Postmodernism.* New York: Routledge.

Lawrence, David. 1991. "Fleshly Ghosts and Ghostly Flesh: The Word and the Body in *Beloved.*" *Studies in American Fiction* 19, 2:189–201.

Lemert, Charles. 1990. "The Uses of French Structuralisms in Sociology." In *Frontiers of Social Theory: The New Synthesis,* ed. George Ritzer, 230–54. New York: Columbia University Press.

———. 1994. "A Classic from the Other Side of the Veil: Du Bois's *Souls of Black Folk.*" *Sociological Quarterly* 35, 3:383–96.

———. 1995. *Sociology after the Crisis.* Boulder, Colo.: Westview.

Lemert, Charles, ed. 1993. *Social Theory: The Multicultural and Classic Readings.* Boulder, Colo.: Westview.

Lepenies, Wolf. 1988. *Between Literature and Science: The Rise of Sociology.* Trans. R. J. Hollingdale. Cambridge: Cambridge University Press.

Levine, Lawrence. 1977. *Black Culture and Black Consciousness: Afro-American Folk Thought from Slavery to Freedom.* New York: Oxford University Press.

Lévi-Strauss, Claude. 1963. *Structural Anthropology.* Trans. Claire Jacobson and Brooke Grundfest Schoepf. New York: Basic Books.

———. 1966. *The Savage Mind.* Chicago: University of Chicago Press.

Lichtman, Richard. 1982. *The Production of Desire: The Integration of Psycho-analysis into Marxist Theory.* New York: Free Press.

Lipsitz, George. 1994. *Dangerous Crossroads: Popular Music, Postmodernism and the Poetics of Place.* New York: Verso.

Litwack, Leon. 1979. *Been in the Storm So Long: The Aftermath of Slavery.* New York: Vintage.

Lubiano, Wahneema. 1989. "Taking Seriously the Writing and the Tears: *The Color Purple* and Genre Appropriations." Paper presented at the Institute on Culture and Society, Carnegie-Mellon University, June 15–22.

———. 1991. "Shuckin' Off the African-American Native Other: What's 'Po-Mo' Got to Do with It?" *Cultural Critique* 18 (Spring):149–86.

———. 1992. "Black Ladies, Welfare Queens, and State Minstrels: Ideological War by Narrative Means." In *Race-ing Justice, En-Gendering Power: Essays on Anita Hill, Clarence Thomas, and the Construction of Social Reality,* ed. Toni Morrison, 323–63. New York: Pantheon.

———. 1993. "Standing in for the State: Black Nationalism and 'Writing' the Black Subject." *Alphabet City* 3:20–23.

Lukács, Georg. [1918–1930] 1971. *History and Class Consciousness.* Trans. Rodney Livingstone. Cambridge, Mass.: MIT Press.

Maci, Guillermo. 1986. "The Symbolic, the Imaginary and the Real in Luisa Valenzuela's *He Who Searches.*" *Review of Contemporary Fiction* 6, 3:67–77.

Magnarelli, Sharon. 1988. *Reflections/Refractions: Reading Luisa Valenzuela.* New York: Peter Lang.

Marcus, George. 1994. "The Official Story: Response to Julie Taylor." In *Body Politics: Disease, Desire, and the Family,* ed. Michael Ryan and Avery Gordon, 204–8. Boulder, Colo.: Westview.

Marcus, George, and Michael M. J. Fischer. 1986. *Anthropology as Cultural Critique: An Experimental Moment in the Human Sciences.* Chicago: University of Chicago Press.

Marcuse, Herbert. 1955. *Eros and Civilization: A Philosophical Inquiry into Freud.* New York: Beacon.

_____. 1969. *An Essay on Liberation.* New York: Beacon.

Martinez, Zulma Nelly. 1986. "Luisa Valenzuela's 'Where the Eagles Dwell': From Fragmentation to Holism." *Review of Contemporary Fiction* 6, 3:109–15.

Marx, Karl. [1844] 1975. "Economic and Philosophical Manuscripts (1944)." In Karl Marx, *Early Writings,* trans. Rodney Livingstone and Gregor Benton, 279–400. New York: Vintage.

_____. [1867–73] 1976. *Capital: A Critique of Political Economy.* Vol. 1. Trans. Ben Fowkes. New York: Vintage.

_____. [1888] 1970. "Theses on Feuerbach." In Karl Marx and Frederick Engels, *The German Ideology, Part One,* ed. C. J. Arthur, 121–23. New York: International Publishers.

Marx, Karl, and Frederick Engels. [1888] 1973. "Manifesto of the Communist Party." In *The Revolutions of 1848. Political Writings,* vol. 1, ed. David Fernbach, 62–98. London: Penguin Books with New Left Review.

May, Samuel. [1856] 1861. *The Fugitive Slave Law and Its Victims.* New York: American Anti-Slavery Society.

McDowell, Deborah E., and Arnold Rampersad, eds. 1989. *Slavery and the Literary Imagination.* Baltimore: Johns Hopkins University Press.

McElroy, Guy C. 1990. *Facing History: The Black Image in American Art 1710–1940.* San Francisco: Bedford Arts in association with the Corcoran Gallery of Art.

McGuire, William, ed. 1988. *The Freud/Jung Letters: The Correspondence between Sigmund Freud and C. G. Jung.* Trans. Ralph Manheim and R. F. C. Hull. Cambridge, Mass.: Harvard University Press.

Mills, C. Wright. 1951. *White Collar.* New York: Oxford University Press.

_____. 1959. *The Sociological Imagination.* New York: Oxford University Press.

_____. [1959] 1963. "Culture and Politics." In *Power, Politics and People: The Collected Essays of C. Wright Mills,* ed. Irving Louis Horowitz, 236–46. New York: Oxford University Press.

_____. [1960] 1963. "The New Left." In *Power, Politics and People: The Collected Essays of C. Wright Mills,* ed. Irving Louis Horowitz, 247–59. New York: Oxford University Press.

Minh-ha, Trinh T. 1989. *Woman, Native, Other: Writing, Postcoloniality and Feminism.* Bloomington: Indiana University Press.

_____. 1991. *When the Moon Waxes Red: Representation, Gender, and Cultural Politics.* New York: Routledge.

Mitchell, Juliet. 1974. *Psychoanalysis and Feminism.* London: Penguin.

Mitchell, Juliet, and Jacqueline Rose, eds. 1982. *Feminine Sexuality: Jacques Lacan and the École Freudienne.* London: Macmillan.

Mobley, Marilyn Sanders. 1993. "A Different Remembering: Memory, History, and Meaning in *Beloved.*" In *Toni Morrison: Critical Perspectives Past and Present,* ed. Henry Louis Gates Jr. and Kwame Anthony Appiah, 356–65. New York: Amistad.

Moglen, Helene. 1993. "Redeeming History: Toni Morrison's *Beloved.*" *Cultural Critique* 24 (Spring):17–40.

Mohanty, Satya P. 1993. "The Epistemic Status of Cultural Identity: On *Beloved* and the Postcolonial Condition." *Cultural Critique* 24 (Spring):41–80.

Molotch, Harvey. 1994. "Going Out." *Sociological Forum* 9, 2:221–39.

Morrison, Toni. 1970. *The Bluest Eye.* New York: Washington Square.

_____. 1973. *Sula.* New York: Knopf.

_____. 1977. *Song of Solomon.* New York: Knopf.

_____. 1981. *Tar Baby.* New York: Knopf.

_____. 1987a. *Beloved.* New York: Knopf.

_____. 1987b. "'Five Years of Terror.' A Conversation with Miriam Horn." *U.S. News & World Report,* October 19, 75.

_____. 1989. "Unspeakable Things Unspoken: The Afro-American Presence in American Literature." *Michigan Quarterly Review* 28, 1:1–34.

_____. 1992a. *Jazz.* New York: Knopf.

_____. 1992b. *Playing in the Dark: Whiteness and the Literary Imagination.* Cambridge, Mass.: Harvard University Press.

Morrison, Toni, ed. 1992c. *Race-ing Justice, En-gendering Power: Essays on Anita Hill, Clarence Thomas, and the Construction of Social Reality.* New York: Pantheon.

Mouffe, Chantal. 1992. "Feminism, Citizenship, and Radical Democratic Politics." In *Feminists Theorize the Political,* ed. Judith Butler and Joan W. Scott, 369–84. New York: Routledge.

Mullen, Harryette. 1992. "Runaway Tongue: Resistant Orality in *Uncle Tom's Cabin, Our Nig, Incidents in the Life of a Slave Girl,* and *Beloved.*" In *The Culture of Sentiment: Race, Gender, and Sentimentality in Nineteenth-Century America,* ed. Shirley Samuels, 244-64. New York: Oxford University Press.

Nelson, Cary. 1987. "Men, Feminism: The Materiality of Discourse." In *Men in Feminism,* ed. Alice Jardine and Paul Smith, 153–72. New York: Methuen.

Newfield, Christopher. 1996. *The Emerson Effect: Individualism and Submission in America.* Chicago: University of Chicago Press.

Nicholson, Linda J., ed. 1990. *Feminism/Postmodernism.* New York: Routledge.

Orphée, Elvira. 1985. *El Angel's Last Conquest.* Trans. Magda Bogin. New York: Ballantine.

Ortiz, Alicia Dujovne. 1986–87. "*Buenos Aires* (an excerpt)." Trans. Caren Kaplan. *Discourse* 8 (Fall/Winter):73-83.

Owens, Leslie Howard. 1976. *This Species of Property: Slave Life and Culture in the Old South.* New York: Oxford University.

Partnoy, Alicia. 1986. *The Little School: Tales of Disappearance and Survival in Argentina.* Trans. Alicia Partnoy with Lois Athey and Sandra Braunstein. Pittsburgh: Cleis.

Patterson, Orlando. 1982. *Slavery and Social Death.* Cambridge, Mass.: Harvard University Press.

Payer, Cheryl. 1974. *The Debt Trap: The IMF and the Third World.* New York: Monthly Review Press.

———. 1982. *The World Bank: A Critical Analysis.* New York: Monthly Review Press.

Peri Rossi, Cristina. 1989. *The Ship of Fools.* Trans. Psiche Hughes. New York: Readers International.

Pfohl, Stephen. 1991. "Postmodernity as a Social Problem: Race, Class, Gender and the 'New World Order.'" *Society for the Study of Social Problems Newsletter* 22, 3:9-14.

———. 1992a. *Death at the Parasite Cafe: Social Science (Fictions) and the Postmodern.* New York: St. Martin's.

———. 1992b. "Postmodern Pittsburgh: New World Disordered Conventions?" *Society for the Study of Social Problems Newsletter* 23, 2:4-8.

Pietz, William. 1993. "Fetishism and Materialism: The Limits of Theory in Marx." In *Fetishism as Cultural Discourse,* ed. Emily Apter and William Pietz, 119-51. Ithaca, N.Y.: Cornell University Press.

Pion-Berlin, David. 1989. *The Ideology of State Terror: Economic Doctrine and Political Repression in Argentina and Peru.* Boulder, Colo.: Lynne Rienner.

Pratt, Mary Louise. 1992. *Imperial Eyes: Travel Writing and Transculturation.* New York: Routledge.

Pratt, Minnie Bruce. 1984. "Identity: Skin Blood Heart." In *Yours in Struggle: Three Feminist Perspectives on Anti-Semitism and Racism,* ed. Elly Bulkin, Minnie Bruce Pratt, and Barbara Smith, 11-63. New York: Long Haul Press.

Rawick, George. 1972. *From Sundown to Sunup: The Making of the Black Community.* Westport, Conn: Greenwood.

Reed, Ishmael. 1976. *Flight to Canada.* New York: Random House.

Reich, Wilhelm. 1970. *The Mass Psychology of Fascism.* Ed. Mary Higgins and Chester M. Raphael, M.D. New York: Farrar, Straus & Giroux.

———. 1972. *Sex-Pol: Essays 1929–1934.* Trans. Anna Bostock, Tom DuBose, and Lee Baxandall. Ed. Lee Baxandall. New York: Vintage.

Rhodes, Jewell Parker. 1990. "Toni Morrison's *Beloved:* Ironies of a 'Sweet Home' Utopia in a Dystopian Slave Society." *Utopian Studies* 1, 1:77-92.

Rickles, Laurence A. 1988. *Aberrations of Mourning: Writing on German Crypts.* Detroit: Wayne State University Press.

_____. 1991. *The Case of California*. Baltimore: Johns Hopkins University Press.

Rigney, Barbara Hill. 1991. "'A Story to Pass On': Ghosts and the Significance of History in Toni Morrison's *Beloved*." In *Haunting the House of Fiction: Feminist Perspectives on Ghost Stories by American Women*, ed. Lynette Carpenter and Wendy Kolmar, 229–35. Knoxville: University of Tennessee Press.

Robin, Régine. 1980. "Toward Fiction as Oblique Discourse." *Yale French Studies* 59:230–42.

Robinson, Cedric J. 1983. *Black Marxism: The Making of the Black Radical Tradition*. London: Zed Books.

Rock, David. 1985. *Argentina: 1516–1982*. Berkeley: University of California Press.

Rose, Jacqueline. 1983. "Femininity and Its Discontents." *Feminist Review* 14:5–21.

_____. 1986. *Sexuality in the Field of Vision*. London: Verso.

Ross, Andrew. 1988. Introduction to *Universal Abandon? The Politics of Post-modernism*, ed. Andrew Ross, vii–xviii. Minneapolis: University of Minnesota Press.

Ross, Dorothy. 1991. *The Origins of American Social Science*. Cambridge: Cambridge University Press.

Rubin, Gayle. 1975. "The Traffic in Women: Notes on the 'Political Economy' of Sex." In *Toward an Anthropology of Women*, ed. Rayna Reiter, 157–210. New York: Monthly Review Press.

Rubio, Patricia. 1989. "Fragmentation in Luisa Valenzuela's Narrative." *Salmagundi* 82–83:287–96.

Rustin, Michael. 1991. *The Good Society and the Inner World: Psychoanalysis, Politics and Culture*. New York: Verso.

Sánchez-Eppler, Karen. 1993. *Touching Liberty: Abolition, Feminism, and the Politics of the Body*. Berkeley and Los Angeles: University of California Press.

Scarry, Elaine. 1985. *The Body in Pain: The Making and Unmaking of the World*. New York: Oxford University Press.

Schatzman, Leonard, and Anselm L. Strauss. 1973. *Field Research: Strategies for a Natural Sociology*. Englewood Cliffs, N.J.: Prentice-Hall.

Schirmer, Jennifer. 1988. "'Those Who Die for Life Cannot Be Called Dead': Women and Human Rights Protest in Latin America." *Harvard Human Rights Yearbook* 1: 41–76. Cambridge, Mass.: Harvard Law School.

Schor, Naomi. 1987. *Reading in Detail: Aesthetics and the Feminine*. New York: Methuen.

Schwarz, Roberto. 1992. *Misplaced Ideas: Essays on Brazilian Culture*. Ed. John Gledson. New York: Verso.

Scott, James C. 1990. *Domination and the Arts of Resistance: Hidden Transcripts*. New Haven, Conn.: Yale University Press.

Scott, Joan W. 1992. "'Experience.'" In *Feminists Theorize the Political*, ed. Judith Butler and Joan W. Scott, 22–40. New York: Routledge.

Seidman, Steve. 1991. "Postmodern Anxiety: The Politics of Epistemology."
    Sociological Theory 9, 2:180–90.
_____. 1994a. *Contested Knowledge: Social Theory in the Postmodern Era.*
    Cambridge: Blackwell.
_____. 1994b. "The End of Sociological Theory." In *The Postmodern Turn:
    New Perspectives on Social Theory,* ed. Steve Seidman, 119–39. Cambridge:
    Cambridge University Press.
Sekora, John. 1988. "Is the Slave Narrative a Species of Autobiography?" In
    Studies in Autobiography, ed. James Olney, 99–111. New York: Oxford
    University Press.
Sekora, John, and Darwin T. Turner, eds. 1982. *The Art of Slave Narrative:
    Original Essays in Criticism and Theory.* Macomb: Western Illinois
    University.
Sheridan, Alan. 1980. *Michel Foucault: The Will to Truth.* New York: Tavistock.
Showalter, Elaine. 1985. *The Female Malady: Women, Madness and English
    Culture 1830–1980.* New York: Pantheon.
Shumway, Nicolas. 1991. *The Invention of Argentina.* Berkeley: University of
    California Press.
Silko, Leslie Marmon. 1977. *Ceremony.* New York: Viking Penguin.
_____. 1991. *Almanac of the Dead: A Novel.* New York: Simon & Schuster.
Simpson, John, and Jana Bennett. 1985. *The Disappeared and the Mothers of
    the Plaza.* New York: St. Martin's.
Slotkin, Richard. 1973. *Regeneration through Violence: The Mythology of the
    American Frontier, 1600–1860.* Middletown, Conn.: Wesleyan University
    Press.
_____. 1985. *The Fatal Environment: The Myth of the Frontier in the Age of
    Industrialization, 1800–1890.* New York: Atheneum.
Smith, Dorothy E. 1987. *The Everyday World as Problematic: A Feminist
    Sociology.* Boston: Northeastern University Press.
Smith, Mark C. 1994. *Social Science in the Crucible: The American Debate
    over Objectivity and Purpose, 1918–1941.* Durham, N.C.: Duke University
    Press.
Smith, Valerie. 1987. *Self-Discovery and Authority in Afro-American Narra-
    tive.* Cambridge, Mass.: Harvard University Press.
_____. 1990. "'Loopholes of Retreat': Architecture and Ideology in Harriet
    Jacob's *Incidents in the Life of a Slave Girl.*" In *Reading Black, Reading
    Feminist: A Critical Anthology,* ed. Henry Louis Gates Jr., 212–26. New
    York: Meridian.
_____. 1993. "'Circling the Subject': History and Narrative in *Beloved.*" In
    Toni Morrison: Critical Perspectives Past and Present, ed. Henry Louis
    Gates Jr. and Kwame Anthony Appiah, 342–55. New York: Amistad.
Sollers, Philippe. 1994. "Nouvelle nuit, nouveau brouillard." In *Les Dispari-
    tions,* ed. Amnesty International, 9–16. Paris: Amnesty International.
Sommer, Doris. 1991. *Foundational Fictions: The National Romances of Latin
    America.* Berkeley: University of California Press.
Sontag, Susan. 1977. *On Photography.* New York: Dell.

Spillers, Hortense J. 1987a. "Mama's Baby, Papa's Maybe: An American Grammar Book." *Diacritics* 17, 2:65–81.

_____. 1987b. "Notes on an Alternative Model: Neither/Nor." In *The Year Left 2: An American Socialist Yearbook,* ed. Mike Davis et al., 176–94. London: Verso.

_____. 1989. "Changing the Letter: The Yokes, the Jokes of Discourse, or, Mrs. Stowe, Mr. Reed." In *Slavery and the Literary Imagination,* ed. Deborah E. McDowell and Arnold Rampersad, 25–61. Baltimore: Johns Hopkins University Press.

Spivak, Gayatri Chakravorty. 1985. "The Rani of Sirmur: An Essay in Reading the Archives." *History and Theory* 24, 3:247–72.

_____. 1987. *In Other Worlds: Essays in Cultural Politics.* New York: Methuen.

_____. 1989a. "The Political Economy of Women as Seen by a Literary Critic." In *Coming to Terms: Feminism, Theory, Politics,* ed. Elizabeth Weed, 218–29. New York: Routledge.

_____. 1989b. "Who Claims Alterity?" In *Remaking History,* ed. Barbara Kruger and Phil Mariani, 269–92. Seattle: Bay Press.

_____. 1992. "Acting Bits/Identity Talk." *Critical Inquiry* 18, 4:770–803.

_____. 1993. *Outside in the Teaching Machine.* New York: Routledge.

Starling, Marion Wilson. 1988. *The Slave Narrative: Its Place in American History.* 2d ed. Washington, D.C.: Howard University Press.

Sterling, Dorothy, ed. 1984. *We Are Your Sisters: Black Women in the Nineteenth Century.* New York: Norton.

Stuckey, Sterling. 1987. *Slave Culture: Nationalist Theory and the Foundations of Black America.* New York: Oxford University Press.

Taussig, Michael. 1987. *Shamanism, Colonialism, and the Wild Man: A Study in Terror and Healing.* Chicago: University of Chicago Press.

_____. 1992. *The Nervous System.* New York: Routledge.

_____. 1993a. *Mimesis and Alterity: A Particular History of the Senses.* New York: Routledge.

_____. 1993b. "Schopenhauer's Beard; or, The Public Secret." Paper presented at the University of California, Santa Barbara.

Taylor, Diana. 1990. "Theater and Terrorism: Griselda Gambaro's *Information for Foreigners.*" *Theatre Journal* 42, 2:165–82.

_____. 1991. *Theatre of Crisis: Drama and Politics in Latin America.* Lexington: University Press of Kentucky.

Taylor, Julie. 1994. "Body Memories: Aide-Memoires and Collective Amnesia in the Wake of the Argentine Terror." In *Body Politics: Disease, Desire, and the Family,* ed. Michael Ryan and Avery Gordon, 192-203. Boulder, Colo.: Westview.

Timerman, Jacobo. 1981. *Prisoner without a Name, Cell without a Number.* Trans. Toby Talbot. New York: Vintage.

Travis, Molly Abel. 1992. "Speaking from the Silence of the Slave Narrative: *Beloved* and African-American Women's History." *Texas Review* 13, 1–2:69–81.

Turkle, Sherry. 1992. *Psychoanalytic Politics: Jacques Lacan and Freud's French Revolution.* 2d ed. New York: Guilford.

Valenzuela, Luisa. 1976. *Clara: Thirteen Short Stories and a Novel.* Trans. Hortense Carpentier and J. Jorge Castello. New York: Harcourt Brace Jovanovich.

_____. [1977] 1979a. *He Who Searches (Como en la Guerra).* Trans. Helen Lane. Elmwood Park, Ill.: Dalkey Archive.

_____. 1979b. *Strange Things Happen Here.* Trans. Helen Lane. New York: Harcourt Brace Jovanovich.

_____. 1983. *The Lizard's Tail.* Trans. Gregory Rabassa. New York: Farrar, Straus & Giroux.

_____. 1985. *Other Weapons.* Trans. Deborah Bonner. Hanover, N.H.: Ediciones del Norte.

_____. 1986. "Dangerous Words." Trans. Cynthia Ventura. *Review of Contemporary Fiction* 6, 3:9–12

_____. 1988a. *Open Door.* Trans. Hortense Carpentier et al. San Francisco: North Point.

_____. 1988b. "Symmetries." Trans. Christopher Leland and David Rieff. *Grand Street* 8, 1:35–44.

_____. 1992. *Black Novel (with Argentines).* Trans. Toby Talbot. New York: Simon & Schuster.

Van Der Zee, James, Owen Dodson, and Camille Billops. 1978. *The Harlem Book of the Dead.* Dobbs Ferry, N.Y.: Morgan & Morgan.

Weiss, Rachel, ed. 1991. *Being América: Essays on Art, Literature and Identity from Latin America.* Fredonia, N.Y.: White Pine.

Weschler, Lawrence. 1990. *A Miracle, a Universe: Settling Accounts with Torturers.* New York: Pantheon.

Wideman, John Edgar. 1994. *Fatheralong: A Meditation on Fathers and Sons, Race and Society.* New York: Pantheon.

Williams, Patricia. 1991. *The Alchemy of Race and Rights.* Cambridge, Mass.: Harvard University Press.

Williams, Raymond. 1977. *Marxism and Literature.* Oxford: Oxford University Press.

Wilson, Henry. 1879. *History of the Rise and Fall of the Slave Power in America.* Vol. 2. Cambridge, Mass.: Riverside.

Yanuck, Julius. 1953. "The Garner Fugitive Slave Case." *Mississippi Valley Historical Review* 40:47–66.

Yúdice, George. 1991. "Testimonio and Postmodernism." *Latin American Perspectives* 18, 3:15–31.

Žižek, Slavoj. 1989. *The Sublime Object of Ideology.* New York: Verso.

Index

Italicized page numbers refer to illustrations.

Avery F. Gordon is professor of sociology and law and society at the University of California, Santa Barbara, and visiting faculty at the Centre for Research Architecture, Goldsmiths College, University of London. She is author of *Keeping Good Time: Reflections on Knowledge, Power, and People* among other works.

Janice Radway is professor of literature at Duke University and past president of the American Studies Association. She is the author of *Reading the Romance: Women, Patriarchy, and Popular Literature* and *A Feeling for Books: The Book-of-the-Month Club, Literary Taste, and Middle-Class Desire.* She is coeditor with Kevin Gaines, Barry Shank, and Penny von Eschen of the forthcoming anthology, *Reconfiguring American Studies: The New Analytics,* and with Carl Kaestle, of *Print in Motion: The Expansion of Publishing and Reading in the United States, 1880–1940.*